THE FALL AND RISE OF MODERN ITALY

L'aiuola che ci fa tanto feroci . . .
                              —Paradiso

THE FALL
AND RISE OF
MODERN ITALY

SERGE HUGHES

THE MACMILLAN COMPANY, NEW YORK

COLLIER-MACMILLAN LTD., LONDON

The Macmillan Company, New York
Collier-Macmillan Canada Ltd., Toronto, Ontario
PRINTED IN THE UNITED STATES OF AMERICA

For Betts, looking up from
"the road down there."

ACKNOWLEDGMENTS

The problem with thanking all those who have helped the author in the preparation of this work is that the list is too long, and individual acknowledgments would add one more chapter, a chapter that would be of interest only to those mentioned therein. I will try to express my gratitude to most of these people in other ways. It would be inexcusable, though, to make no mention of Katy Canevaro and Nando Fabro of *Il Gallo*, and above all of Mrs. Vittoria Bonfante, whose fine, solicitous reading of the manuscript spared the author a great deal of necessary, but undoubtedly less affectionate, criticism.

CONTENTS

INTRODUCTION

In 1968, Italians will go to the polls to decide whether the present Christian Democrat–Socialist government will remain in power for another five-year term. The decision matters. If the Center-Left coalition, a radically new political orientation, wins by even a narrow margin, Italy may be on the way to achieving the most stable and democratic government in its century-old history as a modern state. If that coalition is defeated, political Italy will once again be polarized between an Extreme Right (right-wing Christian Democrats and Liberals) and an Extreme Left (Communists and dissident Socialists). Italian politics has experienced such polarization before, and the results have not been felicitous. In the coming instance, they will be not only unfelicitous but crucial.

For many reasons, however, we in America, despite our current well-disposed and fashionable interest in things Italian, have so far not responded to the urgency of the present political moment in Italy. Excellent books and articles by experts on various aspects of Italy's political present and immediate past continue to appear, but in general, the predominant interest of Americans in things Italian centers rather on the meaning of the latest Antonioni film, the changing role of sex in Moravia's novels, and the dips and swells of the Italian economic miracle. Politically, we prefer that Italy show no signs of recurrent Fascism and that it not go Communist; but beyond that preference we are not sure what we ought to think about Italian politics. We are similarly vague as to how things got to this point. Fascism, we feel, was long ago, and wrong—but the road leading to fascism and away from it seems to us, more often than not, hazy and hard to recognize.

There are both good and bad reasons for this prevailing vagueness. Our two-party system makes us impatient with the intricacies of the Italian party system, which since its beginnings has been anything but clear-cut and easily analyzable; and our sound pragmatic sense, which has done so much to keep us on the right side of sustained coherence, tempts us to dismiss most political philosophy as mere ideology. Besides, when all is said and done, it does not appear that the study of Italian political problems can contribute much to the solution of our own.

Occasionally we find it hard to overcome the suspicion that in so thinking we have drifted into the shoals of oversimplification; in general, however, we overcome those misgivings. Thus, in spite of remarkable work, especially in the last twenty years, by Italian and non-Italian historians on the history of Italian parties, we continue to avoid hard thinking on the place and meaning of those parties; in particular, we continue to harbor the haziest of ideas about the meaning of Marxist-Socialist parties. Indeed, with respect to Italian Socialist parties, a knowledge of which is indispensable for an understanding of modern Italy, we tend to become particularly adamant. Ill at ease with theoretical Marxism, and inclined to believe that any Marxist party is all one with the international Communist structure or conspiracy, we approach all Marxist-Socialist parties with suspicion, almost as a matter of principle. Our misgivings are firm; and precisely because they are firm, we do not look closely at Italian socialism, which from its beginnings in the 1890's to the present time has always been Marxist. When the Italian Socialist Party was first founded, it was organized as a Marxist party, and after Fascism and World War II, it was reorganized again as a Marxist party.

This cavalier attitude of ours toward the problem of Italian political parties and Italian Marxist parties in particular will not disappear overnight. For a long time to come, foreseeably, political Italy, in the popular American view, will continue to be the dark side of the moon. In the meantime, though, one observer of the Italian scene has decided that it is time to light his small candle, to cast some light on the twists and turns of ideas and events that have led from the Italy of the 1890's to that of the 1960's.

In the course of producing this work, and while mulling over the peculiar problems of the relations of Socialists first with the Liberals and later with the Christian Democrats, the author has stumbled into what may in some quarters be considered "a new interpretation of modern Italian history." He is both excited and somewhat embarrassed by this, and at the outset he would like to make a few quick disclaimers, in case the book should fall into the hands of scholars. The author respects scholarship, even pure scholarship, and he has no doubt that in the pressure of research he has missed several important articles, and somewhere overlooked at least one relevant tome. He nonetheless stands by the conclusion that forced itself upon him as the manuscript pages heaped up on his desk: although the history of modern Italy is usually looked upon as one unit until World War I, as another unit with Fascism, and still another since Fascism ended, these units are actually only handy subdivisions. Though appreciative of the indispensability of such practical divisions, even though they are arbitrary (this study makes use of the prevailing, almost canonical, historical divisions), the author has concluded that modern Italian history consists basically of two periods, and that the pivotal point that separates one period from the other lies in our time, in the early 1960's. From this perspective, Italy from the 1890's to the early 1960's emerges as an initial phase in which first Socialists and Liberals, and then Socialists, Liberals and Catholics failed to work out a minimum of collaboration; Italy from 1963 on appears as the second phase in which that collaboration has so far succeeded, if ever so precariously. This study, of necessity, concentrates for the most part on the first phase.

Whether original or not, however, this interpretation of Italian history accounts for the peculiar chronological delimitations of this work, why fascism both is and is not considered central, and why what preceded and followed it seem to this writer more decisive in Italy's national development.

In this moving toward and away from the totalitarian experience, a number of very perceptive Italians, in complete disagreement among themselves, have not minced words in branding what they considered the most abominable failings of their people. Outsiders match but do not surpass the vehemence of the charges hurled by the Marxist Labriola, the Liberal-Marxists Rosselli and Gobetti, the Liberal Croce, and the Catholic Sturzo. In anti-Italian spirit, the Italians have few peers, and today, as yesterday, their affectionate hatred and anguish endure. They are quite naturally incapable of the detachment of outsiders who, studying the same political-moral failings, have concluded that Italians, though a marvelous and fascinating people, have a curious ineptness for politics.

Preferring, for purely autobiographical reasons, the self-criticism of Italians to the criticism of outsiders, the author has sought detachment in two ecumenical platitudes: that political ineptness is a common trait uniting all countries, and that passionately committed partisans in a political struggle are apt to exaggerate the failings of their people. This attempt at equanimity, however, should not be interpreted as historical impartiality. The author has taken sides. He has never quite understood the notion of history "as it actually happened," and sees no reason why in history, any more than in life, one should confuse political wisdom and political skill, the raw fact of success and political-moral success.

Precisely because politics, as the superbly ironical definition would have it, is the science of the possible—that is, a science with indeterminable limits—the author does not feel compunction for the seeming disorder in this work and for the constant shuttling from small politics to politics in a larger sense, from electoral statistics to philosophical disquisitions on the nature of economics, from ideology to political philosophy, from religious sociology to religion. No doubt a study made through a smaller, more controlled aperture would have given a surer outline, a greater clarity of perspective. In excuse, the author would like to suggest that the historian's work ought not be confused with that of the political philosopher or the sociologist or, *tout court*, the philosopher. It is the function of the historian, working on frescoes rather than cameos, to give witness to the comic-tragic need of knowing "more than we need to know"; and if the notion of history as *magister vitae* means anything at all, it probably means that a historian can tranquilly savor a certain amount of disorder, consoled by the certainty that something worth doing is worth doing badly, and that in history as in life, a good amount of disorder and unevenness is a sign of vitality.

But because politics is more than the sum total of political men, parties and suprapersonal forces, the author has taken occasion to parallel this story of Socialists, Liberals and Catholics with that of Benedetto Croce, the thinker who left an indelible mark on two generations before and during fascism, on those for whom political values were absolutes with absolute rights, and those for whom politics was nothing of the sort. Marxist-Socialist and Liberal doctrine would not have been quite what they were had not Croce, who was not at all primarily political, taken politics very seriously in theory and practice.

The "political" Croce, in general, has not been very much appreciated abroad. Croce the philosopher, the author of the *Esthetics*, the historiographer and literary critic, has received and continues to receive the lion's share of attention among us. As far as political thinkers of this period are concerned, we tend to focus principally not on Croce, but on Gaetano Mosca (whose theory of the political elite has become very popular among us today as the theory of the "power structure"), and Vilfredo Pareto, with his very spacious synthesis of sociology and economics. Both thinkers have much to offer and both have often seen more clearly into the political-economic process than Croce. Neither one, though, was a participant in a Liberal-Marxist dialogue in the dramatic and telling way that Croce was, and as theoreticians of liberalism, neither Pareto nor Mosca had the scope or range of Croce. Don Benedetto alone is the *magister vitae* of several generations of liberal-oriented Italians of this period.

And yet for all of this, the Neapolitan philosopher remains a particularly elusive figure. A man of many parts, Croce is and is not the same thinker before fascism, during it, and after; and because, in spite of the voluminous work dedicated to the philosopher, this complicated truism is not yet generally appreciated, the author has thought it worthwhile stressing. There is a likelihood otherwise (and particularly among us and in other English-speaking countries) that a one-sided appreciation of Croce as the embodiment of the Liberal "no" to fascism would imperceptibly give way to a view of Croce as the archetype of a subtle conservative with no real concern for the commonweal; and the last condition of Croce would no doubt be worse than the first.

In laying his penultimate card on the table before starting—for the introduction is hardly the place to give it all away—the author would like to candidly own that he is neither a Socialist nor a Crocean, but that like Croce, he considers a concern for politics indispensable, though not primary. This study is evidence of that persuasion. Those who believe that politics is but one dimension of life ought to think hard about its nature and workings if they care to lend weight to that conviction. There are all sorts of implications and assumptions in this approach, needless to say, which the reader will want to test according to the criteria of his own notion of plausibility. The author has no quarrel with readers who do to him what he has done to others. He would like to express a word of caution, though. The categorical imperative should have its limits. If his ideal reader were to put his meditations down in writing and put some order among those thoughts, by the time he finished, he too, God forbid, would have written a book.

PART ONE

SAND CASTLE

1890-1925

I

THE LONG RESTLESSNESS

OF LIBERAL ITALY

There are Italians today who are convinced that not to have lived before World War II is not to have lived at all. They may be right. There are others who feel that not to have lived before 1914 is not to have lived at all. They too may be right. Nostalgia encourages tangled judgment, varying in sophistication and insight; and in times of national stress and strain, as in the Italy of the 1960's, a longing for the recent past is not stamped with patronizing condescension, but is usually conceded certain rights. Indeed, a degree of nostalgia has become quite common and respectable among Italians—one of the "consolations" of the times. Like a vest of late-nineteenth-century cut worn beneath a dacron-and-wool jacket, nostalgia has its place in the style and outlook of today's Italians. In fact, considering the pressures of this decade, there is the likelihood that nostalgia in one form or another will continue to appeal to them for a long time.

Those who lived in the years before 1914 would have been perplexed at the thought that anyone in the 1960's would long for their world. They, especially those in the generation of 1890, certainly did not at the time consider theirs a privileged state. The vast majority, in fact, had no doubt that they were living in very bad times. They were disillusioned. They were resentful and exasperated. When they muttered, as Italians traditionally do, "*Si stava meglio quando si stava peggio*"—"We were better off when things were worse"—they did so without ironical overtones, without a trace of the equanimity of an "It was the best of times, it was the worst of times" mood. They had a host of good reasons for their lack of equanimity.

From the beginnings of the unification of Italy in about 1815 to the culminating entry of Italian troops into Rome on September 20, 1870, the Risorgimento—meaning the Resurgence, or Uprising—for the relatively few who actively participated in the movement, appeared as a cause that would not experience anticlimax. In 1859, Count Camillo di Cavour set the firm foundation of the new state with the annexation of Lombardy, Emilia and Tuscany to the Piedmontese kingdom of the house of Savoy (the kings of Sardinia). A year later, 1860, Garibaldi with his *Mille*, his one thousand followers, conquered the South and virtually doubled the territories of the emerging nation. In the same year, troops of Victor Emmanuel II took over the Papal States of Umbria and the Marches in central Italy. In 1866, Venice and a part of Venetia came under Italian dominion. The occupation of Rome seemed the last upward thrust of a movement that gave no sign of arching.

But after some twenty years of post-Risorgimento rule, even the most ardent patriot admitted to faded illusions. The business of governing with authority and justice was harder than the expulsion of the Austrians from northern Italy and the occupation of papal Rome. In the 1870's, the cry of Risorgimento leaders, "Now that we have made Italy, we must make Italians," had the ring of exuberant self-assurance; a generation later it was heard less frequently, and then more with bitter irony than with confidence. By 1890, it sounded like an empty slogan or adolescent braggadocio. Italians were not united, and the numbers of the indifferent had not lessened perceptibly. If there was any recognizable change, it lay in the fact that their wait-and-see attitude had become more hostile, less passive.

The indifferent—the largest class in Italy, and one that cut across all economic and cultural divisions including peasants, the middle class, and a substantial segment of the landed aristocracy—had never been won over to Risorgimento ideals. From their beginnings, those ideals had flourished among only a small part of a small middle class, and twenty years later they had not gained wider acceptance. In the prodigiously varied Italian class structure, the new nation remained very old. In 1890, as in preceding centuries, the unity of Italy continued to be largely cultural, that of the few who saw in classical culture and in Italian literature since 1300 a common patrimony. In all other respects, however, there was no bond of interest common to all classes. The Piedmontese aristocracy did not have the same outlook and values as the Tuscan, and neither had much in common with southern aristocrats; it was very much the same with the other classes. The peasant of the North was quite different from his counterpart in the South, and the differences were more decisive than the similarities. Members of the southern middle class had been very active in the Risorgimento, but twenty years of Liberal rule had not brought about a fusion of their interests and values with those of the northern middle class, of which Cavour was the most gifted representative.

More telling yet, the position of Catholics actively interested in politics and deferential to the political counsels of the Pope continued to be one of uncertain and limited approval. There were very few staunch, believing Catholics of independent mind like Bettino Ricasoli, who in 1861, despite intransigent papal hostility to the new Italian state, chose to succeed Cavour as prime minister. True, Leo XIII had softened the Vatican's stand toward the group in power, but by and large, the mood of the papacy was still that of Pius IX and of his *non expedit*, a directive that instructed the faithful with a vocation for politics to confine themselves to the local level. In this restricted sphere, politically active Catholics drew closer to the Liberals, and indeed were often indistinguishable from them. There were Catholics with Liberal political leanings, as there were Liberals with private Catholic convictions.

Whatever support the government gained from this convergence of interests was offset by the still uncompromising stance of the Pope toward the alleged political philosophy of the new Italy. In the 1890's, the attitude of the Vatican to the Law of Guarantees was precisely the same as when it was passed in 1871. Leo XIII made it clear that this law, which laid down the terms under which the new state of Italy would respect the territorial and spiritual sovereignty of the Vatican, was Caesar's idea of what was his and what was God's. The papacy never formally recognized the Law of Guarantees, though it did submit to its provisions. Both Pius IX and Leo XIII, however, made it plain that there were limits to the practical concessions they were willing to make. In the 1890's the restitution of the city of Rome to the Popes was no longer a real issue, but the Vatican stood firm in its contention that the state had no right to legislate on spiritual matters, that on this principle there was no room for compromise. The papacy remained adamant in particular on its application to the education of the young. Leo XIII took a fresh and active interest in the moral-political problems of the times and the *Rerum novarum* of 1891 was a precedent-shattering encyclical that ultimately opened up new possibilities for Catholic attitudes toward politics within and without Italy. At the time, however, there were no repercussions of the encyclical in the practical political sphere among Catholics in Italy, and none on the official traditional papal policy toward the new Italy.

How many Catholics considered what the Pope had to say politically relevant or acceptable is hard to say. Not all Catholics supinely deferred to pontifical wishes: The 1860 referendum in the Papal States attested to the overwhelming preference of the citizens of those regions for Victor Emmanuel II. Italian Catholics knew how to distinguish between the black-and-white language of pontifical doctrine and the give-and-take necessary in dealings between two strong adversaries. Strengthened with this type of wisdom, a great number of believers holding very divergent political views managed to come to some sort of compromise in which they felt no less Italian than Catholic.

In this respect, twenty years of Liberal rule based on Risorgimento ideals brought about a softening of attitudes in some quarters, but hardly in all quarters: Masons in 1890, as in 1860, regarded themselves as the custodians of freedom, dedicated to the destruction of superstition and clerical obscurantism, or its synonym, Catholicism; nor was there any dearth of Catholics of equal fervor who considered themselves the defenders of God and Church against the apocalyptic Beast of the atheist Risorgimento state. Fortunately, relations between Catholics and Liberals were not consistently on this level, but even in instances where they improved perceptibly they did not change drastically. There were still Catholics who recalled with pride that at the height of the church-state conflict in the 1870's a Piedmontese bishop refused the last sacraments to a Catholic in Cavour's government unwilling to retract his support of certain Liberal measures; and there were Masons who glowed when they reminisced about how Garibaldi had called the Vatican, *senza peli sulla lingua* (without circumlocution, a square mile of dung).

More serious, though, post-Risorgimento Italy not only failed to raise perceptibly the level of religious polemics; it also further complicated the Catholic problem. Catholics were not in outright opposition to the new state, but neither did they give it their wholehearted support; and in this peculiarly indecisive stance, *vorrei e non vorrei* of sorts, they were the most striking anomaly in a very anomalous state. There were Catholics openly willing to work with Liberals and vice versa, just as there were undercover groups of Liberals and Catholics working toward official reconciliation between church and state. Each time these groups appeared to be making some progress, however, they were invariably disavowed by one or both of the parties.

But compared with the problem of growing division among the Liberals, the complexities of the Catholic problem appeared almost picayune. Risorgimento Liberals closed ranks and made a sterling show of unity against the Austrians and the Pope, but in dealing with the multifaceted domestic problems of unified Italy, they ran into a beehive of difficulties. In a very short time, divisions that had been discernible even in the heart of the Risorgimento struggle— conflicts between monarchists and republicans, between the King and Garibaldi, between federalists and the proponents of a strong central government—now reasserted themselves, and in a much sharper form.

Zeal for the republican cause of Mazzini dwindled after his death in 1872, but did not wholly abate. The Republicans, though numerically weak as a party in Parliament in the 1890's, still had a following. As before, their accusation that the ruling Liberals had betrayed the revolution still carried weight, and the charge was reinforced with new evidence. Meanwhile the constitution of the new state was still that granted by King Carlo Alberto to his Piedmontese subjects in 1848, with all its limitations. In that bicameral system the Senate was appointed exclusively by the King. The lower house won real power with its control of finance and the treasury, but in many respects, it too was still under the King's shadow. The very restricted suffrage (2 per cent of the population) worked to the monarch's advantage, since the few represented were those who most concurred with his views, and so did the fact that representatives received no remuneration, which made politics primarily the concern of those who could afford it. The right of Victor Emmanuel II and his successor, Umberto I, to call and dissolve Parliament, and when necessary to rule by decree, destroyed a great degree of initia-

tive and made for a deferential Parliament. Furthermore, the King's
trusted aides were very much a power. They had as much to say in
foreign policy as the party in power, and they could count on the
unqualified aid of the military to maintain domestic order in increasingly restless times. As commander in chief of the armed forces, the
King was in a position to act very firmly when he felt the safety and
order of the country were in danger, and he met with little resistance from any prime minister. In the twenty years from 1870 to
1890 the King and Liberal government exercised these powers again
and again in the name of order, repeatedly violating freedoms guar-
anteed in the constitution, such as freedom of the press and freedom
of assembly. Republicans in particular, who only a few years earlier
had been in the thick of the struggle for unification, were singled
out for persecution, and in 1872 the new state's oppressiveness came
to a climax that outraged all politically conscious Italians with the
Villa Ruffi incident, in which a peaceful, law-abiding meeting of
Republicans near Rimini was broken up and its leaders imprisoned,
charged with conspiring against the state. The new Italy, true, was
monarchist and Liberal, and the Republicans had seen their day; but
the measures employed at Villa Ruffi did not heal still-open wounds,
but rather exacerbated old rancors and perpetuated the disunity that
had long antedated the Risorgimento.

The Republican Party in the 1890's was led in its denunciations of
the government by a most articulate spokesman, Giovanni Bovio, a
man of ample nineteenth-century cut and the author of some bad
romantic plays. Together with the older and much more sedate
Agostino Bertani, Bovio carried on an attenuated Mazzinian policy.
Since times had changed remarkably since the 1870's, the Republicans' attacks on the Liberals in the 1890's often had the support of
former enemies, the Radicals, a group that followed the policies of
the aging Garibaldi, the fiery old leader of the *camicie rosse* (red
shirts). Before his death in 1882, Garibaldi, who never had much
sympathy for the monarchist cause and repeatedly clashed with
both Mazzini and Victor Emmanuel II, took an unqualified stand
against the Liberals and the monarchy. Post-Risorgimento Italy had
disillusioned him, as it had many others. Its leaders, Garibaldi
charged, did not trust the people; they had no interest in implementing the vision for which he had fought. The gist of the General's
indictment was that for them, the central problem of political Italy

was the need of a balanced budget, not the urgent needs of education, literacy, land reclamation and agricultural reform, and—not the least of the General's preoccupations—eliminating clericalism and superstition. Compulsory, universal education, universal suffrage, a firm commitment to the humanitarian, egalitarian principles of the French Revolution—these were the principles to which Italy should be dedicated. Instead, they were being trampled on. Thus contended Garibaldi.

This passionate denunciation of a revolution betrayed found its spokesman after Garibaldi's death in the Radical, Felice Cavallotti—like Bovio, a bad playwright and poet but a vigorous, sentimental, swashbuckling rhetorician. With Bovio and his Republicans, Cavallotti and his party constituted what was known as the Extreme Left, a very small group in Parliament (quite naturally so, given the make-up of the electorate). But it was the only alternative to the two amorphous groups—the Liberal Left and the Liberal Right—that made up the ruling party.

From 1870–76, Liberals of the Right, a group of austere political leaders best represented by the inflexible Quintino Sella, followed each other in rapid succession in the office of prime minister. Despite numerous Cabinet reshufflings, they had to their satisfaction saved the country from the threat of national bankruptcy that followed hard upon the Risorgimento conflict. This success, together with a cautious foreign policy oriented toward Germany and Austria-Hungary, was their great accomplishment. Their achievement, however, made Italy the most heavily taxed country in Europe; this helped explain the landslide victory of the Liberal Left candidates at the polls in 1876. The defeat of the Right, however, was not exclusively attributable to its financial policy, nor was the triumph of the Left an unqualified improvement. In general, the leaders of the Liberal Left were not noticeably superior to those of the Right in political skills, and they were certainly several notches below them in political morality. The Left did pass some urgently needed reform measures and they were not as paternalistically high-handed in decreeing political priorities, but in many respects they tended to substitute a peculiar mixture of self-interest and wordy righteous indignation for the excessive austerity of the Right.

With Agostino Depretis, however, the Left had a talented political leader, who for eleven years, from 1876 to 1887, the year of his death, did his best to erase still further the indistinct lines that separated the Liberal Right and the Liberal Left; thus he ruled with a coalition of both groups that virtually obliterated what was left of the old divisions.

The art with which Depretis achieved his goal was known as *trasformismo*, an untranslatable term that might be defined as the art of winning over opponents and having them share the responsibilities of government by toning down all basic differences. The skill is an old one and hardly the most insidious ruse known to political man; it was a sign of the growing exasperation of the times that by the end of his tenure, Depretis had unjustly become one of the most vilified political men in Italian history.

Trasformismo in a two-party government, and especially in a country such as the United States, works rather well. But there are certain prerequisites that explain the success of the system among us that help account for its failure in the Italy of the nineties. Trasformismo, to work, requires a common political tradition, a common point of view among people and parties. In the Italy of that time, however, there was no such political tradition to bind together the various Liberal factions, much less to bind Liberals together with other groups. Trasformismo also requires a stability based on a moderate degree of prosperity and a reasonably equitable distribution of wealth. Nor can it work where there is a fundamental conflict of loyalties, such as the conflict in Italy between church and state. It presupposes a certain unity of interests, a homogeneity of classes; and Italy, with its remarkable variety of classes and its decentralized city-state history and tradition, was simply the poorest, most sterile soil possible for sustained trasformismo.

Depretis was certainly not to be blamed for recognizing that times had changed, and that in the 1880's, Right and Left were only labels, not distinct positions. Indeed, judged from the vantage point of the present, the acrimonious debates on trasformismo as "the abomination of desolation" do appear overheated characteristics of an age of political anticlimax. It is also true, however, that trasformismo—and many Italians sensed and recognized as much in those years—was a short-sighted solution. The real evil of trasformismo was its encouragement of a specious, hollow political unity. It did do harm in circumventing the pressing problem of post-Risorgimento Italy, united and yet divided—the need for clear political convictions that could distinguish one political party from another.

Because of trasformismo there was not, nor could there be, any "political party" in the modern sense of the term in the Italy of the nineties—no party, that is, with a substantial following, united by a coherent party platform and party discipline, willing to work up to a point with its rivals. In this sense, the Extreme Left (the Radicals and the Republicans) came close, for they shared a coherent party platform, but they had only a minuscule following and absolutely no experience or idea of party unity or discipline. The Liberals were in a better position. They had what the Extreme Left lacked, a substantial following—actually enough of a following so that, with the proper coherence and discipline, their divergent factions could have split into at least two clearly articulated parties. But, alleging the need to defend the newly united Italy from enemies within and without, the many Liberal factions remained one; remained, that is, not a real party but a coalition of groups. In this way they kept their solid hold on Parliament, and as a liberal political force had nothing to fear from any opponent. There was no better device for remaining in power. Over the years, however, the technique became irritatingly ineffectual, and its achievements (for trasformismo undoubtedly accomplished some good) were rightly judged meager in proportion to the price paid.

Depretis initiated some electoral reform, increasing suffrage, in a country of some 28 million souls, from 2 to 7 per cent; he took steps to correct a regional disparity in taxation extremely unfair to the South; and some first steps were also taken in his time toward increased local autonomy. But even the adherents and defenders of trasformismo had more than occasional doubts as to whether those accomplishments justified the practice. There was not one forceful personality of the Right or of the Left who did not feel exasperated at the extremely loose theoretical basis of the Liberal "party," which advocated at one and the same time a tough, unrelenting policy of state primacy over the Church and a reasonable policy disposed to concessions. It urged a prudent foreign policy that toned down the possibilities of colonial expansion, and also one that insisted on expansionism as the sign of Italy's emergence as a modern power. It stressed the primacy of a balanced budget as well as that of agricultural reform. It favored a laissez-faire policy to fledgling

Italian industry while it fought for a measure of state control. It ceaselessly invoked the new united Italy, yet practiced a regionalism of vested interests. This ambivalent behavior of the one political group that had enough followers to become a real party, or perhaps two, largely accounted for the sulphurous denunciations and political disillusionment of the times.

Yet this very sense of importance, this awareness of a painfully unfulfilled need, also marked in a very real sense the positive beginnings of the history of modern Italy. Twenty years of post-Risorgimento rule demonstrated that national unity was fragile, even somewhat fictitious, that Risorgimento *élan* was not enough to weld Italy into a truly united country, or to govern it well. The new nation desperately needed a unity made up of diversity, a unity that only strong parties could provide, parties that would not simply be variations to the right or left of a nebulous liberalism, parties that would not become the instruments of well-meaning, or not so well-meaning, strong men, but that would give voice to profound differences of opinion within the country and construct the framework for a workable coexistence. Though such parties would of course run into many vexing problems, it was still true that the dissatisfaction and restlessness caused by the preparty web in which Italian political life had been caught from 1860–90 signaled definite moral-political progress. The beginnings were naturally humble ones, and Italy would long continue to suffer in particular from one political question mark: the anomaly of Catholics who neither fully entered into nor quite abstained from political activity. But however humble, it was a beginning; in this sense, the work of the Extreme Left, and even more so that of the newly founded Socialist Party, the great political innovation of the time, marked the disillusioned 1890's as the beginning of a new stage in the political experience of modern Italy.

In Parliament, the Socialists had only insignificant numerical strength, but in the country, it was evident even in 1892, when they first constituted themselves as a party, that they needed only an enlargement of the very narrow electorate to increase their representation rapidly. Although there were a few deputies among the Liberals, like the southerner Giustino Fortunato, who were actively interested in what was then called the "social question," and even more among the Extreme Left, only the Socialist Party made the exploitation of the poor and the privileges of the rich its well-nigh exclusive concern. This gave the Socialists one of the essentials of a party: a loyal and increasing following. The Socialist Party was the natural spokesman—indeed, the only one—for the inarticulate, the destitute, the poor, with a thousand and one justified grievances; and the condition of the peasants and artisans was indeed deplorable. Workers in the Lombard rice fields and those in Sicilian sulphur mines labored at least twelve hours a day; the exploitation of child labor was commonplace; and until the mid-1880's all workers' strikes were illegal. Needless to say, such embryonic labor unions as existed were powerless, and they certainly had no say in fixing wages or hours.

Like the Extreme Left, the Socialist Party had the very real disadvantages of having no real party apparatus, discipline or unity. They did, however (and this was very important), have a firm, definite outlook on life and politics—a Marxist outlook—and they were adamant in their denunciations of trasformismo.

Marxism was many things in many lands, but in post-Risorgimento Italy, the Marxism of the Socialist Party was principally a means of marking off Socialists from the bourgeoisie and the Liberals, the party in power—a marking off that was proper to a legal, law-abiding party. To this end, in 1892, the Socialists broke completely with the Anarchists, who until then had fought off all attempts to distinguish them from Socialists. Of course in an Italy where real parties did not yet exist, the Anarchists were not so very different from other groups fighting the government. All opposition parties had more or less anarchical tendencies, and if the Anarchists stood out, it was perhaps because they theorized their very lack of unified theory. The Anarchists—a striking assortment of discontented and indignant members of many classes, despairing idealists of all ages, frugal artisans, authors of unpublished manuscripts, the bored and the frustrated—were proud of their claim to represent the most vehement expression of the prevailing disillusionment. Moreover, since they had a good number of clandestine and semi-clandestine publications, they made their boasts and their laments heard. Some who considered themselves authentically anarchistic proclaimed that the only effective action against the tyrant state was armed insurrection. Others sharing the same conviction but less fond of violence, emigrated to Brazil, where they established an uncorrupt, peace-loving Anarchist colony. Still others, with little faith in terrorism or rebellion, boldly hoped—and their vision was considered a kind of madness—that they might yet see an Italy with an eight-hour day, universal suffrage, and like blessings.

The moving spirit of the Italian anarchists, Enrico Malatesta, a legend in his lifetime, was a worthy successor to the Russian Anarchist, Mikhail Aleksandrovich Bakunin, who in the 1870's had found a large and enthusiastic following in Italy. Yet in 1874, when Bakunin led a revolt to take over the municipal government of traditionally revolutionary Bologna, the results were humiliating. Even before nearing the city hall they were to assault, the plotters disbanded, and the sputtering grand finale was more reminiscent of Offenbach than of Wagner.

In the decades following, revolutionary ambitions continued to dwindle in Italy. In March 1882, to the stunned amazement of his followers, Carlo Cafiero, after Malatesta the most publicized of Italian Anarchist leaders, called for anarchists to run for Parliament instead of blowing it up. In that same year, outraged Anarchists were fond of pointing out, Cafiero literally did go mad. In contrast, Italian Anarchists were busy abroad. Santo Casino's assassination of the French president, Sadi Carnot, in 1894, and Michele Angiolillo's murder three years later of the Spanish prime minister, Antonio Canovas, showed that terrorism was more than a speculative persuasion among Italian Anarchists. But within Italy in the 1890's, anarchist violence was generally no threat.

Nevertheless, considering the swollen reputation rather than the real accomplishments of Anarchists in Italy, Italian Socialists had much to gain in making a clean break with them. But the new party did more than break with the Anarchists; it also did its utmost from its very beginnings to show that where it was strongest it was also peaceful and law-abiding. In Emilia-Romagna, the rich farmland area of central Italy where there was a centuries-old tradition of bloody conflict between peasants and landowners, Socialists were the voice of moderation. Their most respected leader, Andrea Costa, founder of the first Socialist newspaper, the famous *Avanti!*, so named in honor of the German *Vorwärts*, was an ex-Anarchist from that region, and as the first Socialist to be elected to Parliament he, far more than the great landowners, stood for restraint and reasonableness. Camillo Prampolini, another prominent Socialist from the same region, was another pillar of moderation. He dedicated himself with dubious success and admirable fervor to Socialist evangelization, to the preaching of a socialism that was peace-loving, lawful and morally superior to the Catholicism of the peasants of Romagna.

The Socialists' break with the Anarchists and their decision to be unequivocally lawful brought the party not only within the law but also close to the Extreme Left. Undoubtedly, the Socialists would have moved closer yet, and the entire history of modern Italy would have been quite different, had Italian socialism not been Marxist, with all the intransigence that that implied toward enemies, and even toward friends. But Italian Socialists had to be particularly on guard against doctrinal compromise. They were aware that doctrinal vagueness had ruined the Liberals; it had led them logically to a trasformismo that had contributed to a political pragmatism concerned only with the party's continuance in power. Doctrinal Marxism conceivably would be of some help in warding off any danger of assimilation into trasformismo—remote as that possibility seemed in the 1890's.

The problem of how intransigent the Socialists would or could be, however, the extent to which they ought to collaborate with the Extreme Left, for example (from the Marxist point of view, an irreducibly bourgeois coalition), was at the time of the party's beginnings an almost absurdly speculative problem. The central Socialist problem in the 1890's was hardly a question of the extent to which philosophical principles could be endangered by political compromise. The problem for the Socialist Party was much simpler. It was a question of survival. For in 1887, after the death of Depretis, the Liberals had chosen Fransesco Crispi as his successor, convinced that he was the one man who could check the increasing popularity and strength of the Extreme Left.

To the Socialists, Crispi, a grand old man of the Risorgimento, an ex-Mazzinian conspirator active in the planning of Garibaldi's invasion of Sicily, embodied the most dangerous of all possible forms of trasformismo. Though almost seventy years old, Crispi was the rival in eloquence and sheer animal vitality of Bovio and Cavallotti. Like them, he too inveighed against corruption, lack of party principles, and the apathy and creeping pace of the new Italy; and as a member of the heroic generation of the Risorgimento, he was inspiringly impatient for the new state to become both an exemplar of social justice and a nation respected by all its neighbors. Crispi's past explained why the Liberals had settled on him; but it was also known that the choice had been facilitated by the autocratic leader's habit of judging the boundary between the legal and illegal, not by constitutional definition, but by his own personal judgment.

Ostensibly, Crispi appeared to have all the virtues that these years required. In the field of foreign policy, for example, his views were generally considered sound. Though he advocated colonial expansionism, colonial ambitions did not blind him to the necessity of bringing to a close a particularly unfelicitous adventure in Ethiopia initiated under Depretis, and indeed by 1889, Crispi signed the Treaty of Uccialli, restoring good relations with the Negus of Ethiopia. In the matter of foreign alliances, he acted with similar prudence. A notorious Francophobe, Crispi moved much closer to the other members of the Triple Alliance, which had been initiated by the Liberal Right. A great deal was made of Crispi's encounters and secret talks with Bismarck, but in spite of all the conjectures and admiration evoked by the Prime Minister's bellicose posturing, the much heralded agreements with Germany never amounted to anything substantial.

Crispi also effected changes in domestic policies, pushing through measures to increase regional autonomy, to make the office of mayor elective and to improve penal codes and hygiene. In ecclesiastical policy, however, the old Mason, who had very clear ideas about the state as a perfect society subservient to no one, followed a very hard line; accordingly, tensions increased.

In his domestic and foreign dealings, however, the impetuous Crispi showed a tendency to take less and less notice of Parliament, and frequently substituted his own decrees for that body's deliberations. The majority in Parliament by and large was perfectly willing to let him do so, and when he was forced to step down for the first time, in February of 1891, it was due more to his arrogance, his bungling of finances and his personal involvement in the notorious Banca Romana scandal, than to indignation at his treatment of Parliament or his lack of effort toward real party rule.

Thus, four years of Crispi's rule came and went and the misgivings of Socialists and the Extreme Left appeared excessive. Crispi had not turned on them or persecuted them. He recognized their legal status. The Liberals in Parliament, however, were not all glad to see the old warrior leave, and many of them were outspoken in their regrets. They made it clear that they felt far more confident with him than with the two political foes who held office in his absence from 1891–93: the Sicilian aristocrat Antonio di Rudinì and the very middle-class Piedmontese, Giovanni Giolitti. The Liberal majority felt that neither di Rudinì, nor certainly Giolitti, could deal with the ominous growth in these years of the power of the Sicilian *fasci:* unions of workers and peasants that protested the abominable working conditions in the sulphur mines, the starvation wages paid to agricultural workers and all the evils of absentee landownership. Even more, they protested the hold of the middle-class administrators, the *capeddi*, on the peasants. Di Rudinì did not receive much parliamentary support in dealing with the problem, and when Giolitti made it clear that he did not intend to make any show of strength even after peasants clashed with police, he was eased out under the convenient excuse that he too was involved in the Banca Romana scandal. The last thing that Parliament and the King believed wise or necessary was a capitulation to the peasant-worker demands, demands that from their point of view were outrageous, reflecting in part a dangerous anarchist trend, and in part the machinations of a separatist movement that made use of the Anarchists. Neither the King nor the majority of Liberals in Parliament paid any heed to the repeated warnings of Giustino Fortunato, an enlightened southern Liberal, that economic conditions in his region were appalling, and that emigration from the South, which had virtually doubled between 1870 and 1890, had now risen to a frightening 275,000 a year. Instead, they noticed that Anarchists were active in the increasingly violent unrest in Sicily as were members of the Extreme Left parties and also the Socialist, Giuseppe de Felice. In their eyes, these enemies of the Liberals now appeared as enemies of the state.

There was no better man to deal with this situation than the forceful Crispi. Called back to office, the old ex-conspirator showed precisely what he could do about the "outrageous" agrarian reforms that the peasants, for once turning the tables, had imposed on the southern landowners. Crispi was absolutely convinced that the peasant revolt was an outright assault on the unity of modern Italy; he also believed it to be part of a giant conspiracy involving France, czarist Russia, and even the Vatican. In January of 1894, therefore, he dispatched 50,000 troops to Sicily, declared a state of siege, and proclaimed martial law. Shortly thereafter, in the same month, uprisings occurred in the North in Lunigiana, near Massa Carrara, a traditional Anarchist stronghold. Again Crispi moved, in the same expeditious way.

Having clamped down on the Sicilian uprising with martial law, Crispi imposed lengthy jail sentences on those Socialists, Republicans, and Radicals who had taken part in it. He was hardest on the Socialists. He put absolutely no stock in their claim to be separate and distinct from the Anarchists; he saw them only as a threat to the unified Italy which it was his mission to defend. The leading role of the Socialist de Felice in the Sicilian revolt confirmed Crispi in his estimate of what could be expected from Socialists, so that in 1894 he abruptly declared the Socialist Party illegal.

As a consequence Crispi was hailed as the savior of the country. More popular than ever, he proceeded to make up for past faults by dedicating himself completely to balancing the budget. In general, he was so appreciated that he might have remained in power longer had he not attempted to deal with foreign policy in the same authoritarian way he had handled the Sicilian uprising.

When in 1896 a disagreement arose with the Negus of Ethiopia over the interpretation of the Treaty of Uccialli, Crispi moved to solve the differences with guns rather than with arguments. Respectful, though, of the aversion of northern industrialists for colonial wars, and not wishing to risk the strain of still higher taxes on the country, he put pressure on the military, instructing them to make up for shortages in war matériel with valor and daring. It was not to be the last time, regrettably, that a modern Italian leader would act in this fashion, nor the last time that the consequences would be catastrophic. Heeding his advice, the former Garibaldian general, Oreste Baratieri, confusing courage and brashness, led his troops into the Battle of Adowa. When the smoke cleared on March 1, 1896, some 6,000 Italians lay dead on the field.

The defeat stunned Italy. It marked the dead end of the series of misadventures—not only financial and colonial, but matrimonial as well (the passionate patriot was a bigamist)—that forced the Prime Minister to step down.

It was an oblique victory for the Extreme Left and the Socialists; there would probably have been no victory at all had Crispi won his

African gamble. The Prime Minister's fall was not the outcome of domestic issues, the way he handled the Sicilian revolt or dealt with the Extreme Left and the Socialists. Ethiopian tribesmen and an ostensible national preference for monogamy had far more to do with his loss of support than any action of his political opponents. The Extreme Left had as little to say in Parliament after Crispi's downfall as before, and Parliament's new concessions to reform were confined to granting amnesties to those involved in the Sicilian uprising, initiating a small degree of land reform in Sicily, and choosing once more a less authoritarian prime minister, Crispi's old enemy, di Rudinì. The Sicilian marchese, it was hoped, might be the man to rebuild the Liberals' national popularity.

But it soon became clear that di Rudinì did not even have the support of his own party. The Extreme Left attacked him for the slow pace of his reforms, and conservative Liberals attacked him for his speed. Meanwhile, peasants' and workers' protests and uprisings, particularly in central Italy, were again on the rise. To the nonpolitical, it seemed that Parliament understood only the language of protests and demonstrations, and it had to be made clear that the peasant-worker uprisings demanded more than the fall of Crispi and the accession of a more moderate prime minister.

In the aftermath of the Sicilian revolt and the defeat of Crispi, then, the opponents of the Liberals, the Extreme Left and the Socialists, faced a problem: Both stood to gain by the mounting unrest, but they obviously had to emphasize the fact that they did not instigate violence, that their own quarrel was not with the state but with bad government. Socialist leaders in particular had to protest vigorously. They did their utmost to make it clear that their Marx was not the revolutionary Marx feared by Crispi, even to the point of leading him to make oblique approaches to the Vatican for a possible alliance in defense of God and country. But for many Italians, the distinctions between the Marx of the barricades and the Paris Commune and the moderate Marx espoused by Italian Socialists were negligible. In the 1890's, therefore, the Socialist Party's pressing need was to convince Italians of the relative innocuousness of their Marxism.

In the nineties, however, neither the Liberals with their theoretical vagueness nor the Catholics with their official policy of nonparticipation in national politics and their *vorrei e non vorrei* stance, were in a position to smile at the difficulties faced by the Socialists. The Italian political structure of that decade was a large glass house. It ill behooved any group in it to look condescendingly on the efforts of others to work out a firm theoretical basis for a party. The construction of a strong party was a work to which sooner or later all rival parties would have to apply themselves. To ignore that requirement was simply to ensure a future of a bankrupt trasformismo. For it was already clear by the mid-1890's, even to those very much in the rear of the avant-garde, that trasformismo was rapidly exhausting its possibilities. At the turn of the century the need for solid theoretical foundations of political parties was not to be denied. That need was imparting a new shape to old politics.

II

TURATI AND THE TRUE MARXISM
OF ANTONIO LABRIOLA

A surprising number of publications in the Italy of the 1890's dealt with the problems of Marxist theory and practice. None had the popularity and prestige of Filippo Turati's socialist periodical, *Critica Sociale* (*Social Criticism*). It dealt with Italian social-economic problems and discussed Socialist theory. Its tone was particularly felicitous. Sufficiently unacademic to interest the general reader with no taste for sustained abstraction, it displayed just the proper amount of interest in the speculative side of politics to set it several notches above any other Socialist journal. The *Critica Sociale* was a well-balanced publication; in this respect, as in others, it very much reflected the spirit of its founder-editor, a jovial, urbane militant Marxist.

Son of a middle-class Lombard family, Turati had, as a young man, like many of his generation, confused romantic sensibility and poetry, and endowed that confusion with rhyme and meter. Soon enough, however, he realized that poetry was not his vocation and, very sensitive to the currents of the time, began to evince a sustained and perceptive interest in social questions—in particular, problems of penology and criminology. It was only a short step from this to political journalism, from which he progressed to Marxist political journalism, a leading role in the Socialist Party, and the beginnings of a career in Parliament that was to last for some thirty-five years.

Had it not been for his encounter with Anna Kuliscioff, a fascinating Russian emigrée who had been exiled during her university days for nihilistic convictions, Turati would in all probability have remained what he was at heart: a sentimental, humanitarian Socialist. Even after his political conversion, he was more preoccupied with alleviating the sufferings of the poor and the unrepresented than in elaborating the doctrinal foundations of the Socialist Party, and more appreciative of the advantages of Marxism as a unifying social theory than as a total all-embracing truth. In the last analysis, Turati was at best only a Marxist of sorts. Yet his meeting with Anna Kuliscioff (who had converted the Anarchist, Andrea Costa, to Marxism while sharing a ménage with him in Paris) did somewhat complicate his socialistic development. It was not long before he shared Anna's Marxism as well as her affections. His journal, formerly *Cuore e Critica* (*Heart and Criticism*), became the more "objective," "factual" *Critica Sociale*. With good reason, this liaison with Anna, which lasted until her death in 1925, has become a standard example of an authentic Socialist marriage.

As a "scientific" Socialist, Turati did not lose much time in finding the Marxist he most admired—not Kautsky or Bernstein, the official heirs of Marxist tradition, but significantly, the French Socialist and politician, Jean Léon Jaurès. Turati, oriented toward French rather than German culture, responded to the sweeping nineteenth-century gestures of the French Socialist leader, his robust humanitarianism, the overt pragmatism with which he unhesitatingly made any necessary adjustments in the body of Marxist doctrine. Indeed, Turati thought of himself very much in terms of an Italian Jaurès; the opponents who charged him with being a cross between Victor Hugo and Jaurès were not altogether wrong.

There was no room in Turati's humanitarian Marxism for the viciousness of the polemics of Marx himself and his successors and disciples in France and Germany. The *Critica Sociale* opened its columns wide to polemics, but kept them within limits. Though Turati occasionally had misgivings as to the results of such freedom of discussion, at no point did he abandon the policy. He believed that it was the one way to show interested Italians that Marxism was not conspiratorial, tyrannical, or afraid of discussion, and that this justified the risks.

This open airing of Marxist polemics was no doubt a great gesture of intellectual independence. It gave Italian socialism tone. But it did not do away with one stubborn, obtrusive difficulty: Marx's whole critique was concerned principally with industrial economies, economies that had already entered the capitalist orbit, and in the 1890's, as in the 1860's, Italy was indisputably a predominantly agricultural economy, with only the barest beginnings of industrialization. Such an economy, as Stefano Jacini, an extremely perceptive student of the country's rural problems, wrote,

> presented such a variety of facets that far from constituting an economic unity it reflected within it, as no other country in Europe, a most disparate rural economy, with a range such as that one might find from Edinburgh to Stockholm to Smyrna to Cadiz. There were the extensive medieval *latifondi*, cultivated with the most primitive as well as the most modern tools, and small-scale cultivations, also equally varied, ranging in value from five to two thousand *lire* a hectar; there were peasants who owned their small pieces of land and *braccianti*, farm laborers hired on a day to day basis; there were workers who were moderately well-off and others whose life was a bare survival.

Of the three zones of Italy, the central zone—the valley of the Po and the flatlands of Emilia-Romagna—was the richest and most fertile. The South, in spite of the then-prevalent myth of its inexhaustible fertility, was the poorest. It was also the region with the greatest number of surplus laborers, and more than any other part of Italy, had been crippled in the late 1880's by Crispi's unrelenting anti-French foreign policy. The French had been importing extraordinary quantities of grapes from southern Italy because of the ravages of a vine disease in France. To meet the heightened demands, southern growers had wherever possible taken over lands previously used for other crops and concentrated on vine-growing. The closing of the French market to southern Italian grape producers, therefore, had a catastrophic effect on the region's economy.

Contemporary students of Italy's agricultural economy at the end of the nineteenth century have contended that the general situation was not quite as bad as Jacini made it out to be, and that, all things considered, the economy of central and northern Italy was neither better nor worse than that of other European countries. That may be. The fact remains, however, that it was the injustices of Italy's agricultural system that gave rise to the Italian Socialist Party, and it was the agricultural sector of the economy that provided that party with its core following. Nevertheless, southern Italy, where the plight of the peasants was most desperate, had only islands of socialist activity, principally in Sicily. The first Socialist Congresses were quite properly held in Emilia, and quite understandably the great concern of the Socialist Costa was the establishment of cooperatives to break the economic hold of the large landowners on the peasants and *braccianti* (day laborers).

If the agricultural economy was wobbly, industrial Italy was hardly more sturdy. A census taken in 1861 showed that out of 25 million inhabitants some three million were employed in manufacturing; among these, women outnumbered men. The most important industry was silk—Italy produced twice as much as France, its nearest European competitor—but it was mostly piecework turned out by women at home. Industries organized along more modern lines, the mechanical industries, for example, were few in number and small in size. The Breda ironworks, heavily subsidized by the government, was the largest industrial complex in the country. There was no chemical industry to speak of, and Lombardy, Venetia and Piedmont, which are the industrial heartland of modern Italy, were still for all practical purposes undeveloped. In all respects, twenty years after the formation of the Italian nation, products "made in Italy" were still largely produced by artisans.

In the 1890's, therefore, Italian Marxist-Socialists were still awaiting the capitalistic phase in Italy's economic development. That is to say in those years the Socialist Party was faced with the problems of interim politics and interim ethics. It was difficult enough to maintain that, on the one hand, Socialists were and would remain law-abiding, and on the other, that the parties of the bourgeoisie and that of the proletariat were irreconcilable; but it was even more difficult for Socialists to decide among themselves which policies they should approve and fight in Parliament. It was not altogether clear on what grounds they were to sanction or condemn measures leading to industrialization. For example, should they support an austerity program that put national solvency above all other goals, one that, in providing the basis for capitalism (primarily through the establishment of a national railroad network), made the greatest demands on those who could least afford it, the southern peasantry and small landowners? Or should they make agricultural reform their primary objective, and consider progress toward capitalism secondary? A Marxist party, in the abstract, assumes the existence of an industrial proletariat. Had such a class existed in the Italy of the 1890's, a great many perplexing problems would no doubt have been eliminated.

Yet Turati, leader of the Socialists in Parliament, did not let the insolubility of the actual situation overwhelm him; he acted with as much coherence as was possible under the circumstances. To begin with, he temporized. At the time of the Sicilian revolt of 1894 Turati and the deputies of the Extreme Left denounced the government for its indifference to the plight of the peasants, for the working conditions in the sulphur mines, and for its collusion with the great landowners. But Turati's indignation was tempered with caution: Marxism did not incite to revolt. It was not Marxist insurrectionary preachings, but the intolerable oppression of the feudal lords that had triggered the Sicilian outbreak. He expressed solidarity with the peasants, and went no further. The main work of the *Critica Sociale* editor, after all, was in Milan, the commercial capital of Italy, pushing ahead the cause of labor unions, and in Rome, organizing a Socialist pressure group in Parliament to promote prolabor legislation (minimum wage, maximum hours, workmen's compensation, etc.), and above all, to work for the enlargement of the electorate, the fastest means by which to increase Socialist power in Parliament. In effect, Turati's attitude toward the government policy that distinctly favored the North at the expense of the South (for it was obvious even then that, for many reasons, industrialization would be centered in northwest Italy) was one of thinly veiled approval. He did not mean to stand by and ignore the plight of the peasants, but he had no real quarrel with the policy favoring the North, so long as decent concessions were made to labor.

On only one point, the question of colonial expansion, did Turati take an unswerving stand: No matter how long and arduous Italy's road to capitalism might be, no matter how badly its political leaders wanted it to catch up with other European powers, there could be no justification for a colonial war. A country which had had Mazzini as a teacher, had heard his pleas for the self-determination of peoples, could have nothing to do with colonial wars; indeed, such a country ought to have little to do with militarism of any kind. Aside from this exception, however, Turati's attitude toward the measures taken by the Liberals to prepare Italy for industrialization was one of cautious, implicit approval.

In all justice to Turati, the Socialist leader did not feel that he could do much one way or the other about the means taken to achieve industrialization. Socialists were numerically insignificant in Parliament, and there was so much they had to do to strengthen their position that they could not afford to get bogged down in the complexities of such a difficult undertaking. They had managed to break all official ties with the Anarchists, but there were still many within the party with an anarchist mentality, and socialism's first and foremost need was to win those people over, to persuade them that no greater harm could be done to the cause than to talk constantly of the imminent collapse of the capitalist structure, and the heroic days of the Paris Commune. No one knew, Turati argued, the hour when capitalism, undermined by its inherent contradictions, would fall of its own weight, but that final moment, when it did come, would not be hastened by insurrection and violence. For Turati, the Marxist dictum that capitalism would not collapse until it had exhausted all its means was the last word. He embellished the concept and stamped it with his own sensibility when he warned that only at that moment of collapse, "the moment when the bud, come to its full growth, would burst forth," would a last thrust, a decisive moment of "violence," be proper. There was nothing to indicate that that moment was imminent, but a great deal to point to what Italian Socialists could do to hasten it. Socialists had to educate the masses politically. They had to learn party discipline and present a united front in Parliament, rather than represent provincial interests. Above all, Socialist leadership had to remain united.

In this basic stand, Turati could count on the steady aid of two of his closest friends and collaborators on the *Critica Sociale*, Claudio Treves and Leonida Bissolati. Treves, loyal to Turati to the end in all the parliamentary battles and the later battles fought in exile, added no *esprit de finesse* to Turati's cause, but he was steady and indefatigable. Heavy-handed in polemics, characteristically nineteenth-century in his cult of the natural sciences, Treves' general outlook was more Masonic than Marxist, but in all matters of Marxist theory he willingly deferred to Turati; for him, the chief's enemies were his enemies.

The older Bissolati (he was then in his forties), as moderate as Turati in his Marxist socialism, was of another calibre and temperament. Brought up by a mother who translated Bakunin's *God and the State* into Italian and a father who wrote an account of why he had put aside clerical garb, he was far more complicated than Treves, and was both Marxist and Mazzinian. (In 1895, for example, he refused to take his place in Parliament because of his doubts as to whether he had actually received a majority in a hotly contested election.) As the editor of the Socialist organ *Avanti!* when it moved to Rome—"the lair of the enemy," Bissolati wrote, "the better to spy him out"—he had, as rarely among Italian Marxists, absorbed himself in problems of foreign policy. For him, the Mazzinian principle of self-determination was a yardstick of political morality. In line with this conviction, in 1897 he had called for Italian Socialist volunteers to fight for the independence of Greek nationals revolting against the Turks in Crete.

Of the other contributors to Turati's *Critica Sociale*, the most distinguished perhaps was the economist and sociologist Achille Loria, whose economic theories were as acceptable to moderate Marxists as to enlightened Liberals. Loria stood apart from the rest of the group, but in general he too gave the weight of his authority to Turati's moderate views.

But not all Socialists were willing to follow Turati's lead. The editor of the *Critica Sociale* was not fighting men of straw when he insisted that the first task of the party was to convince all its followers of the self-defeating quality of revolutionary Marxism. From the very beginning, Turati's moderatism met with strong opposition. There was as an example the brilliantly demagogic Enrico Ferri, who was as skilled in political rhetoric as he was in criminology, the field in which as a young man he already acquired an international reputation. A tireless advocate of insurrectionary Marxism, Ferri had a loyal following among small groups in the party; and these groups were among the elements that constantly threatened, even at so early a date, to unseat Turati and take over leadership of the party.

At first glance, in this skirmishing among Marxist theorists and leaders, Turati seemed to have the wholehearted support of Antonio Labriola, a brilliant, sardonic professor of philosophy at the University of Rome, acknowledged by the *cognoscenti* as the country's foremost Marxist theorist. Labriola abhorred the Anarchists, and had been of substantial aid to Turati in expelling them from the party at the Socialist Congress of 1892. He had no use for peasant insurrections and, with Turati, constantly repeated that Socialists had to remember and take into account the fact that Italy had a long way to go before joining the ranks of capitalist economies. In the interim, Labriola agreed with Turati, peasant or anarchist revolts only gave the state and the bourgeoisie further pretexts for crushing every form of Socialist action.

The agreement between Labriola and Turati thus seemed substantial. It was, however, tissue thin; both men concurred that if socialism was to be anything at all in Italy, it had to be Marxist, but having gotten that far, they disagreed more or less publicly (Labriola never contributed to the *Critica Sociale*), on nearly everything else. Differences in temperament accounted in part for the acid tone of the relations between the sarcastic academician and the benignly ironic journalist-politician. No doubt Labriola's utter lack of political gifts (his most notable political achievement was the organization of the first May Day parade in Rome in 1892) strained relations.

But the core dissent was something deeper than temperamental differences or the tensions that usually exist between men of action and men of thought. They did not see eye to eye on the basic meaning of Marx's analysis; they did not look at the problem of Socialist action or the problem of the South in the same way; and the clash between them was in every way as important, and its implications as lasting, as that between Turati and the revolutionary Marxists. At issue was the very idea of a Marxist party and of Marxism itself, and the difference allowed of no compromise.

Labriola's way to Marxism in no way resembled that of Turati. There had been no vague humanitarianism or bad romantic poetry in Labriola's youth, no overwhelming concern for the exploited and those who hunger and thirst after justice. As a young man, he was drawn to philosophy and studied at the University of Naples, an anachronistic citadel of Hegelianism. Soon thereafter, though, like many of his generation in Italy and throughout Europe, he lost all faith in the dialectical idealism of Hegel, and indeed in metaphysics of any kind. He did not lose faith, however, in the primacy of German culture; for some time, he became the advocate of the ethics (not the metaphysics) of Johann Friedrich Herbart, a minor German philosopher of the early nineteenth centry. Labriola felt Herbart's ethical system was the only one that did justice to the moral exigencies of man without relying on any metaphysical system. But gradually the problem of personal ethics became less and less important to him, and his interest shifted to the study of society and suprapersonal forces. By the 1880's he had concluded that the only proper task of philosophy was to put order into the theory of suprapersonal forces, the influences that, he was sure, directed history.

Concern for a philosophy of history, then, was one of the main routes that led Labriola to Marxism; but that concern, like his early philosophical interests, had a double bottom. From his precocious youth to the year in which he committed himself fully to Marxism, Labriola had a passion for politics—and shared with his mentor, the neo-Hegelian Bertrando Spaventa, and Silvio Spaventa, his brother, the former Minister of Justice, a vitriolic hatred for what he considered the betrayal of the ideals of the Risorgimento by virtually all political men of his time. Italy was to be a powerful modern state that made no concessions to petty regional interests, that did away with the bickering of self-seeking political groups, and dealt firmly with the Vatican and believers. In a word, it was to be a truly unified Italy. But the government of the Right fell, largely because of Spaventa's plan to nationalize the railroads, and its defeat in 1876 and the subsequent rule of Depretis and of Crispi had blackened Labriola's spleen. His feelings became still more intense when the Right acquiesced and joined Depretis and Crispi in trasformismo.

All principles, it appeared to Labriola, had left politics. In desperation he joined the Radical Party, which was based on a vague humanitarianism that he abhorred, the doctrine of the rights of man. It was foreseeable that he could not long remain in such a party, and that having left it, he could espouse no socialism but Marxist socialism. When Labriola came to Marxism after his long, progressive political disillusionment, therefore, he came to it with the same sense of discovery and elation he had experienced in abandoning all metaphysics and concluding that in life and history, the only forces that mattered were suprapersonal forces. To him, Marxism represented the parallel development in politics and philosophy, and equally important, a means of legitimatizing old deterministic leanings he had

had to abandon (his youthful ideal in philosophy had been Spinoza), but which had never ceased to attract him. Finally, Labriola felt that in Marx, he had found a tough, austere thinker who at no point yielded to the temptation to denounce and attack what *was* in the name of what should be. This was a lesson that Italian Socialists, and indeed all Italians, had to learn. Marx believed that society was ultimately a question of class conflict, and that class conflict was something not to be condemned but to be accepted as iron necessity. Italians had expected too much from the programs of the Risorgimento, and that was why, so argued Labriola, there was so much that was absurd, incoherent and exasperatingly anomalous in post-Risorgimento Italy, which

> has recently acquired all the inconveniences of parliamentarianism, militarism and a new style of finance but which at the same time lacks the fullness of modern production and the attendant possibility of free competition. Prevented from competing with more advanced industrial countries by lack of coal, scarcity of iron, and deficiencies in technology, Italy flatters herself that electricity will give her the means to make up for lost time. . . . A modern state in an almost exclusively agricultural society, and in large part an old-style agricultural society: this situation explains the prevalent restlessness, the feeling of the incongruity of it all. This is the root of the incoherence and the inconsistencies of parties, the facile oscillations from demagoguery to dictatorship, the endless swarms of political parasites, project planners, dream-makers, idea men.

The same point could have been made by Turati; but just as the two men disagreed even when agreeing on fundamental tenets, so they drew utterly divergent conclusions from the same premises. Turati saw that Italy was nowhere near even the beginning of a capitalistic phase. But that knowledge did not exasperate him; he knew how to bide his time, and although he did not always know how the party should behave with respect to the way industrialization was proceeding, he proposed some sensible pragmatic approaches. Labriola, by contrast, never quite learned how to transmute the implications of his theoretical Marxism into practical counsel. As basically uncertain as Turati on Socialist policy toward industrialization, he ran into a maze of difficulties that only illustrated that Marxism had accentuated rather than diminished his utter lack of gifts as a political man. (They also revealed the gigantic rationalization involved in his writing to Engels of his decision to withdraw from practical politics because the times were not right, Italy was not right, and the Italian Socialist Party was not right.)

Although Labriola agreed with Turati that Socialists should act in Parliament and not in the piazzas, he qualified his agreement with a number of caveats. As capitalism grew stronger, he pointed out, it became of necessity more brutal and immoral. Italian Socialists were wasting time in their constant prattle of the "rights of man" and the "rights of workers." Capitalism was not an ethical system. It was, Labriola contended, the inevitable result of massive impersonal forces oblivious to so-called rights; and Italian Socialists ought not make much of or be bridled by the piddling concessions of a terrified bourgeoisie. In a word, Italian Socialists in Parliament should not be drawn into the trap of seeking a reform of the existing system. Socialists in other, more advanced countries, including Germany and England, had fallen into that trap, and the result had been a contamination, a nonsense of "social democracy," of Lassallean appetites, a serious retardation of the proletariat's acquisition of power. Italian Socialists, Labriola felt, had to be on perpetual guard against this sort of petty bribery.

Similarly, Italian Socialists had to take care not to make too much of the Sicilian revolt, which had been hailed by Karl Johann Kautsky, the German Marxist, as the great Socialist event of the year. Obviously, Labriola argued, the problems of the Italian peasantry mattered to the Marxist party. But they were not central and ought not to become so. It was enough that the peasants be neutralized. "Until the peasants are won over," Labriola wrote, "we will always be weighed down by the burden of that peasant idiocy which, precisely because it is idiocy, causes or renews the 18 brumaire and December 2." The Socialist Party was still to be the party of the industrial proletariat, and as such, should have no objections to whatever measures the state took to hasten the advent of capitalism. If an impoverished Italy suffering from a scarcity of raw materials sought to compensate for its poverty through colonial expansion, Socialists should withhold condemnation. Such expansionism had marked the rise of capitalism in other countries, and Italian Socialists would therefore be inconsistent to protest such a policy on the grounds of self-determination and pacifism. A capitalistic Italy would be a great power among other great powers, making its way to the necessary ultimate triumph of the proletariat, which would be the final fulfillment of the dreams of the heroic Risorgimento bourgeoisie.

The sweep of this vision and the arguments of Labriola left their traces on Italian intellectual history and on the history of Italian parties. But in practical terms, Labriola's uncertainty and hesitation as to the extent to which the Socialist Party should dedicate itself to winning humane social legislation for workers, and his fear of falling into social democracy virtually nullified any possible influence he might have had among moderate party leaders and their followers. Similarly, his shame at the role played by the Socialists in the Sicilian uprising, and his desire to dissociate the party from any similar occurence in the future left him without influence on those Socialists eager to alleviate the plight of the peasants. His defense of colonialism shut off the possibility of a following, especially after the disaster of Adowa. The charge that colonialism was a governmental ruse for distracting attention from domestic issues was much more popular and plausible than Labriola's view that expansionism would hasten the advent of capitalism. But perhaps what most decisively destroyed Labriola's chances of directly influencing the Socialists of his day, or at least restricted his influence to the Marxist revolutionaries he professed to despise, was his conviction that the greatest danger confronting Socialists was ultimately that of trasformismo—that through collaboration with bourgeois parties, Socialism would eventually become indistinguishable from them. He repeatedly warned his listeners at the Caffè Aragno in Rome, his favorite informal lecturing place, that Marxism was not, as Turati, a sheep in wolf's clothing, seemed to believe, a quarry from which everyone dug and took home what he liked. Nor was it merely a theory of history. History itself *was* Marxist; that is, it unfolded along the lines discovered by Marx. The party of the proletariat was not a party like any other, but the germ cell of the society of the future. Labriola was bitterly certain, therefore, that ultimately the party would triumph, regardless of the blunders of its leaders.

Despite his firm faith in the eventual ascendancy of the proletariat, however, Labriola was aware that the party could not entirely dispense with the contribution of the intellectuals, even those of bourgeois origins. In 1895, therefore, he published his *Essay on Historical Materialism*, not as a speculative contribution, for his fervor precluded such disinterestedness, but as a weapon for the intellectual aspect of the class struggle. The work is a landmark in the history of Italian socialism. It was the first noteworthy Italian treatment of Marxism and its implications for the country, and the specific problems that the West and Italy were to deal with before the classless society could be achieved.

Economic determinism, he began, does not provide an automatic explanation of every historical phenomenon.

> The economic substructure which determines all the rest is not a simple mechanism out of which institutions, laws, customs, thoughts, feelings and ideologies jump as immediate, mechanical, automatic consequences. From that substratum to all the rest, the derivative process is quite complicated, subtle and tortuous, and not always decipherable.

Marxist historians, therefore, no less than those of any other school, are limited by the tools of historical research—examination of sources, verification of witnesses, approved procedures in collecting and classifying historical materials. Where such documentation is inadequate, the Marxist historian can claim no fuller understanding than any other. Given sufficient information from other sources, however, the doctrine of economic determinism provides the Marxist historian with an additional tool—insight into the ultimate economic causes of historical events. He contended further that history cannot be understood in the light of any single factor, and that no line of investigation, no matter how abstract, is utterly unrelated to other lines of investigation and, in a broader sense, to the structure of the society in which the investigation takes place. There is a reciprocal influence between economic factors and other factors.

In actuality, however, Labriola's defense of conventional historical research did not amount to much. Those historical problems which he conceded were impermeable to the light of economic determinism were invariably insignificant ones. It did not matter very much, for instance, that the ultimate economic source of a Mosaic precept in the Old Testament was unascertainable, since economic determinism has passed definitive judgment on all religions, including that of the Old Testament. Labriola's concessions, therefore, in no way tempered the dogmatism that even today tends to limit the Marxist historian.

With respect to philosophy, Labriola's concessions were no more substantial, and in literature he followed even more slavishly the typical Marxist appraisal of those years. Though amused by naïve Marxists who sought to interpret the *Divine Comedy* through an analysis of the finances of the Florentine wool merchants of Dante's day, Labriola's approach was not much less crude; there is nothing to indicate that in the last analysis his own appraisal of Dante differed substantially from that of the most perceptive Italian Communist theoretician after the Russian Revolution, Antonio Gramsci, for whom the great poet was *"un gran vinto di classe"* (a great man crushed by the class conflict).

All things considered, it was not hard to see why Labriola's economic determinism was so pedestrianly Marxist, why he had lost all real interest in metaphysics and in those experiences that pointed to a dimension in man that eludes deterministic classification. Labriola *had* his poetry, metaphysics and religion—the drama of class conflict and the eventual emergence of the proletariat; he found all other religions superfluous or inadequate.

But Labriola was more drawn to the implications of Marxist analysis for Italy than to the speculative discussion of Marxism. In his discussion of the French Revolution at the end of the essay, he singled it out as a superb illustration of the resistance and dangers that the Italian Marxist party would encounter, and the pitfalls to be avoided in meeting the demands of the long struggle ahead. For those who were conversant with the differences between Turati and Labriola, and who could thus read between the lines, the applicability of his conclusions was instantly recognizable.

The conservative Thermidorean reaction provoked by the Terror demonstrated the inevitability of failure for any revolution that seeks to surpass the limits imposed on it by the social-economic structure of the times. Thermidors would continue throughout Europe; the massive interests of capitalism would not be overcome by occasional revolts. Italian Socialists, therefore, had to keep in mind that indignation could spark revolt, but could not sustain a new order.

The Revolution also illustrated the dangers of that bourgeois ideology that infected even the proletariat: the ideology of human rights, the social contract, the abstract, unhistorical notion of human nature. As an ideology to be used against the old regime, those doctrines had been of some use; but in the emerging Socialist order they were superfluous, and even did substantial harm. Italian Socialists did not sufficiently recognize, as Marx had, that the theory of the ethical state, for example, was but an insidious bourgeois rationalization to perpetuate its power. Its latest variants, social democracy and state socialism, were, if anything, even more dangerous.

Finally, in terms reminiscent of Marx in the *Communist Manifesto*, Labriola once more expressed his ambivalent attitude toward the role of intellectuals in the establishment of the classless society. He very much wanted to win over the intellectuals of a new generation, but he was equally anxious that they should recognize the primacy of the rights of the class conflict over any purely intellectual pursuits. Not to recognize this supremacy was to fail to understand history, ethics and progress, for true progress was only that which hastened the advent of the classless society, and true ethics those that furthered the cause of the proletariat in the struggle with the bourgeoisie. Progress was not, as the eighteenth and nineteenth centuries believed, exclusively scientific and moral, nor was it automatic and irreversible. Thus, even a pre-Marxist or non-Marxist ethic conceived in undoubted good faith retarded progress, for its inevitable political naïveté made it susceptible to exploitation by the bourgeoisie, which would defend itself to the last. In the classless society of the future, ethics would no doubt acquire other and new dimensions; but in the meantime, there was but one course for the moral intellectual: to place his gifts at the disposal of the proletariat.

Labriola hoped to clarify the limitations of the intellectual contribution to the ultimate Marxist mission. He was aware that Marxist proselytism exposed the most well-meaning Socialist to a kind of transcendent irony. During the class conflict, ideas seemed more important than they really were, and the Marxist himself contributed to that illusion.

This ambivalence toward the intellectual, which was perhaps at the heart of his reluctance to put his reflections down in writing, never quite left Labriola. No doubt he would have preferred to be writing, not for intellectuals, but for men with an active vocation for politics. It would have delighted him to know that the day would come when the nineteen-year-old Trotsky, while serving out a political jail sentence, would read his work and admiringly go over its principal points, repeating them to himself again and again. In Italy, though, Labriola did not see or soon expect a Marxist *condottiere* or a Marxist party that would embody his vision. He lived thus in Marxist expectation, as did Turati. In the small area of that common faith, both men sought to make the best of their uneasy alliance and bide their time. Each was convinced that in those evil times, intellectuals drawn to socialism had everything to gain by listening to his voice rather than that of his opponent.

III

LABRIOLA AND THE DEVIATIONIST
MARXISM OF CROCE AND SOREL

It is altogether understandable that in their contrasting versions of
Marxism, Labriola and not Turati was the successful proselytizer,
the one who had something to say to those for whom politics
needed a certain dimension and breadth. Indeed, Labriola's view of
Marxism left its mark on many who ultimately played important
roles in Italian politics—Angelica Balabanoff, for one, a Russian
emigrée. Not as elusively intense and feminine as Anna Kuliscioff,
perhaps, but just as forceful, Angelica was to leave her mark on the
party and on Benito Mussolini, to whom she was very close. Another was Don Romolo Murri, who later organized a Catholic political movement of the Left. Labriola's most immediate and lasting
influence, however, was on men of a philosophical bent, like himself,
interested but not active in politics. Perhaps the two most important
men of this type whom Labriola led to Marxism were the Frenchman, Georges Sorel, and the Neapolitan, Benedetto Croce.

The waspish Georges Sorel, a self-taught, retired engineer fasci-
nated by politics and religion, was a recent convert to Marxism
when he became acquainted with Labriola. As editor of the short-
lived Marxist review *Devenir Social*, to which Labriola contributed,
Sorel was instrumental in having Labriola's commentary on the
Manifesto appear in a French translation. Sorel was as outraged at
the state of France as Labriola was with that of Italy, and like
Labriola, he was prone to employ austere slander and passionate
rebuttal in dealing with opponents. The times were infamous and
decadent, he declared, particularly in France. As late as 1889, he had

believed that conservative principles could save France, but in the
ensuing five years, he concluded that a decadent democracy and a
corrupt Parliament had brought France to its lowest point, and that
only a Marxist party could summon the moral strength and vigor
to revive it.

For Sorel, Marxism was a great "religious" force, a movement
that unmasked the rationalizations of the corrupt bourgeoisie, the
cult of the natural sciences, the idea of perfectible human nature,
the myth of progress. Indeed, he contended, Marxism was the only
political philosophy that could give the modern world an example of
the indispensable moral virtue without which the state could only
succumb to those plutocratic demagogic forces that used politics to
further their own interests. Marxism, he felt, recognized the tragic
dimension of life, the necessity of sacrifice and intransigent action,
of not coming to terms or compromising in the name of expediency
as so many political reformers and parties had done. Finally, Marxism exposed the total inadequacy of political theories based on the
eighteenth-century notion of reason; it grasped the ultimate irrational sources of all sublime moral action. In one of his early works,
The Trial of Socrates, he had defended the Athenians who condemned Socrates, on the grounds that there were deeper values in
life than abstract reason; he viewed the political necessities of his
own time from a similar standpoint. Like many sophisticated intellectuals, Sorel was keenly conscious of the meretricious aspect of
reason, its pliability; Marxism, as he understood it in Labriola,
brought scale and dimension back into the political struggle. It was
the creed of the strong young barbarian whose views of the world
were rooted in something deeper than reason.

In 1895, Sorel was ten years away from his celebrated doctrine of
revolutionary syndicalism, which substituted the idea of uncor-
rupted and incorruptible Marxist labor unions for that of a Marxist
party. He had not yet definitively worked out the theory of myth as
that irrational force and enthusiasm that alone can move men to
revolutionary political change, and which is judged not by any
standard outside of itself, but only in terms of success or lack of it.
The notion of the general strike, the weapon that could paralyze
bourgeois society and bring it to its knees, was still a nebulous thing.
Yet most of the elements of what was to receive polished form in
the *Réflexions sur la violence* of 1906 were already there germinally
in Sorel's thought at the turn of the century. The radical mistrust of

the give-and-take of any form of parliamentary democracy was all-pervasive, and so was the persuasion of the inevitability of corruption of parties that tolerated a parliamentary regime. From the very beginning, consequently, for all of his philosophical sophistication, there was in Sorel an anarchist-insurrectionist streak that won him a following not only in France, but even more, perhaps, in Italian Marxist circles. There the insurrectionary Marxists that gravitated to Ferri—and especially the young Neapolitan Arturo Labriola (no relative of Antonio Labriola, but repeatedly confused with him)—found in Sorel the voice they had been waiting for, the theorist who could vie with Turati or Antonio Labriola. In the last decade of the nineteenth century, however, the first telling attacks on Antonio Labriola's Marxism did not come from the insurrectionary wing of the party. That development was not to come until some ten years later. From about 1898 to 1904 or so, the sharp cutting critique directed against Labriola and a good part of the basic Marxist tenets came from a most unpolitical young Neapolitan scholar, Benedetto Croce.

In contrast to Sorel, Benedetto Croce's interest in Marxism had no long history of past disillusionments. Born into a family of wealthy landowners in 1867, as a very young man he inherited the conservative convictions of his class, and showed little sympathy for southern Liberals and the ideals of the Risorgimento. But after 1883, when his family was killed in an earthquake at Casamicciola, and he was taken in by his uncle, Silvio Spaventa, the ex-minister of justice and brother of the philosopher, Bertrando, he gradually changed his political orientation. It was in the Spaventa household that he learned to appreciate the ideals of the southern Risorgimento, and it was there that he first met Antonio Labriola, a frequent visitor to the house.

It was Labriola the intellectual and moralist, rather than the political thinker, to whom Croce first responded. For one thing the breadth of his knowledge in many areas provided a welcome change from the almost unrelieved political atmosphere of the Spaventa home. More important, Labriola's austere, Kantian-oriented ethics offered the young Croce the moral stability for which he had been groping. It was because of Labriola, he gratefully wrote in his fifties, that he had been spared from floundering in the shallow ethics of Social Darwinism, utilitarianism or hedonism.

After leaving the Spaventa household, Croce settled in Naples, acquiring in a few years a reputation as a promising young historian of seventeenth-century Neapolitan culture. His gift for restricted erudition in a specific academic area did not stifle his interest in more general questions, however, for in 1895, he wrote an essay on the theory of history, *La storia ridotta sotto il concetto generale dell' arte* (*History-Writing as Art Knowledge*), and one on the theory of literary criticism.

Throughout this period, Croce never lost contact with Labriola, but it was not until 1895 or so that he began to share some of his mentor's interest in Marxism. In that year, he published a number of monographs on the Neapolitan Revolution of 1799, drawing heavily on the *Saggio storica sulla rivoluzione napoletana del 1799* (*Historical Essay on the Neapolitan Revolution of 1799*) of Vincenzo Cuoco, a participant whose explanation of the revolution's failure was written in exile.

In Cuoco's view, the failure was due to the excessively abstract nature of theories of revolution. Not recognizing that the soil in which ideas are to take root is as important as the ideas themselves, the revolutionaries had treated ideas as export items, and had acted as if the social and cultural conditions of eighteenth-century Naples were the same as those of eighteenth-century France. They trusted too much in the ability of ideas such as the equality and goodness of man, the moral superiority of republican virtues and the deep sense of justice of a noble, exploited peasantry, to spark and sustain a revolution. Thus, they misjudged the loyalty of the peasants to the king and created lasting enmity between the *ceto medio*, the progressive middle class in a social rather than economic sense, and the enlightened Bourbon monarchy. This analysis, with its critique of eighteenth-century rationalism, minimizing of ideas and corresponding stress on social structure, class allegiances and the progressive role of the middle class, bore some striking resemblances to Labriola's assertion of the primacy of the social process over ideas. From this point of view, Marx could appear as a logical and coherent developer of the insights of the southern Liberal political philosopher.

Marxism's appeal for Croce, however, was not primarily political, but philosophical. The ideas of Marx on the theory of history even more than on politics were what drew Croce to the German thinker and explain why in the same year, 1895, he published at his own expense Labriola's commentary on the *Communist Manifesto*. The effect of the commentary on him was electrifying. "I felt," he wrote in his recollections, "like someone no longer young, in love for the first time, who studies in himself the mysterious workings of that love." Completely unconcerned with that part of the commentary that was a radical critique of Turatian socialism, Croce, who felt an aristocratic contempt for the political Italy of his day, was mesmerized by the scope of the essay, the arch of Labriola's philosophizing. Never had he come across any such sweeping, over-all historical synthesis or philosophy of history, and he was awed.

Yet his own approach to problems, his detached, cumulative reasoning, extremely mistrustful of the sudden leap in logic, was not the way of Labriola. Quite as fervently as Marx and Labriola, Croce also sought the summit, an all-inclusive view of man and nature; but like a seasoned climber, he moved with the greatest deliberation and, unlike either his mentor or Marx, displayed no impatience to be a man of political action.

The first stand that Croce took on Marxist doctrine was an article for the *Archivio Storico* in 1895 (the year of Labriola's commentary on the *Communist Manifesto*), a review of a number of works on the Renaissance philosopher, Tommaso Campanella (1568-1639). Among the works reviewed was one by the well-known Marxist theoretician, Paul Laforgue, a monograph in the *Geschichte des Sozialismus in Enzeln Darstellungen*, edited by Bernstein and Kautsky, the leading Marxist theorists in Germany. Following Labriola's admonition, Croce applied to Laforgue's work the criteria that were demanded not of Marxist historical writing alone, but of any historical writing. He amassed a small but impressive list of Laforgue's sins of omission and commission: his ignorance of original sources, his breezy, cavalier assumptions with respect to Campanella and the historical scholarship devoted to him. On this level, the review remains to this day one of Croce's better critical demolitions. But Croce did not stop there. He went on to pass judgment on the quality of Laforgue's Marxism, a rather bold move, considering the prestige of Laforgue in French Socialist circles, a reputation based on something more than his marriage to a daughter of Marx. Laforgue, Croce wrote, did not grasp the point of Marx's scientific socialism, and what distinguished it from the preceding utopian socialisms. If he had, he could not have viewed Campanella as one of the great predecessors of Marxist socialism. Without saying so in so many words, Croce argued that not all those who cried out for the abolition of private property or for common ownership, or who led peasant revolts, were precursors of scientific socialism. In effect, his critique said clearly, though he would not at that time have used such terminology, that not all who denounced social injustices made straight the way of Marx.

Croce was not the thinker to let such asides as "the pantheism and transmigration of souls in the Kabala are nothing but the metaphysical expressions of goods and their exchange" go by unnoticed, nor did he allow to pass without comment Laforgue's evaluation of Campanella as the philosopher "who unconsciously expressed in his philosophy the imperious needs of the capitalist bourgeoisie." Laforgue, Croce's review said unequivocally, was not a good historian, Marxist or otherwise, nor was he a good philosopher.

The review did not give a clear idea of the limits, if any, of Croce's acceptance of Marxist doctrine. During the following year, however, Croce undertook an intensive study of economic theory, from Adam Smith to the contemporary pure economists of the Austrian school and their Italian counterparts, Maffeo Pantaleoni and Vilfredo Pareto. He subsequently took a firm, but not wholly unequivocal stand in a long essay, *Sulla forma scientifica del materialismo storico* (*On the Scientific Form of Historical Materialism*), in large part a meditation on Labriola's *Saggio sul materialismo storico*. The peculiar tone of some of Croce's conclusions on Labriola's ideas and a certain embarrassed respect for his teacher's sensibilities explained in part, perhaps, why the essay appeared in Sorel's *Devenir Social* rather than in an Italian journal. In French or in Italian, though, the point of the essay was clear: that Marxist doctrine was not what Labriola seemed to say it was. Whenever a claim appeared preposterous, however, Croce courteously insisted that Labriola could not possibly have meant what he actually said.

The last thing that Marx had in mind—so went Croce's argument —was a philosophy of history that explained all history, present, past, and future. *That* had been the intent of the pretentious sociologists of the late nineteenth century, of social Darwinians and the followers of Comte. Their notion of one single force moving all history, in terms of which history could be plotted and traced, was patently absurd. Marx, who had demonstrated the absurdity of that pretense, could hardly have himself advocated any such notion of a philosophy of history. The point of economic determinism, Croce insisted, was to demonstrate once and for all the failure of all philosophies of history. Marx was aware that history was moved by massive suprapersonal forces, but had no intention of using his analysis of those forces to write the history of the future. He himself had argued that communism might be made superfluous by one of the great technological discoveries that accounted for the deepest historical changes.

As for the interpretation of the past, it was true as Engels had asserted: underneath all great social changes is a principle of continuity, the famous "red string," the economic factor. But that truth must be interpreted judiciously. It does not deny (and Croce wrote that it was his understanding that Labriola agreed with him) that history is an interplay of many factors, and that any given point in history has ineradicably individual traits that make it impossible for it to be considered as a predictable phase.

Marxist doctrine, consequently, was neither a morphology of the future, nor a philosophy of history, and only in a very approximate sense was it a valid interpretation of the past; it was simply a useful analysis of contemporary society. It was not original, but the last of the insights of nineteenth-century thinkers; but originality is not the only test of the value of a doctrine. What made Marxist doctrine so useful was its very sensible quality, the admonition not to lose sight of the economic factor, to realize the influence of economics on culture, in its most diversified aspects. For the student of history with an inadequate appreciation of economics, Marxist doctrine was a lens that suddenly disclosed unsuspected relations and interconnections. Economic determinism, when used with the insights of other disciplines, Croce concluded, was a highly useful tool.

"Other disciplines," for Croce at this particular point, meant principally philosophy; and in discussing the connection between philosophy and economic determinism he was as assertive and as confident as he had been in the preceding discussions. There was room in doctrinal Marxism, he wrote, for the coexistence of economic determinism as an analysis of society, and for philosophy as an analysis of properly philosophical problems. The two were not mutually exclusive. It only added to the confusion and lack of appreciation of the true meaning of economic determinism for Marxists to apply the principles of economic determinism to philosophical problems.

In a similar way, a clarification was called for with respect to Marxist ethics and ethics in general. Just as there was room for a coexistence of Marxist metaphysics and an independent metaphysics, there was room for the class ethics of Marx and ethics as an independent science. Marx was not interested, Croce argued, in determining a demonstrably and metaphysically true ethics. There was nothing, for example, in Marxist thought that contradicted the philosophical superiority of the Kantian-oriented ethics to which Croce himself adhered. Marx was primarily interested in the use of ethics in the class struggle; the notion of the ethical state, for example, which argued the case for the state as the embodiment of social justice, was of interest to him only as a concept to be combatted in the class struggle, rather than in terms of its intrinsic philosophical value. Marx thus uncovered an essential truth that no theory of ethics could ignore: History is determined not by individual ethics but by supraindividual forces, and these forces are indifferent to ethical values. The individual, therefore, must realize his own relative insignificance and the absurdity of demanding that these forces be subject to the same moral laws that determine his own limited sphere of moral action.

There is a delicate problem involved, however, in assessing the importance of individual ethics in relation to the massive forces that direct history. It is true that the individual ought to have no illusions as to his role in history; but it is equally true that there is no point in excessively minimizing the moral ardor of the individual. It was therefore particularly absurd, Croce maintained, for Marxists to make too much of the inevitability of the ultimate triumph of the proletariat as determined by the forces of class conflict; without zeal, without intense moral ardor, the very progress of society toward that final emancipation would be substantially retarded. In this struggle, moral passion was invaluable, and so basic to Marxist thought, that it made for a slight problem at the heart of the Marxist doctrine of value and surplus value. Surplus value—the difference pocketed by the capitalist between a just wage and the wage paid—was a moral rather than economic concept, and expressed Marx's indignation at how little the laborer was paid for his work. This criticism of a concept that was at the heart of, or at least was central to, Marxist economic doctrine and general philosophical theory was Croce's first direct critique of Marx, and his first foray into criticizing Marx in the German thinker's own field of economic theory. It was a sign of how much Labriola's former student had increased in confidence and dialectic skill in the year since the publication of his review of Laforgue's work.

Having made this central point, Croce concentrated on it in his study of the basic concepts of Achille Loria, the contributor to the *Critica Sociale* who so infuriated Labriola that he denounced him to Engels on charges of plagiarizing Marx. (Engels in turn made the accusation in the preface to the third volume of *Das Kapital*.) The discussion of Loria's philosophy contained nothing new. Loria, like Laforgue, was amusingly vulnerable on the philosophic level. Croce had every right to be amused at the economist's dismissal of Kant, who had admired Rousseau and the French Revolution, as a representative of a feudal age, and his assertion that Kantian ethics were inferior to a naïvely utilitarian ethics of "good" altruism and "bad" egoism.

But the discussion of value, though confined to a long footnote, proceeded on a different plane. The Marxist theory of value, Croce argued, did not conflict with, but harmonized with the theory of the pure economists that value was the sum of sacrifices required for the attainment of a good. The harmony of the two theories of value —and Croce stressed the point—did not mean, however, that the pure economists could dismiss the Marxist concept of surplus value. This Marxist notion, which grew out of a comparison of an ideal society, in which work was the exclusive value, with a society in which work was only a part of value, underscored how little work was esteemed in a capitalist society. Surplus value, for Croce, "remained fixed in the side of capitalist society like a barb." There were many ambiguities and problems involved in this theory of value, but there was nothing at all ambiguous in Croce's repeated judgment on economic determinism. He reduced it to such a degree of coexistence with other theories explaining the workings of society that it lost all value. What began as an attack on the eclecticism and inconclusiveness of Loria, consequently, approached in its conclusion a forthright repudiation of basic Marxist tenets.

Labriola, exasperated and baffled, did and did not understand what was happening; but because he was confident of the absolute truth of Marxist doctrine (even Croce, after quartering it, commended it for its robustness), he answered Croce, though indirectly, in letters to Sorel, who at this time was also posing questions tantamount to repudiations of certain Marxist tenets. Those answers eventually appeared in Italian in 1897 as *Discorrendo di socialismo e filosofia* (*On Socialism and Philosophy*).

The difficulties of economic determinism lay not with the doctrine, but with the cultural level of the times. As a preface to the discussion, Labriola conceded that Marxist theory as historiography or philosophy—Marxist culture, in brief—had not as of that time found impressive champions. It had not found them in part because unusually perceptive advocates could not be won over to any political cause or party when they were simply not there. Marxist Socialism, Labriola pointed out, had fallen on evil times with Jaurès in France and Lassalle in Germany; and in times of reaction, as Engels had suggested, publicists and political philosophers as a group tended to be evasive and conformist. The doctrinal Marxism of the day, at any rate, was acknowledgedly inferior to the original. There was no Marxist historian to continue to work in the splendid cosmopolitan tradition of Marx and Engels. French history, for example, a field in which Marx had found confirmation for some of his most brilliant insights, was now left, Labriola bemoaned, to the archconservative Hippolyte Taine, who interpreted that history with arbitrary canons of right and wrong, a sort of *errata-corrige* of history. And even the German Social Democratic Party, which he admired as the best organized and most doctrinally sound Marxist party, had not come out with critical editions of the collected works of Marx and Engels. Small wonder, therefore, that there was as yet no outstanding philosopher capable of matching Marx's work in politics and economics with similar accomplishments in metaphysics. Too much effort had been squandered on the study of the philosophical predecessors of Marx, a search that often betrayed the complete lack of appreciation of the uniqueness of Marx. And yet, Labriola felt, it was also true that the search for these precursors was not a totally unredeemable error: even when studying the period long before the Industrial Revolution, when the fullness of Marxist doctrine was unimaginable, there was a point in seeking to determine which movements in philosophy contributed in their minuscule way to some fundamental aspects of that doctrine that could only come to its full meaning with the Industrial Revolution. Laforgue and the popular Russian theorist G. V. Plekhanov, who argued that the only basis for economic determinism was atheistic monism, appeared to Labriola crude to the point of error in this connection. Making his own personal philosophical journey a yardstick for progress in philosophy, Labriola suggested (inadvertently lapsing into the language of Loria or Laforgue) that in a proper study of the precursors of economic determinism, a better case might be made for Bruno and Spinoza, whose "heroic dialectic monism had characterized an early heroic bourgeoisie." Of all the tendencies in philosophy, the pluralistic and dialectic tendencies of these philosophers were the most fitting prolegomena to Marx. In any case, however, the entire problem of distinguished philosophical antecedents was, in the last analysis, academic. The crucial need was for a very exact, precise idea of the limitations of *all* philosophy, past, present and future, the realization that economic determinism was itself the last and final philosophy. In still more precise terms, the only specific philosophy proper to Marxist doctrine was the philosophy of work, summed up in the Marxist equation of value and work.

Like Croce, Labriola was convinced that the theory of value was the essence of Marxism, from which all Marxist doctrine derived. But Marxist economic theory, like any other part of Marxist doctrine, took as its point of departure the high point of its immediate predecessors, the classical economists, foremost among them, David Ricardo. Consequently, Marx was hardly remiss (as Croce alleged) in having failed to take into account, as did the classical economists, other possible and actual forms of society. Marx examined those economies that his predecessors considered relevant. Having constructed his theory of value as a model based on the factual, historical reality preceding industrial capitalism and the emerging proletariat, Marx then studied the working of this model in a society in which all the conditions of capitalist production were assumed present and operative. In this society, however, capitalism's inner contradictions multiplied as it increased in strength, and effects appeared to bear little relation to causes; but this was inevitable, and in keeping with the dialectic that ruled the historical process. The maximum of confusion, therefore, occurred when naïve economists, unskilled in the ways of dialectic thought, ascribed the contradictions not to the historical process itself, but to Marx and his analysis of capitalism.

The pure economists whom Croce so respected, Labriola stated categorically, were among such naïve theoreticians. They made the mistake that in effect the practitioners of all disciplines make when they ignore the dialectic at the heart of all reality. Believing they are fixing concepts, they hypostatize reality. He himself had made the same mistake, Labriola confessed, when, as a metaphysician, he had long ago considered the will as an entity. The pure economists, too, hypostatized concepts, only their concepts were not the will, but rent, interest and capital. They never realized that these concepts are not fixed entities but dialectic moments. They compounded this defect, moreover, by constructing hypothetical economies with no foundation in history, economies that were arbitrary constructs; from an essentially unrealistic vantage point, they then passed judgment on the most real of all economies, the Marxist economy. Any line of investigation (except the natural sciences, as Labriola had pointed out in the essay on historical materialism) was arrogant nonsense if it pretended to draw conclusions without taking into account the Marxist dialectic. Economics, like any of the social sciences or the humanities, had to understand the essential role that the class conflict played in its development and its conclusions.

But the pure economists' most fatal error, for Labriola, was exemplified in their basic notion of value. The definition of value as the number of sacrifices required to obtain an end made no distinction between necessary ends and merely pleasurable ends. It was hedonism masquerading as scientific objectivity, and to consider the Marxist theory of value as a subdivision of such a neutral theory of value was nothing less than blasphemy. For work, Labriola argued, was anything but a commodity, a "value" that did not distinguish between need and pleasure. Work was the very heart of the dignity of man. Work was an original, noble, creative force enmeshed in a dialectic achieving its own redemption. It was a many-faceted force that bound together all the activities of men and showed the arbitrariness of the distinctions that up to now had separated the natural sciences and philosophy, arts and techniques. With this idea of work, Marx's dictum that "man knew all that he needed to know" attained the cosmic sweep proper to it; and with it eventually all of humanity, not only a privileged part, would enjoy the fruits of labor, for the day would come when that labor would no longer be perverted and used primarily as a weapon in the class conflict.

All things considered, the points in Labriola's reply added little substantially new to the arguments already adduced in his very first tract on Marxism, the essay on the *Communist Manifesto*. Taking into account, however, his limited interest in abstract economics (and for all of his fervid and earnest dedication to the subject late in life, the idea of the primacy of the economic remained only an intensely speculative conviction, economics being for him in effect not a queen science but rather the handmaid of Marxism), he acquitted himself rather well. In at least one of his points, his case against the value concept of pure economics defended by Croce, he expressed the spirit of arguments still used today against the idea of a pure science of economics olympically indifferent to political forms, whether capitalist or socialist.

If his arguments seem excessively abstract, it must be remembered that economics was always primarily philosophy for Labriola, and it would not be very fair to expect to find in his economic determinism any detailed analysis, not even, for example, of the peculiar form that emerging capitalism was assuming in the Italy of his day. Each country, Labriola knew, made its own way to capitalism, but having made this general enunciation, he was content to let the matter rest. When the government decided after the Banca Romana scandal, for example, despite the gravest misgivings of Liberal economists, to base the expansion of industry on a German-inspired and in part German-financed banking structure that invested virtually all of its capital in long-term loans to fledgling industry, Labriola did not comment on the wisdom of this fundamental change. The philosopher never thought of studying closely the peculiarities of the Italian economic situation in which the state, for good reasons and bad (and to a greater extent than in the more industrialized countries of Europe), through state ownership of railroads, heavy government subsidies to key industries such as steel, and substantial tariff protection, took a very active part in preparing the way for capitalism. There was nothing clear in Labriola's feelings on this state of affairs. On the one hand, he had a proper Marxist fear of the state and detested above all state socialism; on the other, he berated Italian progress in industralization as puny, and placed the blame on an irresolute state.

Yet despite fundamental contradictions and the lack of concern for concrete problems which embarrasses pragmatic Italian Marxist economists of our day, Labriola, with the *Discorrendo*, though add-

ing little that was new, did add something to his stature. He offered
Italian Marxists a body of doctrine that would be without equal
until the time of Antonio Gramsci, the most brilliant theoretician
among the founders of the Italian Communist Party in 1921. Labriola has had his readers in Italy from his own time to the 1960's, as
he will have them foreseeably for some time to come: good men
appalled at the low level of Italian politics, its greater concern for
privileged classes than for the poor; honest men despairing that the
state could ever reform deeply or speedily enough to meet the
demands of social justice. To such readers Labriola had and has
something to say, and it would not particularly matter if virtually
none of them could retrace and make his own Labriola's path to
Marxism, his unique blend of moral indignation and admiration for
determinism on a cosmic scale. There would be enough elements in
his Marxism that could be of use for their particular journey. And
even for the more demanding theorizers of contemporary Marxism—
and a lot of water has passed under the Marxist bridge since Labriola's
time—there would be much of value. The admiration for the dialectic of Engels' *Antidühring* has not perceptibly increased in
Italian Marxist circles; the mistrust for metaphysics of any sort has.
The strong antimetaphysical quality of Labriola's thought, consequently, its basic conviction that social justice is the most meaningful goal of man, and its concentration on rationalization rather than
truth (as marked in Italy as elsewhere today) continue to assure him
readers. Italian socialism's tribute to him, the publication of his
opera omnia, has been in progress since 1959.

But moral passion, more or less intelligent, does not exclusively
account for Labriola's continued meaningfulness. For in a peculiar
way, though possibly not quite the way he would have preferred,
history had vindicated him: that concrete political-economic reality,
the primacy of which he asserted, manifested itself in a state born of
revolution some fifty years ago, today's strong Russian Marxist
state. With the October Revolution Labriola's writings acquired
new meaning; and though the conviction that Russia was the embodiment of the Marxist state was easier to defend in the early days
of the Russian Revolution than later, there have been over the years
enough Italians in good faith, and some in bad, utterly convinced of
its truth. Not all that is Marxist, certainly, is completely acceptable
to the Leninist, but there is enough in Labriola to assure him an

honored place among the great precursors, especially since Fascism. In that period as never before Italian Marxists could point to the strictures of Labriola on social democracy and state socialism as Marxist prophecy verified.

Labriola himself never doubted that his day would come, that the voice crying in the wilderness would eventually be heard. When forced to acknowledge a year after the *Discorrendo* that he had persuaded neither Croce nor Sorel, he satisfied himself with adding to a second edition of that work a page or so directed against Sorel's misinterpretation of the theory of value; several pages of rebuttal to Croce, who from his point of view continued to go further and further afield; and a translation of the celebrated passage of the *Antidühring* on the nature of the Marxist dialectic, as meditation for both Croce and Sorel. Labriola understood with as much equanimity as his temperament allowed, that the mission to at least two bourgeois intellectuals had failed. It had failed, he believed to the last, because of Sorel's radical inability to grasp the point of the theory of value, and Croce's to understand the limitations of all non-dialectic thought. Croce's error, Labriola told him repeatedly, lay in believing that we can know more than we actually can. But there were other considerations which entered into his resolution to withdraw from the polemic. The discussion was taking place under peculiar circumstances both in Europe and in Italy proper. In Germany the divisive debates on authentic Marxist teaching between Kautsky and Bernstein were giving increasing scandal, and Labriola did not want to add the piccolo notes of his polemic with Croce and Sorel to that ominous sound. The incongruity, besides, of advanced discussions on Marxist theory in a country which was so far from the capitalism that the Marxist critique presupposed, bordered on the tragi-comic.

Thus, largely to avoid in any way giving aid and comfort to the enemy, from the time of the *Discorrendo* on Labriola virtually withdrew from further Marxist discussion. In the few years that remained to him, he limited himself to an occasional review and to semi-private meditations such as the monograph he left unfinished at his death in 1904—*Da un secolo all' altro (From One Century to the Next)*, a last look at the meaning of Europe and Italy at the turn of the century. Labriola's last look backward sobered him. All through Europe, and especially in France and England, where social democracy sapped proletarian intransigence and strength, he saw nothing but long, continued corruption. Italy was but a small part of this picture; and there, the long indecisiveness (for Labriola, indecisiveness and corruption were synonymous) would continue as long as many felt that the pace of industrialization was too fast, and just as many felt it was too slow. The prospect, for a while, would not be promising.

Among the developments that most preoccupied him was the rising wave of interest in religion and mysticism among intellectuals. There was no more convincing sign that the tide of reaction was rising visibly in Italy at that very time when his polemic with Sorel and Croce was drawing to a close. That sign alone, the coming Thermidor, was the final reason for his withdrawal.

By contrast, Croce was not at all troubled at the rising tide of reaction that accompanied the polemic. If anything, the Marxist experience had diminished rather than increased his interest in politics. For all practical purposes the end of the polemic brought his Marxist interests to a close. Though he published in 1899 a critique of Marx's law of the tendential drop in profits, his one technical economic analysis, he did not modify any of his main conclusions on theoretical Marxism as a whole. To the last, very much like Labriola, his interest in the concrete economic problems of the Italy of his times was meager and confined exclusively to the speculative. Indeed, in 1901, when he felt sufficiently confident to engage in a polemic with Vilfredo Pareto, the outstanding contemporary economist-sociologist, the discussion was confined to the very speculative concept of value. Croce unsuccessfully sought to convince the economist, who had an ineradicable Genoese mistrust of metaphysics, that he had to revise his notion of value as a mathematically measurable good. Without recognizing the subjective nature of value and its consequent moral connotations, the foundation of his entire theory, argued Croce, was shaky. Needless to say, Pareto made no change in his general theory of value; Croce's argument, if anything, confirmed him in his mistrust of a metaphysical approach to the problem of value, especially that of an idealist-oriented metaphysics.

This exclusive concern for the philosophical approach, for an exhaustive clarity in the speculative foundations of Marxist theory (not crowned with complete success, to judge from the continuing discussions on the true meaning of value in Marx) was perhaps the most evident limitation of Croce's Marxism. Croce, with his analytical clarity, refuted the immodest claims of Labriola, in particular his extravagant claim that economic determinism was the one final interpretation of history; and with that same demanding clarity he also authoritatively put to rest Labriola's arguments for a Marxism that was at one and the same time the very process of history and a knowledge of that process. There is no question, moreover, that Croce disposed of Labriola's arguments that philosophy and ethics were superstructure with similar ease and dispatch.

But if the Marxism of Labriola was transparently that of a passionate, indignant philosopher with all of its palpable weaknesses, there were commensurate shortcomings in Croce's approach, which often replaced a very obvious difficulty with a less obvious one. It is highly questionable, for example, whether Marx, as Croce insisted, actually believed that the class conflict was neither moral nor immoral (a belief Croce himself adhered to even when he no longer accepted the Marxist version of that conflict). It is even more questionable whether the conclusions that Croce drew from the asserted domination of collective supraindividual forces in history led to a more persuasive ethic, or one with fewer problems than the ethics of Labriola. Marxism, Croce concluded in the *Contributo alla critica di me stesso* and reaffirmed in reminiscences twenty years later, taught him that his ethics up to that point had been "abstract," that is, they did not adequately recognize the limitations of individual ethics. Such ethics, in which the ought-to-be was primary, had to be implemented in a historical setting, and the configuration of that landscape was determined by vast supraindividual collective forces, completely free from the primacy of the ought-to-be. Those forces had their rights: "In that fire (of the Marxist experience) I burned my abstract moralism and learned that the course of history has the right to drag and crush individuals." Individuals and collective forces had their respective orbits, but since right was might, there was no point to an individual denunciation of those forces when, as occasionally happened, a collision of the two occurred and the stronger of the two pulverized the weaker.

As an alternative or corrective to a Labriolian-Marxist ethics of the proletariat, therefore, Croce's theory was quite obviously not without its own share of problems. There was a great deal of oversimplification in Labriola's unified Marxist ethics, transparently designed to meet the requirements of a speedy and easeful translation into political terms; but the more sophisticated ethical dualism of Croce, with its unique concession equating right and might, was not a persuasive corrective to that oversimplification.

More surprising and perplexing, though, were Croce's conclusions as to the implication of Marxist theory for the practical politics of a Marxist party. Having made too much of the speculative approach in one area, having overstressed ideas as constituent elements of the Marxist vision, he minimized them to excess in party politics. The Marxist party, Croce argued at the conclusion of his theoretical analysis, should be completely unaffected by the results of the long polemics on Marxist points of doctrine. The party did not have to busy itself with social and economic analysis. Its business was not to understand the world but to change it; and to change it the party needed neither an irrefutable economic analysis of the present nor a philosophy that explained man and the universe. The party ought to recognize that Marx, in Croce's words, was the Machiavelli of the proletariat—that is, the political theorist who taught the proletariat that resoluteness and strength were indispensable to obtain power. With these two political virtues the Marxist party had all it needed. It was unlikely, Croce concluded, "that a movement of the size and intensity of Marxist socialism would be dispersed or absorbed without first leaving a substantial mark on history." The party had a future, and for that future, it could well afford to jettison with impunity the theories that were the subject of constant and unremitting debate.

This paradoxical twist was in a sense a sign of Croce's common sense, a recognition that Labriola had tended to push too far the implications of doctrine for practical politics. The conclusion, however, also revealed the inadequacy of Croce's own idea of the national political realities of the day and what they implied for an Italian Marxist party. Translated into political imperatives, Croce's reduction of all political philosophy to ideology, his notion that a party ought not be concerned with the truth of a political principle but only with its usefulness as an instrument with which to obtain power, had some very peculiar implications.

Neither at this time nor at any other did Croce consider himself a mentor to any political party on its practical politics; but it remained nonetheless true that the conclusions that he drew from his

Marxist experience contained an implicit list of precepts that the leaders of a party ought to follow. The leaders of a well-run, coherent Marxist party, according to this view, were to use Marxist thought itself as an ideology. They could make good use of Marxist doctrine—either in its totality or in any given part; but appreciative of the truism that politics was primarily action directed to the attainment of power, they were not to be unduly insistent on the verifiability of political truths. They were to respect the differences that marked off social philosophy, the province of the thinker, from social change, the province of the political man of action. It did not occur to Croce that Machiavellianism of this type had some of the drawbacks of its prototype, and that in positing and emphasizing a hiatus between political theory and political action, between party leadership and party following, in reducing all operative political convictions to ideology, he was very effectively barring the possibility of a fuller understanding of the nature and function of any Italian Marxist party, present or future.

Even Turati, of all the Marxists the most inclined to use Marxist doctrine as a means to insure party unity, did not consider his notion of the class conflict or his ideal of social justice mere ideology. Nor did those socialist leaders who in good faith accepted most of the Marxist structure. For them Marxism was quite simply true. Men like Bissolati, Treves and Gaetano Salvemini were drawn to Marxism precisely because of their opposition to this brand of Machiavellianism. They regarded the Marxist party as the custodian of a truth that gave meaning to life and politics. For both Turati and Labriola, Marxism, far from widening the gap between party leadership and party following, between political philosophy and ideology, sought to close it.

Because of his brand of Machiavellianism, Croce did not understand or appreciate the aspirations of the best of the Socialist leaders for a politics that abolished the distinctions between political convictions and political practice, a politics that was more than a struggle for power. Even when, at a much later time, he recognized that Marxism did seek to satisfy some just exigencies, he tended to stress the way in which Marxism perverted those exigencies. It is quite understandable, then, that in this earlier period, when he was virtually tone deaf to the legitimate protest note in Marxism, he was unable to comprehend Turati's Marxism and appreciate the good it did. By contrast, these dimensions of the Marxist "faith" that eluded Croce were precisely those to which Sorel most keenly responded. This divergence between the "students" of Labriola was fundamental and lasting, but as so often happens in the case of intellectual friendships, it was not quite recognized by either for years and years.

As late as 1896 Croce wrote that "The French socialist is truly Marxist, perhaps the only Marxist worthy of the name. Sorel does not apply ready-made theories: he has used a great deal of Marx, but if there is a method in his approach, it is that of a complete freedom from any one-sided theory." To the last, Croce admired Sorel for his contempt for humanitarians or sentimentalists, and he wholeheartedly subscribed to the French publicist's critique of those Socialists who stressed analogies between primitive Christianity and socialism, their alleged common concern for brotherhood and community of goods. Christianity, Croce agreed, was anything but a pacifist compromise: it was "a singularly instructive example of social regeneration, of a new beginning or rebeginning," and Socialists, if they concentrated on the proper aspects, could learn much from that history.

Sorel's socialism alone, therefore, according to Croce, was moral. It had nothing to do with "republicans, democrats, followers of the principles of 1789, progressivists, anti-clericals, free thinkers, teachers of the people." These people, Croce believed, were the bane of Italian political life. They were largely responsible for its low level, for its absence of strength or ideals. Talking incessantly of morality, they knew nothing of a morality like Sorel's, "austere, sober, unrhetorical . . . a fighting morality capable of keeping alive the forces that move history and prevent it from stagnating and becoming corrupt." This morality "had no use for universal brotherhood, for those compromises that, satisfying material interests, betray lasting values. From Lassallean socialism, corrupted by these notions, a socialism that disintegrated into Masonry, that talked nonsense of the "duties of society," Croce expected nothing but "*vigliaccheria generale*" (general cowardice).

The publication of Sorel's *Reflexions sur la violence* in 1906 in no way changed Croce's high estimate of the French thinker. That revolutionary syndicalism which bypassed parties and kept intact a moral revolutionary fervor unsullied by any parliamentary compromising appeared singularly desirable to Croce. Revolutionary syndicalism was a welcome alternative to moderate socialism concerned principally with higher salaries. Just as at the end of his increasingly overt polemic with Labriola, Croce wrote that he saw nothing to fear in a proletariat that educated itself for political battle, so in 1906, he saw nothing to fear in a future victory of revolutionary syndicalists, a victory that "was no more frightening than any necessary political development." There were only two qualifications to this approval of Sorelian syndicalism. If that syndicalism was morally superior to all other forms of socialism, it had to prove it by defeating all other socialisms. It had to be, that is, the most powerful as well as the most moral socialism; moreover, it had to reconsider the idea of "myth" as its theoretical foundation.

The Sorelian idea of "myth," that act of faith that could move mountains, and that considered social regeneration more important than any theoretical or practical knowledge, did not allow any philosophy to pass judgment on it. "Myth," the regenerative force, needed no justification outside of itself.

Croce had rejected Labriola's Marxism principally because of a similar denial of the autonomy of ethics and philosophy, and he accordingly and coherently rejected the Sorelian formulation of that notion. Nonetheless he preferred not to stress his critique of that theory. He emphasized instead the area of common agreement. Sorel, for his part, acted much the same way toward Croce: the French thinker could no more reconcile his theory of myth with Croce's notion of the Spirit (in spite of his enthusiastic praise of the system) than Croce could reconcile his philosophy with Sorel's complicated treatment of the Christian notion of faith. To the last, however, Croce disagreed discreetly, out of a sense of comradeship, and very probably because he felt some distress that his appreciation of revolutionary syndicalism was exclusively speculative.

It was all to the good for Turati's cause that the Sorelian conclusion on the nature of true Marxism came some time after the beginning of the Croce-Sorel-Antonio Labriola polemic. It was to Turati's advantage that the impact of those ideas on the Italian Socialist party was not felt until the party survived the high point of the counteroffensive of the reaction in 1898. In the light of that development, those polemics indeed seemed picayune and irrelevant. Such, at least, was the conviction of Turati, who had been conspicuously missing from these speculative polemics, and who de-

plored them as much as he deplored the fanatic coherence of Labriola and Sorel and their acid proselytizing zeal. But by 1898,
Turati was not alone in decrying the excesses of Marxist theoretical
analysis. The political developments of that year, and all the disputants recognized as much, were at least as important as their
theorizing. Once again all three, and even Turati, for the last time
and for radically different reasons, made common cause against a
powerful counteroffensive of militant conservative forces.

IV

THE SEARCH FOR THE MIDDLE COURSE

One year after the unrest in Sicily sputtered to a close in 1897, a new outburst of demonstrations, less organized and much smaller than those of the *fasci*, began to spread throughout the island. The uprisings were not purely of local importance. Starting in the South the unrest began to spiral upward through the peninsula, gaining in size and violence. Not long after the demonstrations in Sicily, similar outbreaks occurred in Calabria and in the Puglie, especially in its capital, Bari. There were many causes for the unrest, but one at least was palpably clear. Wheat was literally the staff of life for the greater part of the population, and its already high price, due to a bad crop, some government bungling, and the impact of the Spanish-American War, had soared again. Having lost hope of bringing their plight to the attention of the country, convinced that Parliament was distant and deaf, the more desperate among the peasants and the middle class expressed themselves in the language of the last resort. Though that language left something to be desired, it was equally true that a deploring majority in Parliament had done little to offer any meaningful alternative. From politically overheated Rome, where demonstrations in January led to the proclamation of a state of siege, to the far less sophisticated Puglie in southeastern Italy, accordingly, violence was the order of the day.

As the disorders crept up to central Italy, into Romagna particularly and the adjacent Marches, blurring the line that marked off violent protest from mob action, it became apparent that they were not going to dissolve on reaching the more politically mature North. The demonstrations, in fact, swept through central Italy, the region many Italians considered the classic limit of the hurricane zone, and continued northward into Lombardy. The violence reached a climax in Milan, the commercial capital of the country. From May 6, to May 10, 1898, there were repeated assaults on government offices and police stations in that city. Fighting was carried on from the rooftops and from behind overturned trolley cars. In the second day of the Milanese revolt, Florence and Naples flared up in a similar way.

Violence on this scale, a good number of conservative Liberals had come to believe, was proper to southern and central Italy. Very little in their political experience, however, had prepared them for the explosion in Milan. After the tragic death in March of the immensely popular Radical leader Cavallotti in the last of his many political duels, and the death in a political demonstration of the son of another very popuar Radical leader, Carlo Romussi, they had anticipated outbreaks, but not revolt. Those Liberals soon regained their confidence, however, if not their composure. The uprising, they reasoned, was proof that their enemies were those of the state, and the state (synonymous with the party in power) had to take whatever measures were necessary for self-defense. From this point of view the fact that some of the anti-government parties involved had not deliberately incited to revolt but had simply made political capital out of the unrest attenuated but did not do away with their criminal responsibility. But whatever the individual party responsibility, Milan appeared damned as either excessively political or politically immature, and in either case the government had but one course to follow. This conviction was shared by Prime Minister di Rudinì, who was certain that the government's wheat policy had had little to do with the turbulence, and because of the grave and pressing danger he acted with singular vigor. In a moment he and the country were long to remember, he declared a state of siege and assigned General Bava Beccaris the task of reestablishing order in the defiant city.

The ideas of the General in dealing with the situation were broadly those of Crispi; and mindful of the charges of irresolution that that fiery old Prime Minister had once hurled against his generals, Bava Beccaris resolved to go to remarkable lengths not to leave himself open to similar strictures. Not confining himself to rifle and small-arms fire, the General used cannon against the insurgents. In his most memorable encounter (attributable as much to poor visibility as to an excess of zeal), his cannon fire utterly routed the enemy —a group of huddled beggars waiting for soup outside a monastery, and the monks within. Not as colorful in other encounters, the General was nonetheless as thorough, and when order was firmly reestablished the mission had been accomplished at the expense, according to official figures which are probably conservative, of some eighty dead and four hundred and fifty wounded.

The General's methods of assuring civil order once the smoke cleared harmonized with the spirit of measures imposed by the government throughout the country. In the aftermath of the uprisings, di Rudinì ordered universities closed, drafted an extra class of conscripts, and made conspicuous display of army troops. The measures that Bava Beccaris applied in Milan were but the last turn of the screw. Military tribunals were set up and every opposition figure of any standing was expeditiously put behind bars. The procedure was carried out without a hint of discrimination: Radicals and Republicans were treated as summarily as Socialists, and Socialists on an equal footing with politically militant Catholics. For the first time, though not the last, leaders of every political persuasion opposing the conservative Liberals—Carlo Romussi of the Radicals, Luigi de Andreis of the Republicans, Don Albertario, a militant Catholic editor, Turati, Kuliscioff, Costantino Lazzari and Costa of the Socialists—found themselves bound together in the common cause of survival, and they united in the founding of the *Lega della Libertà* (The League for Liberty). At stake, though, was something more than their individual liberty, for among the measures decreed by Bava Beccaris was one that suppressed all political publications, from Don Albertario's *Osservatore Cattolico* to the *fasci* Socialists' *Lotta di classe*.

This was the state of affairs in Italy in 1898 at the height of the discussions between Croce, Labriola and Sorel; and the crisis was serious enough to persuade the most concerned, Croce and Labriola, to lay aside their differences for the moment. Discussions of the speculative reconcilability of Marxism and any degree of Liberalism were too obviously absurd during a despotic reaction. Like Turati's Socialists, the Radicals and the Catholics, Labriola and Croce (who defiantly published a talk Labriola had given on academic freedom and government censorship) had a common cause to defend.

Yet even as di Rudinì and Bava Beccaris appeared to be in complete mastery of the situation, the opposition was scoring its first successes. Milan, after all, could not be dealt with as summarily as Sicily. Even under martial law the city remained the political nerve center of the country as well as its tiny commercial capital. It was a center for articulate Socialists and partisans of the Extreme Left and, equally important, for a very influential group of moderate Liberals, whose *Corriere della Sera* was perhaps the most influential daily in the country.

Continuation of di Rudinì's policies required the support of those moderate Liberals. When that support wavered because of the strain the excesses of the reaction (particularly with respect to Don Albertario) put on church-state relations, relations that mattered very much to moderate Liberals, di Rudinì was caught in a dilemma. He could not survive without the moderate Liberals, but neither could he dispense with the support of the violently anticlerical conservative wing of the Liberal Party. After one last failure to obtain further appropriations from Parliament or the king, di Rudinì resigned. By the end of May, revolution and reaction had followed each other in swift succession, and just as rapidly disappeared.

But if the Socialists and the parties of the Extreme Left were strong enough to play a part in the downfall of the Prime Minister, it soon appeared that they were to have far less to say as to the designation of his successor. It was out of the question, of course, considering their limited representation, for them to impose their choice on Parliament. At best, the group could give its support to an acceptable moderate Liberal, one capable of winning the backing necessary for a firm footing in the foreseeably slippery road ahead. But no such candidate presented himself and the crisis was resolved as such crises have been resolved in more recent history, by drafting a candidate with no particular political affiliation, with views ostensibly above all petty party considerations, whose moderate stand assured wide support, and whose role in the recent unrest had actually won him friends. General Luigi Pelloux met these requirements. With some degree of government experience, of known moderate views, admired for his restraint in dealing with uprisings in the Puglie, Pelloux seemed to be the very man Parliament, if not the country, needed. Indeed, when the General formed his first Cabinet, all the optimistic expectations seemed to be borne out. He chose men of the Liberal Left, a sign at least of a willingness to start with new faces. He lifted the ban on political publications and made no move to implement the more oppressive legislation passed under di Rudinì. He smoothed strained church-state relations and actively sought pardons for the political leaders convicted and serving out their sentences—Turati with twelve years, Kuliscioff with two, Romussi with seven, Don Albertario with three.

But Pelloux did not do away with all of di Rudinì's emergency measures. Parties of the Extreme Left continued to work under very close surveillance, and censors kept a close watch on all political publications. In these months, King Umberto decorated General Bava Beccaris for conspicuous gallantry under fire. Pelloux's passive acceptance of such gestures and his toleration of the emergency measures which were not revoked could, up to a point, be justified as marks of a prime minister who had never ceased being a general, with a general's concern for order. Within a very short time, though, before the end of 1898, it became abundantly clear that order was the only clear idea Pelloux had, and that he intended to use every means at his disposal to implement it. Overt in his preference for discipline over even the beginnings of reform, the General (who, like many generals before and since, did not lack a peculiar political skill) eased out the members of the Left in the Cabinet, replaced them with more ductile and conservative members of the Right, and pressed forward with a new ministry that for all practical purposes was again a ministry of the Conservative Right. At his side, as his trusted aide and counselor, Pelloux chose Sidney Sonnino, a member of the Right whose strong influence on the Prime Minister amply justified the designation of Pelloux's tenure as the Sonnino-Pelloux ministry.

Sonnino, whose moral integrity matched that of Silvio Spaventa, had long experience with Parliament and some of the problems of the country. He had a greater interest in concrete political problems than in political theory, and while still a young member of Parliament, had made a name for himself as co-author (with the Catholic conservative, Stefano Jacini) of a report on the economic and social conditions of the South. The study, though not followed by any far-reaching reforms, was nonetheless among the more meritorious services rendered the country by a member of Parliament. No other task, certainly, had given Sonnino as much satisfaction. But with the years, as it became evident that the report would give rise to little actual legislation, Sonnino had despaired of the possibility of serious reform. The low level of parliamentary morality, the instability of Cabinets, the corruption of the deputies, persuaded him as it did many Italians, that parliamentary democracy as practiced in Italy was of little value. Italian politics, oscillating from quasi-dictatorship to quasi-anarchic revolt, Sonnino concluded, showed that the democratic parliamentary form of government made excessive demands on his compatriots; in a word, Italians were not yet ready for it.

The conclusion was substantially that of Labriola, as it would be that of the Fascists twenty years later. It was partly true, partly debatable. But the consequences that Sonnino drew from this partial truth did not allow for debate. He argued that in light of this incontrovertible failure, certain political changes were indispensable. To stabilize the office of prime minister, to prevent the constant shifting of allegiances from one party to another and from one individual to another within a party, the monarchy should be granted even greater power, enough to support the prime minister of its choice. The granting of such power, Sonnino argued, was no more than a return to the spirit of the Italian constitution. Other legislation was equally urgent (here Sonnino's arguments completely convinced Pelloux, who adopted the program without reservation)—legislation to outlaw strikes by public servants, to curb freedom of the press, to grant the government control over public political gatherings. Most urgent of all was legislation granting the government clear powers to disband subversive organizations.

These proposals were not altogether unreasonable. In deploring the instability of the office of prime minister and the constant shifting of party allegiances, Sonnino voiced the convictions of many with radically diverse political outlooks. His attitude on the illegality of strikes by public servants has been and is shared by leaders with no sympathy at all for his basic political ideas. There was even merit in his charge that the press, in particular that of the Extreme Left and of some Socialist groups, on occasion outrageously confused liberty and license. The fact remained, however, that Sonnino's solution of granting greater powers to the monarchy, and specifically to King Umberto, was inept. The king who awarded General Bava Beccaris a medal for distinguished gallantry was not the man to rally the country behind him, or to be trusted with implementing such an explosively dangerous program, particularly the proposal, so soon after the Milan revolt, to ban subversive organizations. Ostensibly the government had in mind that traditional enemy, the Anarchists; but in these years, of all political groups they were among the least successful or dangerous; and there was at the time an anarchist streak in virtually all the opposition parties. Moreover, Enrico Malatesta, the Anarchists' most dynamic leader, had had no part in the Milan revolt. He had been serving a seven-month jail sentence for inciting to revolt with his newspaper, *Agitazione*, in Ancona (the city, in effect, had revolted for two days). After the Milan uprising, instead of being released he was sent to the island of Lampedusa, from whence, to the undoubted relief of the police authorities, he fled and made his way to Malta, and from there to England, not to return to Italy until shortly before World War I.

Since the ban on subversive groups, then, was not really aimed at the Anarchists, it was with good reason considered a sign of the second wave of the reaction, an attempt to do with legal finesse what di Rudinì had done in clumsy haste. Again the pistol was pointed at the Socialists. In 1892, the Socialist Party had for a short period actually been declared outside the law and now it seemed that once more it would be declared illegal—and conceivably for a far longer period. In di Rudinì's time, left-wing Liberals, Radicals and Socialists had all been victims of the reaction, but now there was the possibility that the Socialist Party might be singled out as the scapegoat for all past and present troubles.

Under Turati's leadership the party acquitted itself well in the immediate aftermath of the Milan revolt. At his trial before a military tribunal, the editor of the *Critica Sociale*, who detested violence as much as any moderate and feared it for the harm it could do his party, used truth and found it as effective in politics as any Machiavellian ruse. He was capable of documenting his peaceful, law-abiding Marxism in his writings and even able to document it in his conduct during the four-day revolt. As a consequence, though the government won its conviction on the grounds of a florid phrase in the Socialist leader's oration at the funeral of Cavallotti, calling on citizens to "dismantle the den of iniquity," the Milanese remembered that it was Turati who had pleaded with striking workers at the height of the violence to return to their factories. His conviction, they knew, was manifestly unjust.

Turati's trial, in effect, not only thwarted the attempt to convince the people of the threat of socialism; it actually strengthened the party leader's prestige within and without the party. Before the Milan revolt he had sensibly kept out of the arguments on value and surplus value, the true meaning of economic determinism, and the ultimate dialectical basis of the class conflict, arguments that had absorbed all of Labriola's energies in the discussion with Croce and Sorel. In staying out of them he had arrived at one of Labriola's key conclusions without going through the Neapolitan Marxist's heart-break: for Turati, too, concluded that all these discussions were idle as long as the social-economic condition of Italy, in terms of a modern industrial society, was so retarded. Like Labriola, he had misgivings that all such polemics might be exploited by the reaction. When they were, however, it turned to his ultimate advantage. The affable, easy-going editor of the *Critica Sociale* gave witness to his convictions with a jail sentence of twelve years (though in fact he was released in the 1900 general amnesty after the fall of Pelloux). In jail with Bissolati, Costa, Lazzari and Anna Kuliscioff, Turati won a great deal of sympathy for his judicious pragmatic Marxism. He did not, of course, give a speculative answer to Labriola's charges and objections, but as he served his jail sentence he gave a good practical illustration of Labriola's speculative *"primum vivere deinde philosophare"* (to live first and then philosophize).

Against the new attacks of Pelloux and Sonnino, though, for all his popularity the imprisoned Socialist leader could do very little initially but continue to give witness to the cause. To his relief, however, and to the country's advantage, Bissolati and a number of Socialists were soon thereafter freed and returned to Parliament. Led by Bissolati, Giuseppe de Felice, Camillo Prampolini, and above all Enrico Ferri, they acquitted themselves extremely well in his absence. They were, indeed, indispensable in the resistance that the embattled Extreme Left put up against Pelloux's attempt to win power to rule by executive decree. The Extreme Left resorted to filibustering tactics against the Prime Minister and in those tactics, so congenial to Ferri's temperament and abilities, the Socialists made a contribution out of all proportion to their strength in Parliament.

They were so successful that they drove Pelloux to move—rashly—that an end be put to the debate. That very motion was itself fili-bustered and when the government attempted to take a vote, it was countered by the athletic intervention of Bissolati, de Felice and other Socialists, who overturned the voting urns.

Judged on the basis of these highly dramatic moments alone, it almost seemed that Pelloux and Sonnino had been defeated by the Socialists; but the truth was that, despite their indispensable con-tribution and their edifying defense of parliamentarian rights (a rather uncommon defense in the history of Marxist parties), Social-ists did not play the leading role. When Pelloux was defeated it was because a sufficient number of deputies of the Liberal Left led by Giuseppe Zanardelli, who broke their apathy, withdrew their sup-port, and even more, because in February 1900, the Italian high court declared the executive decrees of Pelloux null and void, and Pelloux abided by the ruling.

The reaction, then, was defeated by the Socialists, the militant Extreme Left, and—most decisive—by a segment of the Liberal Left. Its back was broken. Not even when, on July 29, 1900, to the horror of the country, King Umberto fell the victim of an anarch-ist's bullet in reprisal for his support of Bava Beccaris, did the con-servative wing manage to exploit the occasion and return to power. Although in the general elections held soon after his resignation, Pelloux won by a narrow margin (too narrow to govern), that victory was less significant than the remarkable gains of the Extreme Left and the Socialists. The last hurdle for the Socialists had been cleared. Even without Turati at the helm, the party had weathered the storm. In every way its victory was a ringing vindication of Turati's Marxism, that of a law-abiding, reformist party committed to an unfanatic class policy, sensibly distinguishing between the progressive and reactionary bourgeoisie. Even the mercurial Ferri, so anxious to assert himself, had seen his finest moments in the defense of the moderate cause. It seemed indisputable, therefore, that in the foreseeable future the policy of the party would con-tinue that followed during this period: maintaining the alliance with the Extreme Left, the equivalent of a Popular Front, that was so successful in the elections of 1900. In those elections the Extreme Left rose from 67 to 95 deputies, and the Socialists doubled their representation from 12 to 24. From the twenty thousand votes won in 1892 to the seventy-five thousand won in 1895, the graph of Socialist strength was rising impressively. The party was rapidly asserting itself, and the most dramatic sign of its new stature was the election of the first Socialist mayor of Milan. The times were propitious. For the new King, Victor Emmanuel III, gave no signs of following the political line of his father. After Pelloux's conservative successor, Giuseppe Saracco, stepped down in 1901 after a year in office, the King made no move to oppose the designation of Giuseppe Zanardelli of the Liberal Left as prime minister.

With the appointment of Zanardelli, the breakthrough to a new political orientation was all but complete. Saracco had resigned because of parliamentary protests over his efforts to assist the mayor of Genoa in restricting the power of the *camere del lavoro*, embryonic labor unions in that city. Though Saracco had not resorted to troops to deal with the labor organizations' successful retaliatory strike, his approach had been the traditional conservative one; as prime minister, Zanardelli put a definitive end to a government policy that identified protests with disorders. When peasants went on strike in Romagna during his tenure, the landowners were told to resolve the conflict with bargaining. When Zanardelli failed to find sufficient support for his strong anti-clericalism (his defeat was occasioned by the attempt, heavy with years of failure, to introduce divorce legislation in Parliament), he was followed by Giovanni Giolitti, his minister of the interior, and government policy became even more overtly sympathetic to labor.

To this day, Giovanni Giolitti remains one of the most controversial personalities in Italian politics. Although there has recently been a growing consensus of opinion that he was neither as nefarious nor as upright as his contemporaries held him to be, there is still substantial room for disagreement. Compared to what preceded and followed his long tenure (which ranged with a few interruptions from 1903 to 1914), there is no question but that he did far more good than harm; compared to what he might have done, however, he left a great deal to be desired. At the height of the battle against him his bitterest enemy, Gaetano Salvemini, branded him the *"ministro della mala vita"* (minister of gangsters), and some thirty years later a less politically intense but no less perceptive observer, G. Ansaldo, entitled his study on Giolitti *Il ministro della buona vita*. For Luigi Einaudi, a foremost Liberal economist of the time, Giolitti was a politician with no concern for educating the Italian people to a decent political morality; for Croce, the most articulate theortician of Italian liberalism, he was the finest representative of that liberalism, moral and judicious in intent and works. To his admirers, in brief, Giolitti was the one political man of his generation capable of unifying Liberals, Radicals, Catholics and even Socialists in the pursuit of the commonweal. To his enemies, his success at unifying rival factions had little to do with the commonweal, and was nothing more than pragmatism without principle, having no goal but self-preservation.

The truth of the matter was that Giolitti illustrated the best that trasformismo could achieve in working with fresh forces of the Left, groups that were stronger in the country than in Parliament; but Giolitti did nothing at all to remedy the fundamental lack in Italian political life, the absence of a sense of party identification. Indeed he impeded the emergence of parties. Instead of opposing the Extreme Left and the Socialists, the embryonic parties of the time, he worked very closely with them—in effect, he sought to absorb them in his trasformismo. The danger was very real for the Extreme Left and for the Socialists. Giolitti offered much for Italy and for the Socialist Party, but in working with him, the Socialists did so at the risk of losing their political identity. Collaborating with Giolitti, the party had to maintain its independence and Turati did not expect to find anything resembling a royal road to power in this exhausting work, which was to engage him for something close to eleven years. Indeed, in the early 1900's, on occasions when he and his group in Parliament made common cause with the Prime Minister, Turati was satisfied in simply retaining control of the party against rising criticism within the ranks. It was not easy to side with Giolitti, check dissidents within the party, and hold fast to a Marxist doctrine that distinguished and set apart the Socialist Party from all others—a long and arduous task that began with Giolitti's accession to power in 1903. In that year his conciliatory policy toward labor and the peasantry completely alienated conservative Liberals. Appalled by some thousand industrial and six thousand agricultural strikes, and angered by Giolitti's policy of government aid to the Emilian cooperatives so vital to the Socialists Costa and Prampolini, the conservatives moved to force the Prime Minister's resignation. They were defeated, and among the forces that rallied to Giolitti's defense were Turati's Socialists. In conscience, Turati claimed, he could not withhold support that was but a logical extension of the party policy operative since the Sicilian revolt; and he did not believe that that aid should be refused because the Prime Minister appeared to be stealing the Socialist program or because he found so many parts of the Socialist program acceptable.

Giolitti, in fact, had no quarrel with the greater part of concrete Socialist proposals. Giolitti concurred when Socialists protested that the absence of a stipend for parliamentary representatives openly favored the affluent and left the less affluent very susceptible to bribes. Socialists were right, he agreed, in condemning overcentralization and in demanding increased powers for local self-government. When Socialists argued for the reduction of the national debt, Giolitti, a fiscally conservative Piedmontese, found nothing to object. Nor did he find anything to criticize in another basic Socialist demand, a graduated income tax that would shift the tax burden from the poor and the lower-middle class to the rich. With respect to other social legislation, and in particular workmen's compensation and accident insurance, Giolitti also saw the wisdom of the Socialist cause.

The convergence of views notwithstanding, Turati, on excellent terms with Giolitti, was confident that he could match wits with him. The class conflict, he was convinced, was still a moat wide and deep enough to separate the most liberal of Liberals from the Socialists. So, too, was the ultimate Socialist goal, the socialization of all means of production. Consequently, Turati insisted, the party ought not to be unnerved by Giolitti's maneuvers. Socialists should continue to assist and, if necessary, rescue Giolitti. They could still keep a proper distance, the distance appropriate to a party that respected liberal parliamentarianism but did not consider it the last word in the political evolution of mankind.

Before 1903 was over, Turati illustrated by his own example the limits of a proper, acceptable socialism. When Giolitti assumed power, he provoked a sensation in Socialist circles by inviting Turati to join his Cabinet. The party that three years before had almost been declared illegal and subversive was now asked to join the government of a Liberal prime minister; the small, not well-organized Italian Socialist Party, that did not even distantly resemble its more powerful counterparts in Western Europe, offered a place in the Cabinet! Very quickly, however, this stunned disbelief turned into belligerent indignation. Socialists accused Giolitti of the most diabolical ruse yet in a master plan to destroy the Socialist Party, and Turati gauged properly the intensity and prevalence of this feeling. There was a dark side of the moon in Italian socialism, a part over which the Socialist leader had little control, and he did not want to provoke those elements in the party. For such Socialists, Turati's acceptance of Giolitti's offer of a place in the Cabinet would have been tantamount to a betrayal of the cause; and the very offer, when it became generally known after Turati's refusal, operated to Turati's lasting disadvantage.

In 1898 the mantle of Turati's moderation had covered many then anxious to deny their insurrectionary Marxism. But once the danger had passed, many of those dissidents quickly resumed their old positions, and they soon had a surprisingly strong voice in Socialist congresses. At their insistence, because of their activist zeal, the party proposed two programs: the *programma massimo* or maximalist program, delineating the ultimate goal of the party, the complete socialization of the means of production; and the *programma minimo*, Turati's program, the least the party would settle for in concrete proposals. In 1900, the *programma minimo* seemed very attractive to most Socialists, though not to the point of making the other program superfluous. It became quickly evident that any substantial success of the minimum program appeared paradoxically unrewarding, since it only sharpened appetites and occasioned fear among some Socialists that the party would settle for the achieved ends as a sort of permanent *faute de mieux*.

The situation was just what the revolutionary syndicalists headed by Arturo Labriola had been waiting for. This was Sorel's hour in Italian Socialism, in which he found a following ready to answer the call of revolutionary syndicalism for a new intransigent proletarian aristocracy, an elite willing to endure sacrifices in the name not of higher pay or better working conditions but of an ideal. For Arturo Labriola, in particular, the leading Sorelian theorist in the party, this was the time to challenge Turati for what he considered a deliberate and thorough perversion of Marxism. The Italian revolutionary syndicalist acted confidently, strong with the knowledge that he had the support of a great number of Socialists who were impatient with gradual change and the niceties of Marxist orthodoxy, and who were virtually indistinguishable from the insurrectionary anarchists. Arturo Labriola also knew, though, that to keep this basically anarchist following in line, he had some competent lieutenants such an Enrico Leone and A. O. Olivetti, who capably used the doctrine of revolutionary syndicalism in defense of the South, allegedly exploited by northern capital and industry. These syndicalists periodically reminded Turati that the party had done virtually nothing to right this wrong, that under his leadership Socialists were as indifferent to the plight of the South as Crispi, di Rudinì, Pelloux and Giolitti. In spite of some legislation passed to aid Naples and Calabria, they pointed out, Giolitti had done nothing to change substantially the policy of his predecessors, and the Socialists under Turati had been content with insignificant concessions. What successes Turati had in Parliament, the revolutionary syndicalists charged, were inextricably linked with his silence, his tolerance of this indifference—the price tacitly demanded by Giolitti for his aid and assistance. This also explained why Turati did not protest as forcefully as he should have the workings of Giolitti's electoral machine in the South in the elections of 1903, which were carried out, like preceding elections, with a great deal of bribery, threats and padded electoral lists.

But though some revolutionary syndicalists stressed the problem of the South, most were more concerned with preaching intransigence, abstention from Parliament, revolutionary fervor, and above all, the general strike. Socialists attracted to Marxism for its clear-cut separation of the good people from the bad and for its apocalyptic overtones, dreading the consequences of continued Giolitti-Turati collaboration, gave increasing support to the revolutionary syndicalists; and bolstered by their backing the syndicalists grew bolder. Unable to apply direct pressure on the *Critica Sociale* (Turati at about this time banned Sorel's writings from the publication), much less on Turati's group in Parliament, they were able to protest vociferously in their own publications (principally in Arturo Labriola's *Avanguardia socialista*) and even more decisively in Socialist Congresses, which since 1900 had become extremely democratic and impassioned bouts of rhetoric. Thus in 1904, one year after Giolitti's invitation to Turati, the Socialist Congress at their insistence condemned collaboration by party members with the government.

In the light of this development, Turati did well to refuse Giolitti's invitation, particularly since the revolutionary syndicalists were not alone in their anti-collaborationist stand. Another development within the party matched in importance their growth in power: the sudden rise of Enrico Ferri. Ever since 1900, when Ferri's flair for filibustering won him a national rostrum in Parliament, the dynamic professor of criminal law had become irrepressibly ambitious, and the end of his preaching was to urge Socialists to more active protest, to encourage them to speak more of violence. These exhortations, like those of the revolutionary syndicalists, had their effect. The increasing agitation for a maximum-goal program was the result of Ferri's incendiary rhetoric quite as much as that of the revolutionary syndicalists; and so was the smouldering resentment of many Socialists for Giolittian Italy, a resentment that increased perceptibly once Ferri took over the editorship of *Avanti!* from Bissolati. Directing his journalistic fire against the profit reaped by corporations in the heavily subsidized steel industry, against the "succhioni" (bloodsuckers) in a short time Ferri skyrocketed sales of the paper, and his own popularity as well. There was a solid core of plausibility to his charges, and what truth was lacking was more than compensated for by a willingness on the part of his readers to believe the worst. Ferri was eventually indicted and convicted of libel as a result of the campaign but the judgment of the courts merely confirmed his steadily growing following in their conclusions.

Against Ferri and the revolutionary syndicalists, Turati had all he could do to conduct an effective defensive action with the *Critica Sociale*, in Parliament, and in Socialist Congresses. The chances are, though, that he probably would not have won the day had the revolutionary syndicalists not decided to test the effectiveness of the general strike. On September 7, 1904, public services throughout most of the country came to a standstill. Some parts of the country were paralyzed for four days. On the fifth day, however, services were resumed. The general strike, it appeared, had not hurled a corrupt bourgeoisie into the dust. Instead of an apocalyptic upheaval they had given the country a four-day vacation. True, considering that they did not have the support of most labor unions, the revolutionary syndicalists gave an extraordinary account of themselves; but it was equally clear that they had overreached themselves. For a while, at least, to Turati's immense relief, the party was saved from the irresponsible demagoguery of Sorel and his follow-

ers. As a last touch, moreover, an overflowing of the cup, Turati
had the deep joy not long thereafter of witnessing an ill-considered
move of Ferri that permanently banished him as a political rival.
Two years after the failure of the general strike, during a temporary
withdrawal of Giolitti, who designated the trusted, jovial Alessandro Fortis to act in his stead (neither then nor now has it been
known with any certainty whether Giolitti's resignation was due to
influenza or to his difficulties in pushing through the nationalization
of the railroads), Ferri decided on a singular move. Working
through blocs of Radicals, Republicans, and members of his own
party, the ceaselessly inventive Socialist supported an attempt by
discontented Liberals to organize support for Sidney Sonnino, the
one rival of Giolitti with a chance of unseating Fortis. The choice
was remarkable, but in all justice, Pelloux's ex-advisor was no longer
the political man he had been in 1900. He had quite reversed himself. Now he challenged Giolitti not from a conservative position,
but for not having done enough about the South, decentralization
and educational reform.

The maneuver succeeded and in February 1906, Sonnino came to
power. Ferri, however, did not reap much profit from his short-
lived triumph. After biding his time for three months, Giolitti gave
his supporters the signal to overthrow Sonnino. But even before that
the Socialists, with Turati's wholehearted approval, had forbidden
Ferri to accept any post in the Cabinet; to block him completely,
the revolutionary syndicalists, furious at their ex-ally, persuaded the
party to call on Socialist deputies to withdraw from Parliament,
ostensibly to protest alleged police brutality during a riot in Turin.
Thus, after his three-month spree, Ferri was completely isolated.
Sonnino was in no position to aid him, Giolitti detested him, and
Turati and the revolutionary syndicalists for once saw eye to eye in
their appraisal of him. As a solution to the quandary, Ferri, who was
not without his more felicitous intuitions, decided on a long trip to
South America.

By 1906, Turati thus witnessed the failure of the revolutionary
syndicalists and of Ferri. The time had now come, Turati felt with
relief, to take up interrupted work. But that had to be done with
tact as well as firmness: the editor of the *Critica Sociale* could
hardly betray partisan satisfaction in the misfortunes of his rivals,
since the revolutionary syndicalists were still strong in Socialist

Congresses, and especially since the entire party, not the syndicalists alone, had been hurt by the failure of the general strike. For Giolitti had not let the challenge of the strike pass idly by. A few months after its failure, he called for general elections. Though not many voters had seen the strike as the onrushing wave of an irresistible proletariat and most had made the best of the four-day holiday, in retrospect it seemed to many that the parties of the left should be taught a lesson. A substantial number of Catholics in particular (not the "Catholic vote," for no bloc existed), spurred by a papal encyclical that indirectly relaxed the injunction not to participate in national elections, registered their fears. As a result, the representation of the Extreme Left in Parliament fell to sixty-three members, and the Socialists made only a very modest gain in comparison with their rate of growth in preceding elections, electing only thirty-one deputies in all. This setback, which kept Turati from fully exploiting his triumph over Ferri, also explained the peculiarly muted tone of his victory in the Socialist Congress of 1906. That Congress elaborated a unique Italian Marxist synthesis, the official policy of *integralismo*, which held, in effect, that the revolutionary syndicalists were not blameworthy for their attempted shortcut to the communist society of the future, and neither was Turati at fault for resorting to law-abiding measures for the same end. As a final pacificatory gesture *Avanti!* was assigned to the innocuous non-speculative Oddino Morgari, who avoided Marxist polemics of any kind.

In view of the events of 1898–1906, it is understandable that Turati, like most Socialists who had sought to minimize if not ignore the Croce-Sorel-Antonio Labriola polemic at the turn of the century, showed equal indifference to the changes in Croce's stature. By 1908, Croce was much more than a young and versatile historian of promise with a flair for philosophizing. In *La Critica*, the cultural quarterly that he founded with Giovanni Gentile, a young philosopher friend who introduced him to the thought of Hegel, Croce applied and tested the fundamental parts of his system, including his political insights, in numberless variations. Like the great writers of his generation—D'Annunzio, Pascoli and Pirandello —Croce was extremely prolific (by 1908 the collection of his reviews and essays filled a shelf or two of books); and much more than D'Annunzio, the most cosmopolitan of them, Croce looked abroad for ideas, not to Germany alone but to France and England,

and even on rare occasions to America. Little of cultural interest escaped him, and he earned a firm reputation as a literary critic, a philosopher, a moralist and perhaps above all, as a man of brilliant common sense.

The style of Croce's interests accounted for his growing prestige as much as did their breadth. No philosopher surpassed him in the clarity of his interpretation of Hegel, whose greatness is not usually attributed to the lucidity of his style. Indeed, the Hegelian notion of Spirit with its many intricate assumptions became in Croce's style a proposition as clear as any in Descartes' *Discourse on Method*, an almost commonsense point of departure for any philosophic investigation. When Croce asserted, for example, that philosophy to have meaning had to be Idealism, and dialectic and Hegelian as well, he seemed to be stating self-evident Euclidean postulates. The truth was that there was magic to Croce's style and that magic touched everything that interested him. It was also true, though, that his basically Hegelian orientation, his concern with the one philosophical system which Marx sought to demolish, took away any influence he might have had on the more speculative Italian Socialists of the day.

This virtually complete lack of contact between the philosopher and the leader of the Socialist Party, however, had its malingering effects—for Croce, for Turati, and for the country. Croce would have gained by being more responsive to and appreciative of the sensible aspects of Turati's empirical socialism. He would have learned something from a socialism that diametrically opposed the idea of the hard, unremitting nature of politics, the notion of politics as power without moral qualification, or the exaltation of a Sorelian Marxist ethos. Similarly, it would have been to Turati's advantage had he acquired some of Croce's respect for sustained coherence. Indeed it would have behooved Turati in general to take political ideas more seriously, and certainly those of Croce and Sorel. Turati's notion that the world was big enough for those theorizing on Marx and those guiding a responsible Marxist party was undoubtedly indulgent and benign, but also somewhat glib. As an approach to politics, it was in effect unnervingly similar to a Giolittian appraisal of liberalism as theory and practice, and very reminiscent of the practice of trasformismo.

In 1906, however, the great danger of revolutionary syndicalism appeared exorcised, and as for Croce, the admirer of Sorel, Turati took no notice of him. How dangerous after all, from Turati's point of view, was a speculative revolutionary syndicalist of sorts who was on excellent terms with many Liberals, including the conservative Liberal Sonnino, who in 1907 appointed the Neapolitan philosopher a senator?

The entire period from 1900–1906, then, was a very good period from Turati's point of view; and although he was wrong in believing he had answered the challenge of Giolitti's trasformismo for once and for all, in general he was right in feeling at peace with the world if not with all Socialists. This period was woven of such stuff as nostalgia is made of. Compared to what followed, indeed, nostalgia for these years was singularly proper and understandable, not for Socialists alone but for Croce and a good many Italians.

V

THE INFIRM GLORY

OF TURATI'S HOUR

In the late 1800's, Labriola had remarked that Italy's political corruption and economic scandals lacked scale. Italian capitalism, rich with a thousand forms of petty bribery and wrongdoing, had wasted its talents; it had not yet learned the art of large-scale corruption. Italian capitalism perhaps never became quite as robust as Labriola would have had it, not even by 1914; but for some years before that it was already noticeable, even to the untutored eye, that Italy was entering a new economic phase. The country was visibly, albeit slowly, industrializing. The progress, needless to say, was relative. With an economy that lacked basic raw materials, had come late to the Industrial Revolution and was strongly affected by the ups and downs of its more powerful neighbors, Italy was particularly vulnerable to forces beyond its control. Italy measured its increases in the production of cast iron and steel in thousands of tons, while Germany, France and England were counting theirs in the millions. When all was said and done, as late as 1914 the economy was still primarily agricultural, not industrial.

Yet in spite of the limits and precarious progress of industrialization, it was nonetheless true that the advances of the Italian economy in the first decade of the century were striking. The state had provided the basic necessities for capitalist expansion—a minimum of economic stability, transportation facilities, direct and indirect government support—and industries, particularly those protected by the heavy tariff laws of 1887, began to reap the benefits of that aid. The basic iron industry, for example, expanded from a production of not quite 150,000 tons at the turn of the century to over 700,000 tons in 1914, and in the same period the steel industry went from 60,000 tons to over 900,000 tons. By 1914, too, the two greatest iron and steel complexes joined forces and formed the giant Ilva Corporation, which with the Ansaldo Corporation of Genoa dominated the industry. There was similar progress made in the production of electricity: though "white coal" did not fulfill the exaggerated expectations of many Italians, its production did rise from one hundred million kwh in the late 1890's to more than 2.5 billion (most of it hydroelectric power) in 1914. By comparison, growth in the mechanical industries was not as sure, but the increase in toolmaking machines was impressive, and one corporation, Breda, began to play a dominant role. In shipbuilding, tonnage increased from seven thousand at the turn of the century to almost eight times that by 1914. Among the newer enterprises, the chemical industry was also steadily increasing its output, and Pirelli was making a mark for itself in the rubber industry. The most startling sign of the growth in the economy, however, was the booming automotive industry, which in its first few years saw investments rise from 8,000,000 to 90,000,000 lire. Growth in the less basic industries did not rival this pace, and yet there, too, there was progress. In almost every case these industries showed a tendency to regroup into corporations, in keeping with the new capitalism. Even where that was not so, as in silk (still the chief export of Lombardy, although losing ground to the cheaper and coarser Asiatic silk), the product was no longer produced by artisans at home but in factories. The same was true of cotton, though less so of hemp and wool.

As a geographical configuration of this change, the Milan-Genoa-Turin triangle was emerging as the industrial heartland of the country. There capitalism sunk its strongest roots; and although they were not as yet very deep (witness the recession of 1907, a noticeable setback for iron and steel, the mechanical industries, and in particular the vulnerable automotive industry), those roots were tenacious.

Giolitti, like any political man, willingly assumed credit for this general prosperity; and undeniably he had made his contribution, particularly with the much needed prolabor and social legislation which assured the general stability indispensable for progress. Legislation was passed to improve working conditions in the notoriously unhealthy rice fields of Lombardy and to bar women and children from night work; Sunday was declared a legal holiday; maternity clinics were established. The *camere del lavoro* continued to receive government protection, and although Giolitti was unable to bar the passage of a number of anti-union laws, he did succeed in indirectly assisting labor unions, which by 1906 were organized into a confederation, the *Confederazione del Lavoro*. In this work the able Prime Minister had the assistance not only of the Socialists and the parties of the Extreme Left, but that of a number of Liberals as well, from both Right and Left. But as his government became increasingly supra-party, counting on as much support from Sonnino's faction as from his own, and as the general prosperity increased, Giolitti was faced with some paradoxical consequences. Dissatisfaction among the Extreme Left and Liberals—for not all Liberals by any means followed Sonnino—grew rather than diminished with the prosperity that solidified Giolitti's power, and the tensions between law-abiding and revolutionary Socialists grew.

It was the frequent accusation of many left-wing Socialists at Socialist Congresses (echoed in attenuated form by Roberto Michels, a highly esteemed student of the socialism of those days) that Socialists in Parliament, and especially Turati's group, had lost all contact with grass-roots socialism, that they had become a bureaucratic oligarchy completely enmeshed and indistinguishable from other participants in trasformismo politics.

Turati defended himself well against these charges. The key issue of Giolitti's liberalism, after all, his continuation of state subsidies to growing industry, from a Marxist point of view, was complex; and Marxist writ offered both pros and cons. It was certainly coherent for the leading economic liberals, De Viti de Marco and Luigi Einaudi, to take a firm stand against those policies. According to them, state subsidies were reprehensible. Italian capitalism was not developing in an efficient, profitable manner, nor was it contributing adequately to the well-being of the country. The government, the economic liberals argued, by its policy of protecting the major industries, rendered the country a singular disservice. Because of that excessive aid, the steel industry, safeguarded from all salutary competition, made only scant and ineffectual technical improvements, yielded a very low return, and priced its products so high that it was cheaper to buy imported steel and iron. The same mistake was made in other industries: domestic cloth was more expensive in Italy than abroad, and because of government protection, no more efficient mode of production was in sight. Government monopolies, and in particular the sugar beet monopoly, came in for the same criticism, although this industry was also denounced for accruing profits that were scandalously high.

But the very basis of industrialization, according to the economic liberals, was defective. From the beginning this group had criticized the formation of the *"banca mista,"* the bank that served both as savings bank and investment bank, and they were particularly opposed to having industrial expansion based largely on the loans granted by such banks. The most dangerous part of this system, for them, was the control that banks acquired over industry, the predominance of financial over industrial capital, financial capital that was dependent in numberless ways on the fluctuations of the stock market. With the recession of 1907, they charged, their premonitions were borne out, for then a number of shipping lines and iron-steel combines in grave financial trouble were rescued only at the price of strengthening the grip of such banks on Italian industry.

For the purposes of Socialist strategy, however, these criticisms of the Radicals and economic liberals were a two-edged sword. Socialists could or could not oppose state-subsidized industries as had Ferri with his *succhioni* campaign—but in any case, Turati argued, there was enough to do without becoming panic-stricken and outraged at the idea of continued Socialist collaboration. There was still much to do. In 1904, Giolitti had expressed his sympathy for the Socialist program—for a graduated income tax, a stipend for deputies, meaningful decentralization—but as of 1909 not one of those objectives had been attained. Moreover, the revolutionary syndicalists, after all, had not disappeared with the failure of the general strike of 1904; only three years later, under the leadership of the incendiary Alceste de Ambris, they had made a last violent attempt at a general strike around Parma. The strike failed, and as a consequence the group was virtually excluded from party councils at the Socialist Congress of 1908, which voted to ban general strikes and to condemn strikes by public employees. But the syndicalists, nonetheless, were still active as a group apart, and the revolutionary tension among many Socialists, Turati knew, was still strong. Prolonged collaboration with Giolitti, with all the attendant risks, was called for: the moderate Socialists still had to prove that the party was not revolutionary.

These arguments convinced a good many in the party, but hardly all; they did not convince even some very close to Turati, in particular Gaetano Salvemini, an outstanding personality in the party, equally gifted at journalism and historical scholarship. Given to sweeping statements, as cutting and vitriolic as Labriola, whose works had first introduced him to Marxism, Salvemini denounced Turati's approach as shortsighted and totally inadequate. The conversion to a firm pro-Turatian stand of the *Confederazione del Lavoro*, led by the very able Rinaldo Rigola (150,000 strong in 1906, the Confederation doubled its membership by 1914), did not hush Salvemini's loud dissent, nor did the elections of 1909, in which the Socialists increased their parliamentary strength to forty-two.

The policy of the Socialist Party, Salvemini urged, *had* to concentrate on the South; the party had to make its own the criticisms of such diverse groups as certain revolutionary syndicalists, the Liberals of Sonnino's persuasion, and the liberal economists. The South, all of these groups concurred, was *the* exploited region of Italy. With very limited resources, no appreciable industrialization, and a constantly unstable agricultural economy, the South had had to endure a policy that since Crispi's time had become increasingly oblivious to the sacrifices demanded of the region, until in Giolitti's tenure the plight of the South had become intolerable. Socialists could not be accessory to his maltreatment, which rebounded to the detriment of the entire country. Was prosperity real, Salvemini asked, if it widened still further the gap between the South and the North, and sent emigration figures up to record numbers (two and a half million in 1906)? Was the moral tone of Italian politics raised by Giolitti's use of thugs and all the subtle and unsubtle forms of intimidation in the elections of 1904 and again in 1909? The legislation passed for the city of Naples and for Calabria was pure window dressing, Salvemini charged—the problems of the South could not be dealt with even superficially with a special appropriation or two.

The party, therefore, had its work cut out for it. It should adopt the program of the liberal economists; that is, it should commit itself to a fight against protective tariffs and monopolies, as Giolitti had done to a minimal degree, for example, in lowering the preposterously high price of salt, a government monopoly. At the same time, it should make an equally determined assault on the agrarian bloc, which, like the industrial bloc, had obtained from the government a protective tariff on imported wheat which kept this basic commodity at an oppressively high price. In addition to this program, as their own contribution the Socialists could make universal suffrage an immediate objective of the party, a part of the *programma minimo*. With universal suffrage—and the conviction was a moral passion in Salvemini—the disenfranchised peasantry of the South would wreck Giolitti's electoral machine and free itself from the grip of a reactionary bourgeoisie. With the consequent eventual defeat of the industrial-agrarian bloc, the South, a destitute region forced to pay a double penalty for the nation's tariff policy—outrageous prices for the manufactured goods of the North and diminished exports as a result of foreign retaliatory measures—would no longer be a "colony" of the North.

As thunder and lightning breaking the doldrums of these years, the arguments and exhortations of Salvemini were providential; and regardless of the merits of his arguments, it was to the credit of Salvemini that he kept alive one of the vital elements in the party, the sense of socialism as mission, the advocate of the exploited and inarticulate. A variant of "one-third of a nation ill-housed, ill-fed and ill-clothed," his preaching, more than that of any other Socialist, pointed up the price of prosperity in those years, the ambiguity of a national prosperity concentrated in northwestern and central Italy. In another sense, moreover, Salvemini rendered socialism yeoman's duty: for among the problems that his statistics and sarcasm brought out into the open was the survival, indeed the thriving survival, of deep-rooted anti-southern prejudices not only in trade unions in central and northern Italy but in the Socialist Party itself. A party that based itself on class justice could hardly leave itself open to charges of regional discrimination and prejudice.

Socialists in Parliament, partly because of Salvemini's insights and eloquence, did, when the occasion presented itself during the brief tenure of Luigi Luzzatti in 1909 (in one of Giolitti's characteristic temporary withdrawals) vote against a proposed electoral reform that would have restricted the enlarged electorate to those who could satisfy literacy requirements; thanks to Salvemini, the Socialists realized quite well that the vote would have enfranchised virtually all of northern Italy and left the South, four-fifths illiterate, still disenfranchised.

Salvemini, however, for all his zeal, did not convince Turati or his faction, and universal suffrage and tariff reduction did not become a *sine qua non* of Socialist policy. The majority of the party, admired his maverick spirit but not his ideas or directives. Years later, as a highly regarded opponent of Fascism and historian of modern Italy, Salvemini's view of this moment of Italian Socialist history gained wide currency. It is still very popular today. In this account, Turati cuts a rather poor figure, displaying either criminal indifference to the plight of the South or a slavish attachment to the Marxist teaching of the primacy of the rights of the industrial proletarist. Yet to give Turati his due, he defeated Salvemini on grounds that had nothing to do with the reconcilability of Salvemini's teaching with proper Marxist policy. Turati was quite as willing as Salvemini to fight for universal suffrage (at a Congress in those years when Salvemini declared he would never accept it from the arch-enemy Giolitti, Turati answered that he would accept it from the Pope), but he did not consider the moment opportune. Strong conservative opposition to even the modest proposal of Luzzatti, after all, certainly confirmed Turati's contention that most proposals for substantial electoral reform at that time were mere gestures. History, more important yet, has substantiated Turati's doubts as to the effectiveness of an enlarged electorate or even universal suffrage in solving the problems of socialism or the South; it has judged Salvemini's arguments naïve and utopian. The disagreement, therefore, was not one of principle but of tactics. Considering that when the electorate was enlarged in 1911, the response of the southern peasantry was by no means, either then or in any subsequent elections to this time, as free or as univocal as Salvemini expected it to be, Turati's appraisal of the situation at the time was the more perceptive.

But Turati's position had merits independent of any historical confirmation. Aside from the truism that it was possible to be in good faith and still feel that the much maligned protective tariffs might do more good than harm, there were cogent reasons for modifying Salvemini's judgments on the North and South. Like many zealous reformers, Salvemini occasionally succumbed to a conspiratorial monomania. The South beyond doubt suffered at the hands of the North; but there were reasons for this state of affairs that had nothing to do with the indifference of Italian socialism, or the callousness of Italian capitalism. The problem of the South was not attributable exclusively to the nefarious workings of the agricultural bloc with the industrial bloc. What may be loosely considered a complicated capitalist mentality did develop in the North and not in the South, and it developed there for many reasons, including the geographical proximity of the area to the great markets of Europe, the availability of a better-trained managerial class and a more abundant supply of skilled labor. A great deal of prejudice did exist between North and South, but that did not lessen the relevance of other factors; the roots of that prejudice, in any case, were not traceable exclusively to economic factors but to complicated differences in outlook, in basic values.

In terms of Socialist politics, furthermore, the case for Turati's socialism was singularly persuasive. Turati had no more use for Giolitti's electioneering techniques in the South than did Salvemini, but there was a point beyond which denunciations would have precluded the possibility of any continued Giolitti-Turati collaboration. Turati was well aware of living in a glass house; in case of an open break, Giolitti's counterattack would have exploited the presence of the revolutionary syndicalists in the Socialist Party. A last argument for Turati's case was the truism that Italian socialism in the North had proven to be refractory, difficult to organize and to unify; there was no reason to believe that a broad-based socialism in the South would be any more tractable.

The defeat of Salvemini's bid for a radical realignment, at any rate (though it added to Turati's reputation as a skilled politician and detracted unfairly from his reputation as a moral leader), was not the issue of the day. Nor was the growing Catholic representation in Parliament, though Luzzatti, Giolitti's replacement in 1909, ran into trouble (in spite of Socialist support) for not carrying out an anti-Vatican policy strong enough to satisfy the Radicals and a good number of Liberals. The pivotal issue that brought this brief age of good feeling to a sudden end was, unexpectedly (and not for the Socialists alone), the problem of foreign policy.

All through Giolitti's tenure and during his absences from office, the foreign policy of the government was based on the continuation of the Triple Alliance, operative since the early days of the Liberal Right before 1876. The policy was not always wise or popular. Initiated by statesmen and industrial interests as a means of attenuating French economic domination in the peninsula, the treaty had been backed by King Umberto, an admirer of the forceful German monarchy. But in the first decade of the century, as in its beginnings, the treaty had resolute opponents. It was a point of honor with the parties of the Extreme Left, in particular, to be unyielding in their opposition; and whenever the occasion called for it, Radicals and Republicans staged protests against it as a betrayal of the democratic republican ideals of the Risorgimento. The principal issue with which they could win wide support for their opposition to the alliance was that of *Italia irredenta* (unredeemed Italy). Irredentism may be defined as the nationalistic demand for the annexation of areas beyond one's own borders, in this case, the predominantly Italian cities of Trento and Trieste, where the Austro-Hungarian Empire refused to grant even minor concessions to the Italian majority.

Partly because of this irredentist feeling and partly in the hope that a bit of coolness might make Italy more appreciated by its partners, Italian foreign policy after 1906 was lukewarm to the Alliance. At the Algeciras Conference of that year, called to settle the colonial rivalry of France and Germany at a particularly tense moment, the Italian government showed overt sympathies for the French cause. Germany and Austria both took notice of that attitude. When the Austro-Hungarian Empire moved to annex Boznia-Herzegovina some three years later, the move was made without notifying, much less consulting, the lesser partner in the alliance. The reaction of Italy was quick and predictable. The danger of Austrian "imperialism," the critics of the Triple Alliance alerted the nation, was now clear and pressing. There were Austrian warhawks willing to use Italian irredentism as a pretext for invasion, and the Austrian move eastward was the prelude to an attack upon Italy.

In the crisis, the attitude of the Socialist Party was initially somewhat uncertain. Forthright in its condemnation of all colonial wars and of war as an instrument of national policy, the Socialist Party was not of one mind with respect to the problem of irredentism; many Socialists saw no incoherence in subscribing to the pacifist resolutions of the Second International of 1889 and revering the memory of Guglielmo Oberdan, an Italian patriot executed in 1882 by Austria after he unsuccessfully attempted to assassinate Emperor Franz Joseph in the hope of shattering the Triple Alliance. But the problem of reconciling the claims of nationalism with international socialism, already vexing, was made even more so by Leonida Bissolati, the one Socialist who more than any other of his time dedicated himself to the problems of Italian foreign policy, and did so in the spirit of a Socialist imbued with Mazzinian principles of the right of self-determination of peoples. When the *Avanti!* was reassigned to him after Ferri's escapade, Bissolati made of the newspaper a rostrum for his notion of proper Socialist foreign policy and over the years, his zeal and principles had not changed. In 1897, in his enthusiasm for the ideal of self-determination, he had called on Italian Socialists to volunteer to fight with the Greeks in Crete in their war to free themselves from Turkish rule. Gradually, however, Bissolati's approach became less impulsive, and the change was particularly evident in the very delicate problem of *Italia irredenta*. As late as 1905 Bissolati had worked for irredentism and specifically for the founding of an Italian university in Trieste, through international Socialist channels. He had worked, that is, with the Austrian Social Democrats, in the hope that they could somehow exert some pressure on the Austrian government. But with the passing years, Bissolati's trust and confidence in the effectiveness of international socialism had waned and his apprehension of Germany and Austria-Hungary had increased. The Austrian annexation of Boznia-Herzegovina came as an urgent last warning. As long as Europe remained under the shadow of a militaristic, autocratic Germany and an Austria bent on suppressing all legitimate nationalistic aspirations, a peaceful Socialist Europe, Bissolati was convinced, was inconceivable. A coherent Socialist foreign policy, consequently, had to accept this truth as a fundamental postulate and recognize the cause of self-determination as inseparable from true Socialist interests. A blanket condemnation of militarism as a capitalist ruse to divide the international proletariat, Bissolati argued, did not make sense, nor did deploring useful anti-Austrian or anti-German alliances, particularly anti-German alliances, for Bissolati was convinced that Germany was actively exploiting the strained relations between Austria and Italy. The editor of *Avanti!*, then, in particular after the Boznia-Herzegovina annexation and a good deal of Austrian saber rattling, approved of increased military expenditures and also—the focal point of his Socialist foreign policy—of an alliance between Russia and Italy, of little practical consequence but useful as an anti-Austrian gesture. For Italians who considered Russia the most reactionary state in Europe, to approve an alliance with such a power was to go too far. Objections to Bissolati's idea were vociferous. It seemed to many (and especially to Turati, who had the deepest misgivings) that with his approval of this alliance Bissolati had crossed the Rubicon: he was no longer a Socialist.

This gradual change in Bissolati was of particular interest to Giolitti. Since his failure to induce Turati to join the government in 1903, the Prime Minister had not given up hope of bringing at least one Socialist into the government, and the proper candidate now seemed to be available. In 1910, therefore, Giolitti made his overture to the editor of *Avanti!* Bissolati declined; but he made it clear that he did not do so out of principle, and the invitation and the mode of its refusal were lost neither on Turati nor on the revolutionary syndicalists. At this particular moment, though, after having seen Salvemini take quiet leave of the party to dedicate himself completely to political journalism with his publication, *Unità*, the moderate Socialist leader had no appetite for another showdown. And if Turati had had anything to say with respect to developments in foreign policy, the clash certainly would have been indefinitely postponed. But Giolitti had other plans, and they were directed at a move, already much talked about by 1910, to annex Libya.

There were many reasons why the non-militaristic, non-jingoistic Giolitti resolved on this colonial venture. He sensed the danger of the boredom typical of most periods of prosperity. He knew that the very shakiness of the Triple Alliance and of the general international situation required that if any colonial action were to be taken, it should be taken promptly. But most probably, Giolitti acted out of his awareness that outside of all party politics, and vying with his own characteristic "supra-party" approach, there were restless, vociferous groups, best represented by the Nationalists, who found the achievements of his trasformismo flat and bland, and preached the ideal of a partyless, warlike Italy that could live up to the ideals of a bold, aggressive Risorgimento. To absorb this group in his trasformismo, Giolitti willingly changed his style and usual ways, and in an uncharacteristic fashion spoke a language reminiscent of "manifest destiny."

Giolitti's plan, though undoubtedly adding to his length of stay in office, was perhaps his most serious miscalculation. It presumed that he could afford a rupture with the Socialists, although there was little to indicate that he could. Turati, at any rate, responded immediately to the challenge. Since the time of Crispi's African misadventures and the projected plan for colonization in China that went up in smoke in the Pelloux administration in 1900, Turati had made anti-colonialism a *sine qua non* of Socialist policy. Coming at this point, indeed, Giolitti's colonialism spurred him to that confrontation with Bissolati which he did not want. In the name of anti-colonialism, Turati decided, that showdown with Bissolati was justified. In defense of Socialist pacifism he was willing, in spite of their long, deep friendship, to condemn Bissolati openly.

In this resolve, Turati was aided substantially by Salvemini's documentation in *Unità* that Libya was too poor to alleviate the economic problems of the South. Argument for argument, the moderate Socialist leader's position was certainly as plausible as Bissolati's. He was right in asking why the advocates of self-determination on one side of the Mediterranean abandoned that creed on the more distant shore, and how the occupation of Libya could in any way improve the strained relations between Italy and Austria. But of all his arguments, the most forceful was the twist he gave to one used by the prowar faction; to be great, Turati insisted, Italy did not need to act like other great powers. An increase in greatness implied an increase in responsibility, and Italy ought to act accordingly.

These arguments, naturally, did not persuade Bissolati to revise his basic approval of the war. He did not break with the party at this point, though, and he actually took occasion to condemn severely instances of army brutality during the hostilities. Turati's arguments did not, for that matter, persuade all other Socialists, either. The leader of the old *fasci*, de Felice, hailed the war as the only solution for the perpetually sagging Sicilian economy, and a few revolutionary syndicalists, including Arturo Labriola, also gave their resonant approval. On the left as well as the right, the war issue appeared to have divided the party. To make matters worse, by 1912 the war, though not the *passeggiata militare* (military parade) that Giolitti had promised the nation (it actually dragged on and on), was coming to an official, successful close.

In 1912, or in any time for that matter, the prospects were not bright for any party that condemned on principle a successful war. But Turati was inflexible in his stand, admirably deaf to any small Machiavellian considerations. This, in a sense, was Turati's finest hour. Unfortunately, it was to the country's loss that neither he himself nor many others at the time realized that at the heart of his protest, deeper than any of the avowed Marxist reasons for the condemnation of that war, there was the splendid, decent conviction—by no means orthodox Marxist—that the crime of the Libyan War, as of any war, lay in a violence that inevitably begot greater violence.

This very same admirable defense of principle led to altogether unpredictable and tragically paradoxical consequences in socialism. Among the Socialists backing Turati without reservations in his international stand were a number of revolutionary syndicalists who, because of their active protests and brief stays in prison, had suddenly regained prestige and power in Socialist ranks. It was this very vocal faction that now moved, at the Congress of 1912, against Bissolati and all those who had not fervently denounced the war. Captained by their feverish young leader, Benito Mussolini, that group, against Turati's wishes (he did not care for the inquisitorial tone of the proceedings) sat in judgment on the quality of Bissolati's socialism and that of his followers, among them the promising young Ivanoe Bonomi from Emilia. The friend with whom Turati had weathered the days of Crispi, di Rudinì and Pelloux, the days of the most threatening reaction, was expelled from the party. And that friend, who openly despised the revolutionary syndicalists, and particularly those of the caliber of Mussolini, then moved to found the first important schismatic group, the *Partito Socialista Riformista*, weak in numbers but strong in the quality of its leadership and following.

The unexpected resurgence of the revolutionary syndicalists and the loss of Bissolati was the price that Turati paid for his anti-colonialist, anti-militarist convictions. That price, some political observers believed at the time, was much too high, involving the loss of the very best elements in the party. The revolutionary syndicalists were admittedly stronger than ever before and Turati, in losing Bissolati and Salvemini, had lost two indispensable allies in the fight against them. But Turati was confident that by himself and in spite of the rash impetuousness of the revolutionary syndicalists he could still carry the day, and lead a unified party in the cause of moderate, pacifist socialism. That unyielding adherence to principle, moreover, as is often the case, had some peculiar practical advantages, or at least what certainly appeared to be such in 1912. For with his anti-colonialism Turati had finally found the issue that trenchantly separated the party from Liberals like Giolitti and from the Extreme Left. That cause, in fact, was strong and sturdy enough to distinguish Socialist ideals from even the most advanced and radical reforms of Giolitti, such as the extension of suffrage to illiterates, announced shortly before the Libyan War but first exercised in the elections of 1913, provided they were over thirty and had military service. This unexpected concession, though upsetting and astonishing Salvemini, did not throw Turati off balance. When the euphoria of the Libyan war victory would pass away, and some of its economic consequences would float up to the surface, checking the prosperity that had anesthetized political passion and created an impasse for moderate Socialism, then, Turati hoped, he would spell out his answer to Giolitti's immodest claim that he had "put Marx up in the attic."

VI

WORLD WAR I

Election figures, statistical analysts have meticulously documented of late, are not all that meets the eye. No such analysts were available in Italy after the 1913 elections to illustrate the point for the undiscerning; but a remarkable number of Italians, nonetheless, had little trouble in concluding from the results (and without any conscious parody of Mark Twain) that in politics there were three types of lies—lies, damned lies, and election figures. On the surface the returns indicated a victory for Giolitti and the Liberals. But on closer analysis, it was evident that the margin of victory was extremely narrow, and that the victory was not even that of Giolitti's wing. The lasting divisions between the followers of Giolitti and those of Sonnino and his close friend, the southern Liberal Antonio Salandra, cast a heavy shadow on that triumph; but even more important, the returns left doubt as to whether individual Liberals in a number of cases were Liberals at all. For in that election, so decisive for Italy's future, one new development made for a fundamental change in the practical politics of Giolitti, the Liberals, and indeed of all Italian parties—the Prime Minister's understanding with Catholic groups. The agreement was not with Catholics in Parliament, leaders such as Filippo Meda and Stefano Cavazzoni, who were there as individual Catholics, rather than as representatives of a national Catholic group, but with Count Ottorino Gentiloni, the president of the Catholic Union, a group that was not primarily political but that could make its weight felt in an election. In a "secret" pact with Count Gentiloni, which remained such as long as most Italian secret political pacts, Giolitti, in return for his promise to continue to oppose divorce legislation and discriminatory legislation aimed at the holdings of religious orders, and to defend a degree of religious education in the public schools, won assurance of the support of Catholics.

The election results showed that Giolitti had not miscalculated in making the alliance. No one knew with any precision to what extent Catholics had voted as a bloc; but out of three hundred eighteen elected Liberal deputies, possibly as many as two hundred had been dependent on Catholic votes for election. A sizeable number of those Liberals, indeed, owed more to Catholic than to Liberal votes; that was why in so many instances there was some question as to whether the elected representative was or could be considered a representative of the Liberal Party. The Gentiloni pact, therefore, played an indispensable role in the Liberal victory. It helped check the Socialist advance in the North (the most notable consequence of the enlarged electorate following the electoral reform of 1913), and it maintained the Liberals' hold on the South.

The question remained, however, whether Giolitti could organize a compact following among Liberals, whether he could hammer out a policy equally acceptable to Liberal-voting Catholics waiting for due compensation, and Radicals and Liberals apprehensive of anything with the slightest resemblance to a clerical offensive; and it was not long before Giolitti showed that he was not equal to the task. In seeking to win over mistrustful Radicals with legislation establishing the primacy of civil over religious marriage, Giolitti irremediably antagonized the Catholics, without succeeding in placating the Radicals, who considered that concession picayune. A year after the 1913 elections, consequently, bearing out those who considered them a Pyrrhic victory, Giolitti stepped down and in characteristic fashion allowed his supporters to permit a rival, in this case Antonio Salandra, to assume power. Giolitti assumed that once Parliament and the country realized that Salandra and his group could not solve the problems that had stumped Giolitti, the old Piedmontese would nod to his followers, Salandra would be forced down, and with foreseeably more docile if not more willing allies, he would try his hand again. The only question was the length of time Giolitti would choose to remain out of office. Most Italians, political and relatively unpolitical, did not expect Salandra to succeed where Giolitti had failed.

Certain political parties, however, particularly the Socialists, were determined to prevent any resolution of the consequences of the Gentiloni pact and to place every possible roadblock in the way of Giolitti's return. With fifty-two representatives in Parliament, a stronger representation than the Radicals', the Socialists were a power and a threat. Still incensed over the Libyan war and its aftermath, the temper of most Socialist representatives was similar to that of the revolutionary Marxists who, in protest against Giolitti, the war and "the warmongers," had ripped up railroad ties to prevent the moving of army troops, and of the Socialists who preferred to serve jail sentences rather than a "militaristic bourgeoisie." Aroused still further by the Gentiloni pact, these Socialists had the support of less vehement colleagues who agreed that Parliament was irremediably rotten. As a group they had concluded that the best uses to which Socialist strength in Parliament could be put were abstention and obstruction in order to make clear the quality of their dissent.

Turati had been apprehensive of this mood during and even before the Libyan war, but he had not expected an overwhelming show of strength. He had counted on the good sense and moderation of the newly enfranchised to restrain the extreme wing, among whom were many of his old enemies, the revolutionary syndicalists. There was a place in his plans for an eventual coalition with the Radicals that would effectively undo the advantages accruing to Giolitti from the Gentiloni pact, and in the abstract, considering the precariousness of Giolitti's victory, the project was not without merit. But with the elections of 1913 Turati's plans went up in smoke, and the role he had played in directing the Socialist Party and Socialist policy in Parliament abruptly became a thing of the past. For the revolutionary wing of the party had taken the anti-war stand of Turati, on which he had staked so much, and with it had wrested power from Turati's hands; the elections showed that the majority of newly enfranchised Socialists, particularly in northern and central Italy, considered the revolutionary group, not Turati's, the spokesmen for authentic socialism.

Firmly fixed on the periphery of Socialist power politics, with very limited maneuverability in Parliament and even less in Socialist congresses, Turati from this time on was trapped in a most anomalous position. His influence in the party was significantly reduced, yet he found it impossible either to accept fully the new

Socialist party or to sever himself from it. Nothing appeared more dangerously absurd to him than the new Socialist policy of belligerent abstention in Parliament, but nothing could persuade him that he had any alternative but to wait and hope for the failure of that policy.

Despised by the new Socialists, mistrusted by those within and without the party who were puzzled by his loyalty to a socialism that was the outright denial of what he had fought for during sixteen years, Turati never quite recovered from the blow of the 1913 elections. Since 1893 he had done his share to accelerate the progress of the Socialist Party. He had bested the revolutionary syndicalists and Ferri; he had given Socialist doctrine a respectable tone and a fair degree of popularity; he had managed, with his anti-war stand, to find the one issue that preserved the party's identity and saved it from the threat of Giolitti's all-embracing political pragmatism; and now, when it seemed that he would draw just compensation for all these accomplishments, the party and voters judged him virtually expendable.

At any time, no doubt, the removal of the old pilot would have had serious repercussions for the future of socialism; but at this particular point, at a time when Socialists had to fashion policy against an indirect but forceful assertion of Catholic political strength, that ouster was especially unfortunate. In exploring Socialist approaches to the problem of Catholics in politics, the revolutionary Socialists, the abstentionists, were the most unlikely group to bring about a rapprochement. For this group, the only Socialist policy was violent denunciation; consequently, they were partly responsible, even long before the Gentiloni pact, for the hard, inflexible stand of Pope Pius X toward Socialists, and his restricted notion of the proper duties of Catholics in politics.

Not out of any political naïveté but from the conviction that the Liberals were the least of all political evils, the Pope had encouraged politically oriented Catholics to some form of alliance with them. The Gentiloni pact, inconceivable without his approval, was but one step in this direction. Another was his approval of the *Opera dei Congressi,* a network of Catholic organizations on the parochial level that participated indirectly in local and national politics, working under the direction of the hierarchy. These organizations were undoubtedly a far cry from a political party, but there was something reminiscent of strong party discipline in the Pope's dealings with them. When the *Opera dei Congressi* in 1904 showed signs of impatience with episcopal guidance, the Pope ordered it disbanded. In 1909, he proceeded just as summarily with Don Murri, the young priest who for a while had followed Antonio Labriola's academic courses at the University of Rome. Don Murri's vigorous anti-Liberalism and his very small party, the *Lega Democratica Italiana*, whose political program sought to compete with left-wing Liberals and moderate Socialists, displeased the Pontiff. Don Murri, he instructed, was to resign the party leadership and the direction of the small group's newspaper, *Cultura Sociale;* and on Don Murri's obstinate refusal, the Pope had him defrocked.

Vigorous action of this type, though perhaps explainable in terms of clerical discipline and the Pontiff's resolve to keep Catholics politically united, did little to improve relations between Catholics and Socialists. By acting in a way that was more autocratic than authoritative, the Pope made it virtually impossible for Catholics to argue persuasively that their acceptance of papal infallibility in matters of faith and morals in no way impinged on their freedom of political action. In approving of collaboration with the Liberals alone, the Pope seemed to confirm the contention of moderate as well as revolutionary Marxists that the Church and its members were irrevocably committed to the preservation of a bourgeois *status quo.*

Accordingly, by 1913 the arguments and the political maneuverings between Catholics and Socialists had become a vicious circle, confirming each side in its appraisal of the other. For most Socialists, for whom politics alone mattered, the Pope and the Catholic hierarchy were more or less conscious lackeys of the bourgeoisie; for the majority of Catholics, for whom the doctrinal truths of religion were primary, the Socialists were more or less conscious embodiments of the Antichrist. Although these positions had been expressed before the Gentiloni pact with varying degrees of intensity and (especially on the Socialist side) vituperativeness, in 1913, with the advent of the revolutionary wing to power, the expressions became more violent yet, particularly on the Socialist side.

Turati, whose anti-clericalism and anti-Catholicism were moderate and decent, for whom the belief in the goodness of man and in the power of common sense and the natural sciences was an adequate substitute for the Christian experience, had never been able to control the extreme anti-clerical elements. Too many *reductio ad absurdum* misunderstandings of Catholic and Socialist positions had been operative for too long a time for any one man to do much, perhaps, at this juncture. Still, at the very moment when Socialist and Catholic political strength was picking up momentum, it would have been all to the advantage of the country, certainly to that of the Catholics and even more to that of the Socialists, if Turati's brand of anti-clericalism and anti-Catholicism had predominated. Instead, the Socialist Party's rising star was a fiery young rhetorician from Romagna, Benito Mussolini. As the editor of *Avanti!*, Mussolini, who had undeniable demagogic journalistic gifts, made a signal contribution to the party's new virulence. By comparison, the anti-clericalism of some of his predecessors seemed that of earnest dilettantes.

There were, however, other fundamental changes in the party that were as important as the intensified anti-clerical, anti-Catholic campaign. The new Socialists subjected the idea of the party and its structure to a thorough transformation. As the culmination of an abusive debate of the sort that has ceased to be shocking since the Lenin-Trotsky and Kautsky-Trotsky polemics, but which in the pre-Russian Revolutionary era was as yet unheard of, the new group, with Mussolini acting as the voice of Marxist righteousness, excommunicated Bissolati and his followers. The charge was collaboration with the bourgeois enemy, Bissolati's approval of the Libyan war, but it was no secret that that did not rankle as much as the nineteen seats that Bissolati and his group had won in Parliament. Mussolini also read a number of Masonic Socialists out of the Party in the same mood and manner, and with the pretext that the Masons were a secret organization intent on using the Socialist Party for private ends. Once again it was no secret that those expelled included a number of the most esteemed Turatian and independent moderates in the party, such as the very popular Genoese, Orazio Raimondi.

With the last vestiges of moderation stripped from the party, the leaders, and Mussolini in particular, waited for the occasion to inaugurate a stronger Parliamentary policy than abstention. Resentment for the Libyan war was obviously an ideal starting point for incitement to revolt, and of all the regions in Italy, none appeared more smoldering and sullen in its hatred of Parliament and government than Romagna, the province from which Mussolini came.

There one of his young Socialist friends, Pietro Nenni, was calling out to the *braccianti* for insurrection, for a socialist republic. His cry was echoed by the redoubtable anarchist Malatesta, back from England to try to do in the Marches what anarchists had failed to accomplish in Sicily and Milan.

The material these men were working with was extremely combustible, and in March 1914, with the outbreak of an anti-draft demonstration in Ancona, the long-awaited violence erupted. Throughout Romagna the cry went up for revolt against the warmongering government, the lackey Parliament, the servile army and the exploiters of all classes. The violently revolutionary *braccianti*, who had nothing to lose, and the more conservative peasants took up arms against each other. In the cities, paralyzed by a general strike, mobs looted and ransacked, and the royal insignia was stripped from virtually all government buildings and monuments. Some twenty years after the wild dream of Bakunin, the red flag of anarchy did fly above the City Hall in Bologna, the capital of the region. Ancona declared itself an independent commune, and Romagna, not to be outdone, declared itself an independent republic. For one week, *Settimana Rossa* or Red Week (the term referred to the anarchist origins of the upheaval, and had nothing to do with the still non-existent Communist movement), an entire region successfully defied the central government; and—the most heady symbol of success—the general sent to quell the insurrection was forced to hand the rebels his sword.

Against the threat of chaos, Salandra, with the approval of Parliament and most Italians, who were terror-struck by the revolt, sent some 100,000 troops into the region, twice the number Crispi had sent to Sicily to quell the uprising of 1894. In a matter of days order was restored. Malatesta managed to escape the police and once more fled the country; Nenni was arrested and imprisoned. Mussolini, whose exhortations to revolt in *Avanti!* were considered by many, including himself, as major factors in the upheaval, was admonished and left free. The government did not consider his role important.

Although the scale of the uprising precluded comparision with past upheavals, it did not seem afterwards substantially different from past unsuccessful general strikes. There were the customary brandished threats, the sudden storm, and then the usual abrupt and

total suppression. It appeared that Mussolini and the new Socialist
leadership, like the revolutionary syndicalists in 1904, had overreached themselves. They had achieved one principal objective—a
crisis in the government that pointed to Salandra's resignation—but
at a very high cost. Having made common cause with anarchists
they had raised the ghost of early Socialist days, the question of
whether there was any meaningful distinction between anarchism
and socialism, and the answer to that question suggested by Red
Week was not likely to draw new adherents to the party. One year
after their strongest showing in national elections, the Socialists, by
their abstentionist policy in Parliament and their involvement in
Red Week, appeared to have lost for some time to come the advantages of twenty years of Turati's leadership. By the same token,
though, they also seemed to have prepared the way for Turati's
return.

Unquestionably, the analogies with 1904 could not be stressed;
1914 was not 1904, and Turati felt the absence of the support
of Bissolati and his group, now constituted as the *Partito Riformista Italiano* (the Reformist Socialists) and of individual supporters among the expelled Masonic Socialists. Nonetheless, Turati
seemed remarkably farsighted in his decision to endure, rather
than break with the party. After the setback of Red Week, it was
conceivable that the party would have to revise basic policy; and in
the event of any reversal of Parliamentary abstentionist policy,
Turati would have his one real opportunity to regain lost ground.
After the resignation of Salandra and the expected reaccession of
Giolitti, it even seemed plausible that Turati might work with
Giolitti on the thorny problems of a common Socialist-Liberal policy toward the emerging Catholics.

All these conjectures and hopes were short-lived. The month of
Red Week was also that of Sarajevo and the outbreak of World
War I. From this month on, that catastrophic event, and not the
problem of revolution or the consequences of the Gentiloni pact,
determined the structure and future of the Socialist Party and of all
parties.

The first instinctive response of many, if not most Italians to the
new conflagration, coming but two years after the Libyan war, was
fear and a singular lack of enthusiasm. The African venture had
taught some hard lessons. The memory of casualties was still fresh,

and the dead had been from all classes and parties. Though most newspapers carried the usual glowing accounts of Italian heroism and valor, returning soldiers had brought with them other and equally accurate versions of incredible bungling in logistics and criminal blunders in the distribution of inadequate war matériel. The war had not been the military parade promised by Giolitti. Even he had since reconsidered the caliber and possibilities of Italian war potential. Bewildered, like all Europeans, at the suddenness of the new war, relieved at not being involved, most Italians felt that patriotism, common sense, humanitarianism and enlightened self-interest all argued the case for neutrality. True, foreign policy in recent years had been cool to the Triple Alliance, and German aid to the Young Turks during the Libyan war had strained relations somewhat between Germany and Italy. But Libya had been won and anti-German feelings had faded. Similarly, although during Crispi's last tenure, anti-French feelings had reached a fever pitch in 1897 with the Aigues-mortes incident when French workers attacked immigrant Italian laborers, there were no strong anti-French feelings in 1914.

Anti-Austrian feeling, however, was another matter. The Radicals, whose traditional policy called for the deliverance of *Italia irredenta*, Trento and Trieste, saw in that war an opportunity to redeem their compatriots, and with singular coherence, so did the Reformist Socialists Bissolati and Bonomi, with whose cause Salvemini now allied himself. With the exception of Salvemini this group had approved the Libyan war as a needed check on growing Austrian ambitions, and in their eyes, Italy had a moral obligation to enter the war against despotic reactionary forces that denied the principle of self-determination, and were irremediably feudal, anti-democratic and anti-Liberal. All Europe, not Italy alone, they felt, had everything to lose by a victory of the Central Powers, whose triumph would be a blow to the entire Socialist movement.

Those who pleaded this cause, however, were few, and ranged against them was an imposing array of forces—the military, Giolitti himself and virtually all other political parties. The military men realized that the demands made upon Italy in case of intervention would be far greater than those made upon her in the course of the Libyan war; moreover, although this was obviously less generally known, they were particularly apprehensive about the possibility of secret diplomatic maneuverings that conceivably would let them know only at the last minute what battle plans they were to draw up against which enemy. Giolitti, who had had his fling at nationalistic rhetoric with the Libyan war, was acting more in keeping with his convictions and general outlook in 1914. He made no reference to the Italian equivalent of manifest destiny. The war, he urged, was a cautionary tale—a final bloody chapter in a long economic and military rivalry, and though he expected a German victory, that persuasion did not make him alter his public neutralist stand. Any advantages the war might bring Italy, the old statesman was convinced, would come only at the bargaining table, since both sides were willing to concede much to insure Italy's neutrality. In general, this was the stand of most Liberals, who deferred to Giolitti's judgment, and of the Catholics. As nationalistic as their co-religionists elsewhere in Europe, Italian Catholics saw no reason to intervene. Some had sympathies for Catholic Austria, others for Catholic France. The Pope himself, who, it was commonly held, died of heartbreak over the conflict, rose high above nationalistic sympathies. The famous reference to war as "senseless carnage" was that of his successor, Benedict XV, but he would have subscribed to it completely. As a Christian and an Italian, Pius X believed that neutrality was the only policy.

Italians, then, were generally committed on a remarkably long and varied front to neutrality. This was true of most parties, and vehemently true of the Socialist Party. From the very outset, following its Libyan war policy, it took an absolutely intransigent stand against intervention. A war that was fought exclusively over economic interests, one in which the bourgeoisie used nationalism to divide the international proletariat, was not one in which the Italian proletariat could or should participate. The example of French and German Socialists, who managed to reconcile their international ideals with nationalistic fervor, did not sway the party. Under the leadership of the new command—Mussolini, Lazzari and Nicola Bombacci—the party intended to keep faith with authentic international Marxism. It had everything to gain by doing so. In spite of the failure of Red Week, it could resume its violently anti-war stand (no longer dangerous now that it was shared by most of the country) and bring the troublesome, potentially dangerous Turati into line. The old Socialist, in fact, had no place to turn with the outbreak of the war. The basis of the revolutionary Marxists' anti-war spirit, part and parcel of their intent to demolish the present political and economic structure stone by stone, was not the basis of his; nor did he share their vitriolic hatred of Bissolati and Salvemini. Despite these differences, and Turati's awareness that an anti-war stand was much less complicated during a colonial war than it would be during a general conflagration, he had no choice but to close ranks: for him, the Socialist Party was still the only party with a coherent anti-war platform. With the outbreak of the war, therefore, the Party for the first time in its history had a cause that was at once the common cause of the country, and yet, because of the particular basis of its anti-war policy, a cause that set it off from every other party. The party, it seemed, had never been more successful than it was in 1914 in the task of being *in* Liberal Italy and yet not *of* it, joining in a common work and yet retaining its identity.

Conscious of that achievement, it stood rocklike in its commitment, even after the most clamorous and sensational defection in the history of Italian Socialism, that of Benito Mussolini. Eight months after the outbreak of hostilities, in November 1914, to the stunned amazement of his closest collaborators, Lazzari and Balabanoff, Mussolini declared himself in favor of intervention on the side of the Allies. To the Socialists, his move seemed unbelievable. Mussolini, to all appearances, had all that he wanted: a devoted folowing, the confidence of the party, the absence of any powerful enemies within the ranks. The future was his and he had discarded it, flung it away like some old and useless thing.

Even more incomprehensible, his grounds for intervention were virtually those of the one group that the Socialists particularly abhorred, the Nationalist Party, which had of late immodestly claimed credit for the Libyan war. With a relatively small following composed largely of the disillusioned and resentful among the middle class, the military and Southern aristocracy, that party preached the mystique of nation above all parties, the cult of action, and an Italian variant of *Deutschland über alles*. Initially they had clamored for intervention on the side of the Central Powers, but since the fact of intervention appeared more important to them than its rationale, they reconsidered and adopted instead the more popular cause of intervention for *Italia irredenta*. From the point of view of

Lazzari or Turati, an alliance with a party of this sort was virtually incomprehensible, but the defection of Mussolini suddenly became transparently clear to them when they linked his recent acquisition of the newspaper *Il Popolo d'Italia* with rumors of French interventionist bribe money. The betrayal then became the very latest confirmation of the ultimate economic basis for all action. Mussolini's claim that he defected because he had concluded that international Marxist pacifism was a dead cause was too suspiciously simple for Socialist minds accustomed to the primacy of economic determinism.

After excommunicating Bissolati's excommunicator, therefore, Lazzari and his group realigned their forces, shaken but tenacious custodians of a cause they meant to defend to the last. All things considered, though, the shock had been greater than the loss. Only a small number of revolutionary syndicalists followed Mussolini. For the great majority of Socialists, the ex-leader was an apostate, an untouchable. With a handful of followers, it did not seem likely that he could do much for his own cause or that of the interventionists.

Six months later, however, in May, massive demonstrations in principal cities in favor of intervention on the side of the Allies—the days of *Maggio glorioso* (Glorious May)—showed that even though Mussolini's defection had been without any appreciable consequences, some new steps toward involvement had been taken behind the scenes. It was inconceivable that the demonstrations could have taken place without encouragement and approval in high places; that certainty caused near panic among the anti-intervention parties, especially the followers of Giolitti. It did not matter to the anti-interventionists that they could not prove their case. (Not until the end of the war was it known that the secret treaty of London of April 26, 1915, had persuaded Salandra, Sonnino and the king that the country's best interests lay on the side of intervention.) Too many demonstrations were occurring at too fast a pace. In spite of the highly charged eloquence of D'Annunzio, back in Italy from France, urging Italians to immediate intervention in the name of a heroic, mighty Italy, a substantial number of those who heard the poet and witnessed the crowds concluded with frightened humor that the art of organizing spontaneous demonstrations was making remarkable progress.

But since piazza demonstrations were not the equivalent of a declaration of war by duly constituted authorities, most anti-interventionists, including the Socialists, were still hopeful that the mounting sound and fury would turn out to be nothing but foam dashing against cliffs. The majority in Parliament, after all, was steadily neutralist and so was Giolitti who, though he had temporarily absented himself (as he was wont to do in times of crisis) from Parliament, was still the real power. When Giolitti rushed to Rome to determine the meaning of the demonstrations, it was generally expected that whatever it was that was happening would come to a stop. Soon after his arrival in the capital, Giolitti found over three hundred calling cards from Liberal deputies attesting to their confidence in him and signifying their immediate availability should he decide to return to power.

Precisely at this moment, however, when he spoke for the Italian people and for most parties more than at any other moment in his long tenure, Giolitti failed them. Perhaps out of pique at not having been consulted by Salandra on the secret negotiations, or out of a sense of exhaustion and acquiescence, or out of a conviction that matters had already gone too far to change course, perhaps even to some degree out of a monstrous willingness to let the fortunes of war determine the fate of those who had chosen intervention, Giolitti deferred to their decision. Salandra, who had handed in his resignation, was reappointed, and with Giolitti's acceptance of the *fait accompli*, the last interventionist wave submerged all dissent. On May 24, 1915, by an overwhelming majority that included virtually all of those three hundred Liberals who had offered their support to Giolitti, Parliament declared war.

Neither then nor in the course of the war did Giolitti conceal his misgivings and complete lack of enthusiasm for intervention, but his hostile detachment was of little value; he never regained that indispensable majority in Parliament and the country that had been his for over a decade. Having made the *gran rifiuto* in 1915, Giolitti ceased to be a power in the country and in his party. He still had much of value to offer Italy, and on at least one occasion in the postwar period, he offered a valid alternative to a disastrous political stalemate. Yet even in that crisis, as in all maneuverings from 1915 on, Giolitti moved with limited mobility and an uncertain following. The weight of the 1915 refusal was much too heavy ever to shrug off.

And so Italians took their allotted places, most of them far more out of a sense of duty than enthusiasm, and hoped and worked for victory. The fighting, centered along the northeast frontier, was fortunately a holding operation, a minor theatre of the war that did not require offensive action. Nonetheless it proved to be exhausting. The apprehensions of the military were amply borne out. The Libyan war had depleted military supplies. Italian industry was woefully inadequate for the demands made upon it, and Italian soldiers had to make do with equipment that was substantially inferior to that of their enemies and their allies. In some cases soldiers were equipped with 1890 vintage rifles.

Contrary to Salandra's expectations of a very short war (a calculation that had played a large part in his decision to intervene), there were no signs of an imminent Allied victory. On the contrary, one year after Italy's entry into the war, the Central Powers unleashed a massive offensive on the eastern front. The low morale and the fears of that new offensive accounted only to a minimal degree for Salandra's fall in May 1916. Political considerations played a more central role. Salandra had flaunted Liberal responsibility for the war, and his cabinet was virtually one-party at a time when the very survival of the Liberal Party was dependent not only on Radicals but on the aid of other parties and groups. In not very splendid isolation, consequently, the Liberal Party under Salandra had to bear the full brunt of responsibility for the deterioration of the war effort. Salandra had called it the Liberal Party's war, and the opposition parties did not intend to let him forget it.

The new government that followed was headed, after long deliberation, by the innocuous old Liberal, Paolo Boselli, who was supported by a Cabinet that included representatives of all parties, including the Reformist Socialists of Bissolati, who had served as a volunteer in the Alpine troops in spite of his almost fifty years, and the Catholic, Filippo Meda. For the first time, a Cabinet took into account the existence and the strength of all parties, those who had been actively interventionist from the very beginning and those who were not; all parties, that is, save one—the Socialists.

Virtually all of the fifty votes cast against the declaration of war on May 24, 1915, came from Socialists, and after one year of war nothing had occurred to make the party leadership reconsider its policy. Contemptuous of Parliament, Giolitti and Salandra, whom they regarded as equals in duplicity and criminal irresponsibility, the Socialists remained in Parliament as a reproach and an obstacle to a government they considered the embodiment of cynical indifference to the will of the people and the commonweal. They were not alone, of course, in their resentment; but unlike other groups, they never came to terms with the *fait accompli*.

Their program was to oppose but not sabotage the war, and they set about implementing it in a number of ways. In the municipal administrations in which they held power, and particularly in the great cities such Bologna and Milan, they carried out their duties correctly but with little enthusiasm for the war effort. In the army they served, when drafted, with varying degrees of zeal, accounting for an impressive number of sacrifices in the name of a love of country that was not quite bourgeois patriotism, and for an equally impressive share of the striking number of defections. In Parliament they stood by. At a low point in civilian and military morale in 1915, Giuseppe Modigliani (all the more significantly since he was not of the revolutionary wing of the party) had stood up in Parliament to warn his peers that the government had to see to it that this was to be the last year in the trenches. Backing him up forcefully was the secretary of the party, Lazzari, who barred any Socialist collaboration in war committees of any sort.

This show of party discipline in Parliament was particularly aimed at Turati and his followers who, though in outward solidarity with the leadership, did on occasion betray a weakness for what Lazzari and his lieutenants, Giacinto Serrati and Nicola Bombacci, considered *petit bourgeois* patriotism; a weakness that sometimes almost lapsed into a willingness to do something for the war effort. Yet the party leadership had little cause to worry about Turati. Together with many Italians, the old moderate Socialist had not gotten over or forgiven the acquiescence of Giolitti and his followers to the *fait accompli*. He did not have much stomach for the intensity of Lazzari's leadership, his attacks on the institution of Parliament and bourgeois patriotism; but he felt that for all of his misgivings, he had no choice but to remain in the party and accept party discipline, in spite of the ominous turn the war had taken.

For by 1917, the war was going very badly. In spite of the American entry in April, a new German offensive in the east was sweeping everything before it, and a major Austrian offensive on the Ital-

ian front appeared unavoidable. Tight restrictions on domestic goods
and a growing wheat shortage gnawed at civilian morale until, after
two years of war, in the summer of 1917, anti-war riots erupted in
Turin, culminating in an official count of forty-one dead.

As a partial consequence of uncertainties, fears, war fatigue, tactical military blunders and superior Austrian arms and strategy, on
October 24, 1917, Italian troops suffered the disastrous rout of
Caporetto, involving the hundred-mile retreat of some 700,000 men.
The catastrophe (the Austrian offensive actually endangered Milan,
the nerve center of the war effort) stunned the country, and in the
panic and confusion, Italians resorted to the instinct always operative in such crises, that of recrimination. The generals accused the
soldiers of cowardice, the Socialists accused the generals of criminal
stupidity and sadism, Parliament berated the mild Boselli, Liberals
accused the Socialists of *disfattismo* (defeatism), of having completely sabotaged the war effort, and Benedict XV (who had spoken
of "useless carnage") and the neutralist Giolitti both came in for
their share of denunciation. Once having vented their spleen and
panic, however, Italians of almost all parties and convictions then
acted with singular vigor, heroism and purpose. The forceful Vittorio Emanuele Orlando replaced the very tired Boselli, and Marshal
Armando Diaz replaced General Luigi Cadorna, an unpopular leader
among the troops, as commander in chief. Fighting with a new
spirit, the armed forces held the line, and one month later the Austrian offensive was stopped at the Piave River. The fear of defeat
roused by Caporetto had given sudden unity and life to a war-
weary, divided people.

Yet the new spirit that bound the country together did not quite
sweep up with it all parties and factions. At the time of Caporetto,
Turati and Treves rose in Parliament to attest to their undying
loyalty and willingness to fight the enemy to the last, but they spoke
for themselves and for many Socialists, not for the party leadership.
Even at this critical moment, the party had its reservations. The
leaders, most of whom had been jailed at one time or another on
charges of *disfattismo*, for defeatist anti-war propaganda and activity, were loathe to lay aside even temporarily in the name of an
emergency their convictions on Parliament and the war. Caporetto
notwithstanding, they still believed that the war was of and for the
bourgeoisie. They were furious at the ex-socialists, Bissolati and the

far less important Mussolini, then a soldier on the northeastern front. It was because the government and many parties hammered away at the accusation of treason that Caporetto and its immediate aftermath still found these Socialists intent on opposing, though not sabotaging, the war.

As the country and the Socialists in the midst of this disaster sought to assess individual responsibilities, news of the October Revolution reached Italy. One enormous, irrefutable fact loomed out of the first garbled reports: the Marxist state was no longer a theory. Russian Marxists had made their frontal assault on the bourgeoisie, and the Marxist state was a reality. Erupting at this particular moment, the Russian upheaval electrified the leaders of the Italian Socialist Party. As the only Socialists outside of Russia who had clung to their anti-war, anti-bourgeois commitment all through three years of war, that leadership did not hesitate as to what course they had to follow. A number of independent Socialists, among them Raimondi and Arturo Labriola, who went to Russia soon after with French and Belgian colleagues to seek to dissuade Lenin from pulling out of the war, were reviled and covered with abuse as idiots and shameless agents of an imperialistic bourgeoisie. As for themselves, the leaders of the Italian Socialist Party had no doubt as to what was demanded of them: the cause of the first Marxist state was also their cause.

After Caporetto, the chances that the party might somehow, in spite of itself, tone down the anti-war stand that had progressively alienated it from many Italians and from other political parties, were rather remote; after the October Revolution they vanished altogether. Nor did the party shrink from the consequences of its commitment when new developments on the Italian and eastern fronts triggered fears that the Russian withdrawal from the war in December, 1917, would leave Italy to bear the brunt of a massive offensive along its northeastern frontier. From October 1917, on, the party had a cause that vindicated beyond its wildest dreams that anti-war policy with which Italian Socialists alone among their confreres in Europe had kept faith; and that cause, quite as much as developments in Italy, determined from this point the shape of Socialist policy.

VII

TEMPEST AND TWILIGHT

The Russian withdrawal from the war and the German offensive that followed notwithstanding, by the spring of 1918, the war took a decisive turn in favor of the Allies. By the following summer, a counterattack on the western front steadily pushed the Germans back, and in the eastern sector, Allied forces turned the tide. In October, Bulgaria called for an armistice, and soon after Turkey followed suit.

In this upsurge of forces, in this last mighty offensive, Italian troops contributed their share of fighting spirit and their share of dead. Though the all-out Austrian attack did not materialize in 1917, the Austrians did launch a last offensive some time later. The assault was repulsed; in the same month that Bulgaria and Turkey capitulated, the Italian army won the decisive five-day battle of Vittorio Veneto. As the war on both fronts drew to a close in November, the Italian flag flew above Trento and Trieste and throughout *Italia irrendenta*.

The war was over. After three years of bloodshed, in a conflict that according to official estimates took the lives of some half-million Italians, an exhausted people—elated and resentful—laid down their arms. The victory that months before had appeared remote and a year before had seemed virtually impossible was a reality, and Italians assumed their place at the conference table at Versailles.

At home the time had come to turn once again to the problems laid aside "for the duration"—Socialist parliamentarian abstentionism, increasingly serious Liberal divisions, and an emerging Catholic political force. The war had not made these problems less difficult, and quite understandably, therefore, the Liberals preferred to concentrate their energies on easier and more politically profitable issues—in a word, on a very successful peace treaty which in this uncertain hour might rally all political groups around them.

Yet it became swiftly apparent that a firm, all-inclusive sense of national unity was operative only in the hour of desperate need. Victory could not and did not blot out the divisions that had separated parties before and during the war, and indeed the peace settlement itself became a divisive issue. Not even the struggle to have the secret Treaty of London recognized (Wilson's refusal to consider it binding provoked widespread and lasting anti-American feeling) was catalyst enough to unite all parties.

Orlando and his foreign minister, Sonnino, moreover, did not see eye to eye on details of territorial compensation on the Adriatic coast, and particularly with respect to Fiume, a city not mentioned in the Treaty of London but which Italy claimed in the name of that principle of self-determination that had been invoked to deny her other regions. As a member of the wartime cabinet, Bissolati, incredibly coherent, was so uncompromisingly committed to the principle of self-determination that when Italy was assigned German-speaking territories north of Trento the old Alpino resigned in protest.

In Salandra's phrase, Italy had entered the war on grounds of *sacro egoismo*, that is, on the sacred right of the country to consider its own interests uppermost; and interests, obviously, were all one with territorial aggrandizement. Having failed during the war to win over most Italians, this view—excessively idealistic for some, repugnantly over-realistic for others—failed even more resoundingly in the war's aftermath. There was no common denominator *sacro egoismo* that could bracket together the nationalism of Bissolati with that of various Catholic groups and that of the Nationalists. These latter groups were divided among themselves and divided against the Liberals. So, indeed, were the Socialists, among whom the interventionism of Bissolati, of Mussolini and of the great number acquiescing to the *fait accompli* had virtually nothing in common. All these groups, however, were determined not to let the Liberal bourgeoisie use nationalism as the ideological defense of their vested interests and power.

Exasperation with the flag waving of the Liberals, consequently, was not confined to the Socialists, nor was it the result of any one party discipline. Many of those politically uncommitted who had fought and survived the war with no clear idea of what they had fought for, made their way to some form of nationalism, but an equally substantial number did not. A good part of the intellectual youth, especially, found no balm at all for its anguish and irresolution in the various sophisticated versions of Salandra's *sacro egoismo* then prevalent, not even in the most sophisticated version of all, that of the *maestro di vita*, Benedetto Croce. Croce in these years was at the pinnacle of his popularity and prestige; but with respect to his political philosophy, there were signs that the younger intellectuals admired and respected it, but never accepted it as a guide for their own political action.

Before the war, in about 1911, Croce, like Sorel, lost all enthusiasm for revolutionary syndicalism. His acceptance of the doctrine had been conditional—the test of its ethical superiority was to be its success in action—and when that condition was not met, he quietly put his hopes aside. Politics, at any rate, had become more and more a peripheral interest, and because the party in power in no way interfered with his freedom of thought or his work in philosophy, history and literature, and seemed able to balance such traditional freedoms with judicious reform, his appreciation of Italian liberalism, and in particular, of Giolitti, gradually increased. No other political party in Italy, after all, embodied quite so completely or so safely Croce's essential political requirements, needs he felt all the more deeply since his disillusionment with revolutionary syndicalism: the state, he believed, was in its simplest terms the party, the group in command with the power and right to make absolute demands on its citizens in all matters except basic convictions on the nature and conduct of life.

Of all Liberal leaders, Giolitti appeared to Croce an unsurpassed illustration of the truth of this analysis of the state. Even the Prime Minister's very narrow range of interests, which made him unpopular with many cultured and half-cultured Italians, was for Croce a sign of a healthy awareness of the limitations of the political man. In politics (the conclusion, though he never acknowledged as much, evidently had something to do with his disillusionment with Sorel's doctrines), there was very little need for general ideas. The best politics was a judicious pragmatism, with a *laissez-faire* attitude toward speculative problems and a sensible non-Utopian concern for social justice, a recognition that some forms of injustice were unavoidable, unexorcisable concomitants of the stresses and strains of any body politic. Parties, accordingly, ought not to regard themselves as custodians of the one true ideal of justice, but should act with sensible pragmatism and recognize candidly that their primary function was to serve as an indispensable instrument for the strong political leader. Once again, therefore, Giolitti served as a superb practical demonstration of a truth. Not a party man in the strict sense of the word, not much interested in philosophical problems, committed completely to a pragmatic notion of the commonweal, and bent on inserting new forces such as Catholics and moderate Socialists into an ever-expanding notion of the state, the old Prime Minister seemed an exemplar, an embodiment of every one of Croce's essential theoretical conclusions on political matters.

Croce's theory of politics, no more a reconciliation of the demands of justice and the commonweal with a hard identification of might and right than was Machiavelli's thought, was generally unconvincing, especially for many of his younger readers. It was impossible for them to see in the prosaic, astute Giolitti a fresh political ideal with which to move mountains. As an ideal, an incarnation of political wisdom, he had the appeal of a middle-aged man with rimless glasses. The same thing could be said of Croce's notion of the party as a purely technical instrument. For many of the younger readers of *La Critica*, Giolitti's unheroic acceptance of the *fait accompli* was not inspiring, nor was the war itself. Salandra's Liberal Party could command their obedience but not their enthusiasm. Croce's tardy acceptance of the war, too, did little to increase his popularity with the generation that went to fight in the trenches. Italian youth, if it had to die, wanted to die for a cause, and Croce's rejection of the "naïve" ideal of self-determination and his denial of any clash of cultures and supra-economic values (at one point he called the war a "Marxist" war) repulsed them. Croce took strong exception to the vicious bombastic nationalism of D'Annunzio and the Nationalists; yet his own nationalism was in the last analysis not very different.

The war, Croce wrote, demonstrated once and for all that

the state could never admit to being wrong, it could acknowledge no force superior to itself but the sword of the victor.

The state is like an arrogant man who yields only to another arrogant man stronger and more fortunate than he. The state is brutal in its dealings with the weak, deferential toward its equals, timidly respectful of the stronger. States are collosal brutes, concerned only with living, and willing to accept anything in order to survive.

When Croce argued that "we owe our country our lives but not our souls," a distinction with which he sought to preserve the rights of the person against the state, or when he urged that, in a conflict between love of country and love of higher cultural values, the only thing for the sensitive, intelligent combatant to do was to make an act of faith in the mysterious ways of history and in the immortality of superior cultural values, it seemed obvious to many that his political thought was almost indistinguishable from D'Annunzio's peculiar erotic-mystical nationalism, or Mussolini's even more bizarre nationalist socialism.

In the immediate aftermath of the war, these cumulative doubts as to the perspicacity of Croce's liberalism grew stronger and though his name continued to add luster to the Liberals of his generation, a noticeable number of the politically oriented of the new Liberal generation, like the southern deputy, Giovanni Amendola, sought to elaborate a liberalism that avoided the shoals of Croce's nationalism.

At the end of the war, then, the notion of *sacro egoismo*, whether in the form advocated by Salandra or in the different versions of Giolitti and Croce, had become an insolently meaningless cause, one utterly incapable of uniting the country or the Liberal Party. It was certainly not the instrument with which Orlando, a forceful wartime leader, could in any way counterbalance the centrifugal forces that were ripping the Liberals apart. After a number of particularly stormy sessions at Versailles and threats that Italy would help herself to what was due her, Orlando, in disagreement not only with the Allies but also with his own foreign minister, Sonnino, resigned. A southern Liberal with strong Radical leanings, Francesco Saverio Nitti, took his place.

The crisis, ironically, was precipitated by the issue Orlando had banked on to win solid national support—the insistence on Italian possession of Fiume; and that problem turned out to be as thorny for Nitti as it had been for his predecessor. For three months, argument went on fruitlessly, until on September 12, 1919, in the first direct challenge to the authority of the Italian state made in the name of nationalism, the poet-soldier Gabriele D'Annunzio, with a force of some one thousand men, invaded Fiume, assumed command of the city, and defied the government, the Allies and Yugoslavia to expel him.

The move did not come as a complete surprise. The almost fifty-year-old poet, a black patch over the eye he had lost in a wartime aviation accident, had accustomed Italians to his variants of the *beau geste*. Since 1915, his political activism (no doubt stimulated by the King's request that he return from France to harangue crowds for the *maggio glorioso* demonstrations) had grown perceptibly. Through the war, from his first pamphlet-dropping flight over Vienna to his last florid war communiqué announcing the final victory, he managed to keep a place in the eyes if not in the hearts of his countrymen. The irresponsible invasion of Fiume was in that "grand" tradition. Working closely with high-ranking military personnel, D'Annunzio in Fiume was living the role of the *condottiere* and finding it infinitely more to his liking than literature. The armed poet had a cause and a following, and he was elated at having put the Liberals and Nitti in an impossible position. Fearing national repercussions, both were unwilling to take decisive action against him. They solved the dilemma by publicly decrying the illegality of the invasion, but at the same time making it clear that they considered it morally justifiable, and privately assisting him. Without realizing it, that is, they did all they could to undermine their own position and destroy the respect of the armed forces and the country for the legitimate government.

Compared to developments within the country, however, D'Annunzio's invasion of Fiume was insignificant. Reversing the direction of a booming war economy is always painful, and in the chaos of 1919, Italy was reeling from the effects of the peace. During the war, industry had expanded impressively: from 1916 to 1918 the capital assets of the Ansaldo industrial empire rose from 30 million lire to 500 million, that of the Ilva group, from 30 million to 300 million, Breda from 14 million to 110 million, and Fiat from 17 million to 200 million. But in 1919, as a result of a worldwide recession and the raising of tariff walls that made impossible any substantial increase in the export of Italian manufactured goods—industrial stocks had shown signs of extreme instability. Industry, however, could not put the entire blame on circumstances beyond its control. In a number of cases, industry was so anxious to reinvest very high war profits to avoid taxation that it did so without any real concern as to whether any market existed, and then worsened a bad situation by falling back upon the banks it controlled and seeking to utilize the savings of depositors for its own survival. An increasing number of industries went into bankruptcy, and unemployment rose to over two million in 1921. Inflation soared, paper money in circulation increased from eleven million to nineteen billion lire and the gold content of the lira dropped from sixty gold centesimi to nineteen. The number of industrial strikes (316 in May alone) increased prodigiously. White-collar workers and civil-service employees also repeatedly went on strike. Peasants, driven to desperation by the rising price of wheat and the tightened restrictions on emigration, particularly to America (by 1921 the U.S. had slashed Italy's annual quota from 800,000 to 280,000), again and again rioted and took over big landowners' estates.

A willful leader might perhaps have been able to survive chaos of this sort, but Nitti's forte instead was irony and a rather abstract approach to economics. He stressed that the country had to produce more and consume less, a point that would have been persuasive had there been a foreign market for its products. He spoke of the need for a great program of government-subsidized public works, and for the nationalization of the sugar, power and fuel monopolies. Not one of his more intelligent proposals proved acceptable to Parliament, with the exception of the creation of a national police force, the *guardie regie*, to deal with the mounting violence and disorders. Twenty-five thousand strong, the guard was still inadequate for the reestablishment of order. In the light of all these difficulties, Nitti would have needed at least the passive support of Giolitti to remain in office. But Giolitti and he were implacable political enemies and after the first post-war elections in 1919 it was obvious that Nitti's days were counted. Giolitti and his followers, and the Catholics as well, were tacitly biding their time, and after Nitti reshuffled his cabinet in vain for the third time, Giolitti acted.

Thus, in June, 1921 (it was to be the last time), Giolitti once again assumed power in full revolutionary climate. In every way, the problems that confronted him were maddening and without precedent; and to deal with them Giolitti had only the bare majority of 252 seats, which the Liberals had won in the first post-war elections of 1919. With that tenuous, very divided majority, the old statesman set out to reestablish order, break the impasse in Parliament, and steady the economic situation. These were the immediate objectives, but another end was just as vital: the solution of the problem that had so greatly contributed to his downfall in 1913. He had to fashion a policy acceptable to the Radicals, the Liberals, and—just as important—the Catholics.

By 1921, however, the difficulties involved in this task had multi-plied prodigiously, and particularly with respect to Catholics. No longer a loosely organized group, the Catholics in the post-war Par-liament were an organized party, the Popular Party, the second strongest in the land, holding a hundred seats and polling 1,750,000 votes.

Undoubtedly, the party could not have come into being without at least the tacit approval of the successor of Pius X, the Genoese Benedict XV. The new Pope did not share his predecessor's view of politics or his fears of involvement. An independent party of Catho-lics, he reasoned, responsible for its own actions, was a desirable, sensible development. Such a party would not do away with the recurrent charge that in the last analysis the Pontiff had a very special place in the counsels and moves of any party inspired by Catholic political principles; but at least not every calculated or inept move on their part would be attributed to pontifical meddling in politics. Furthermore, the leader of the party, Don Luigi Sturzo, was particularly well qualified from the Pope's point of view to direct a party whose relations with the Vatican were delicate and complicated. A deeply pious, cultured priest with a wealth of prac-tical political experience on a regional and municipal level, and a national figure in Catholic Action, the fifty-year-old Sturzo was forceful and discerning. He was also the man to reconcile a Center-Left politics reminiscent of Don Murri (with whom he had worked closely since the uprisings of 1898) with the requirements of pru-dence and sacerdotal obedience.

From today's point of view the fact that a priest directed a Cath-olic party in post-World War I Italy no doubt appears disconcert-ing. For some it is sufficient *prima facie* evidence of the bad faith of

a Pontiff who tightened his hold on Catholics in politics while officially stressing the political neutrality of the Vatican. The truth of
the matter, however, is far less Machiavellian. Don Sturzo was *not*
imposed on the party. He imposed himself on it by sheer strength of
personality and political gifts, and in any case the conservative
Catholic lay leaders in the party, who were in most cases to the
right of Giolitti (Filippo Meda adequately represented this predominant group), wanted Sturzo, and actively sought and were
dependent on the support of hierarchy and Pontiff. As questionable
as it may seem to have a priest, under a vow of sacerdotal obedience,
as leader of a Catholic party, the fact remained that the appointment
of Sturzo was not a papal plot. The laity, quite simply, was very
"clerical." A laity that was docile but not excessively deferential did
not yet exist in Italy. The clergy, the hierarchy and previous popes
had their share of responsibility for this unhappy state of affairs—
but so did a laity that chose to be extremely submissive to a smoth-
ering clerical paternalism, even when Benedict XV encouraged
them to a greater show of independence.

All things considered, the party's designation of Don Sturzo as
Party Secretary was fortunate for both Catholics and the country.
Don Sturzo was, as a political man, extremely competent technically. He had been working on plans for an independent Catholic
party as far back as the late 1890's, and by January 1919, when the
party was officially founded, had given ample evidence of his organ-
izational skills. The new party, the *Popolari* (Popular Party), was
strong, with a network of numerous agricultural cooperatives, a
great number of Catholic mutual aid societies and an initial official
membership of no less than 1,200,000 members. Furthermore, the
old friend and collaborator of Don Murri, with the implicit approval of the Pope, had managed to commit a party, in which most
members were in effect Liberal conservatives, to a program that
vied with the Socialist program as much as the times and circumstances permitted. Generally not too radical in its demands for industrial reform, that program—concerned with regional autonomy,
agricultural reform, state-recognized Catholic schools, and above all
decentralization—was not that of a narrow confessional party, but
one in many respects acceptable to a good many enlightened moderate Socialists. Indeed, in a number of respects the party's objectives were not very different from those of Salvemini (whose anti-

clericalism was particularly vehement and often overwrought), since Don Sturzo, an enlightened Christian and a member of the Sicilian upper-middle class, was as conversant with the problems of the South as any political man of his day.

The program of the Popular Party in some respects was also, obviously, close to that of Giolitti—but here Don Sturzo drew the line. He had little use for what he considered the callous pragmatism of Giolitti, and he was determined to hand the Liberal leader the last definitive setback, to settle accounts with him for many old scores, and in particular for Giolitti's alleged failure to live up to the obligations he had incurred toward the Catholics under the Gentiloni pact.

The struggle between Don Sturzo and Giolitti, consequently, was intense and unrelenting. Initially, once back in power in June 1920, Giolitti managed, very much over Sturzo's objections, to persuade members of the Popular Party to join his very representative Cabinet (which included among others the now Independent Socialist Arturo Labriola as Minister of Labor), and having scored this initial success, he went on to others. With a relatively broad base of support, he rapidly achieved some remarkable results, particularly in foreign policy. On D'Annunzio's refusal to withdraw from Fiume, he dispatched a battleship to the port city. The poet still refused and the battleship opened fire. Within a matter of hours D'Annunzio capitulated, putting an end to an adventure that at one point awoke in the anarchist Malatesta visions of Fiume as the base of an anarchist insurrection that would spread throughout Italy. In a similar show of strength, Giolitti renounced Italian claims to Albania and ordered the withdrawal of troops that had become involved in an extremely unpopular war against rebels there.

But in dealing with domestic problems, the Prime Minister was much less successful. His legislative program, which called for extremely heavy taxes on war profits, a stiff income tax, inheritance taxes and a constitutional reform limiting the powers of the monarchy in foreign policy, ran into repeated snags in Parliament, until developments outside of Parliament finally made the passage of the program a virtual impossibility.

Starting in May and continuing into September, principally in Lombardy and Piedmont, more than 160 factories were violently taken over by workers, who raised the red flag of the Soviets above the buildings and shouted their determination to hold out until the industrialists would meet their demands for a greater say in management. There was little enough chance of success, since technicians and managerial personnel did not participate in the strikes; but what chance there was, was destroyed by divisions among the workers themselves, some of whom did not join in the factory occupations voluntarily. There were even instances of workers shot by their co-workers for deviationist activity. In those overheated times, though, sheer panic was the general reaction to what seemed to be the first step in the imminent dictatorship of the proletariat. Coupled with the threat of a nationwide rail strike, the factory occupations seemed part of a two-pronged attack that was to raze to the ground the country's entire capitalist structure.

Giolitti, however, did not call out the national guard as the industrialists insisted. Management, he felt, was not as panicky as it pretended to be, nor was it beyond taking advantage of the situation to deal a real setback to labor and the Socialists. Working closely with the ex-revolutionary syndicalist Arturo Labriola, the Minister of Labor, the Prime Minister forced both sides to come to a negotiated settlement that, had it been implemented, would have opened new ways to Italian capitalism, and would have given an unprecedented voice to labor. With equal dispatch, by brandishing the weapon of instant mobilization, the old Prime Minister settled the national rail strike that threatened to paralyze the country.

Yet despite these successes, Giolitti did not win increased support in Parliament; he lost the support of the more conservative deputies among the Liberals and *Popolari*, appalled at the concessions he made to labor after the occupation of the factories, and he picked up no new support from among independent Liberal deputies or the followers of Nitti. Most crippling, there was no progress made at all in the indispensable objective of winning over the less conservative elements among the Popular Party. When, in an attempt to win moderate Socialist and Radical support, he proposed legislation considered discriminatory against religious orders, calling for compulsory declaration of holdings, he alienated the Popular Party completely. Blocked at every turn, Giolitti called for new elections. Many protested, especially Amendola, who denounced the move as illegal, but Giolitti was determined. Only by running on a wide fusion ticket, a "national bloc," did he expect to win a sufficiently large majority to govern with stability. His often dubious alliances, including one with the Fascists, were certainly the most daring in the old leader's career. This was a climactic moment for all the parties of pre-Fascist Italy, and in particular for the Socialists, or as they were now known (in honor of the Bolsheviks), the *Massimalisti* (Maximalists).

Since the elections of 1919, when the Socialists emerged as the strongest opposition party in the land with one hundred fifty-six representatives in Parliament and a popular vote of 1,440,000, they had played a waiting game. Outside of Parliament, the party was a power: their membership reached almost two million, they held power in over 2,500 communes, the daily circulation of *Avanti!* exceeded 300,000, and the General Confederation of Labor had grown from a pre-war strength of 320,858 to over one million in 1919.

All through 1919 and 1920 the Maximalists moved about in the euphoria of all Socialist parties after the October Revolution. When the King addressed the inaugural session of Parliament in 1919, the belligerently anti-monarchist Socialists, members of the Russian Third International, walked out singing the *Internazionale*. In only a matter of months, it seemed certain, all Europe would turn Marxist; and the Socialists, who had solemnly decreed at the Party Congress of 1919 that the pre-revolutionary period theorized by the Congress of 1892 had come to an end, lived in daily expectation of the final triumph of the revolutionary proletariat. The signs were all about: the bankruptcies, the spiraling number of unemployed, the complete inability of any group in power to maintain order. Any doubt on that score seemed a sign of either obtuseness, excessive prudence or bad faith. The great industrial empires, Ilva and Ansaldo, were tottering. The number of unemployed had passed the two million mark. The great industrial interests were caught in a vicious circle of their own making, falling back on the banks which they had taken over and bringing those banks down with them. The representatives of industry in all parties, the friends of *Confindustria* (the Confederation of Industries, the equivalent of the American Association of Manufacturers) turned against Nitti and Giolitti when they attempted to reform Italian capitalism, and in so acting, they seemed to bear out completely the Marxist analysis of capitalism's ultimate decline.

In this rushing darkness the Maximalists, completely coherent in terms of their own logic, concluded that they had but one course to

follow in Parliament, the abstentionist policy Socialists had adhered
to since 1913. Restricting still further the maneuverability of the
two strong rivals, Giolitti's followers and the Popular Party, that abstentionism, the Socialists were confident, would telescope the last
phases and hasten the paralysis of Parliament to which both Giolitti
and the Popular Party were contributing on their own with their
refusal to collaborate with one another.

As a result of this policy and their accurate appraisal of the situation in Parliament, the Maximalists took scant notice of minor parties of ex-Socialists. These parties, in fact, were not at all numerically important. Bissolati and Bonomi retained only a very meager
following in the 1919 elections, partly because of their interventionism; Salvemini, with his supra-party group, the League for the
Democratic Renewal of the Country, and his veteran's party, which
also sought to be above parties, had not done much better. The same
was also true of Benito Mussolini who, drawing on support from
Nationalists and *arditi* (World War I Italian commandos, many of
whom had invaded Fiume with D'Annunzio), had organized a small
following of his own. That new-born group, which was to be
known as the Fascists, with its vague socialism and equally vague
but intense nationalism, won no parliamentary seats at all in the
1919 elections, and in Milan (the only city in which the Fascists ran
in the municipal elections), they received some five thousand votes
to the Socialists' 170,000 and the 74,000 of the Popular Party.

In spite of the Maximalists' firm grip on the situation, however,
by 1921 they felt the change sweeping through Europe: the
mystique of the Russian Revolution was beginning to wear thin. In
Poland, the armies of the "liberating" Russian Marxist state were
defeated; in Hungary, the Communist regime of Bela Kun, after a
short tenure, folded up; and in Germany, the great hope of all
Italian Socialists, the failure of the Spartacus revolt and the murder
of Rosa Luxemburg and Karl Liebknecht marked the end of the
dream of the great German Marxist state.

In Italy, too, the climate was gradually changing. Capitalism's
"imminent" funeral was repeatedly postponed, and though the system was not powerful enough to withstand all its centrifugal forces,
it did manage to ward off increasing attacks made upon it, and
proved sturdy enough to resist Giolitti's efforts at radical reform.
That dogged resistance played its part in the all-important Socialist

event of the year, the first major split in the party that since 1919 had been waiting for the whirlwind to blow the last clinging fruits off the branches of nearly uprooted trees.

The first crack in party unity occurred in January of 1921, some months before the special elections called by Giolitti, and it was a substantial reversal for the Maximalists and for Serrati, who had taken over party leadership, a schism of notable proportions. At the party congress at Leghorn, a group of delegates, representing 48,000 Socialists (more qualitatively than numerically significant) broke away from the party under the leadership of Amadeo Bordiga, a Neapolitan engineer and editor of the newspaper *Soviet*. The splinter group fully subscribed to Lenin's twenty-one points and constituted itself as the Italian Communist Party, the "authentic" Marxist Socialist party.

It would be a serious, though in fact frequently made, mistake to consider the formation of this party a servile response to an authoritarian Moscow *diktat*, a form of socialist treason. The Maximalists admired Soviet Russia as much as did the Italian Communists; and though from the very beginnings the new party required singular deference to Moscow directives, it nonetheless originated with and expressed purely Italian needs—it was the voice of a group concerned not with imported Russian communism, but with the Italian problems of an Italian Socialist party. Though indistinguishable from a Communist party in ends, the Maximalists were, from the vantage point of the founders of the new party, insufficiently revolutionary, and at the time of the break that judgment was every whit as important as the question of deference to Russian leadership. The Communists were bitterly exasperated by Serrati, by his "do-nothingness," his indecisiveness, his pseudo-revolutionary mood that was more satisfied with disorders than with concrete accomplishments, and above all—and this was their most passionate charge—his alleged crushing of popular insurrectionary initiative, as in the party's condemnation of the factory occupations. The Maximalists, the Communists accused, spoke as if Parliament were of no account, but concurrently counted their successes only in Parliament and acted as if the conflict would be settled principally there.

These points were effectively made not only by Bordiga, but by a Turin group—a new breed of Socialists represented by Palmiro Togliatti, from a middle-class Genoese family; Umberto Terracini, the future president of the first Constituent Assembly after World War II; Angelo Tasca, who was to be the first "deviationist" in the group to challenge the Stalin line; and their leader Antonio Gramsci, a sickly, intense young Sardinian in whom Serrati had placed great hopes, and to whom he had assigned the editorship of the Turin edition of *Avanti!*. All of these men were university graduates. Gramsci, with his newspaper *Ordine Nuovo* (1919–20), had already won a reputation as *the* Marxist-Leninist intellectual of the day. All of them at this time were as appreciative of the needs of cultural warfare as they were of the need of absolute party discipline.

At no point, then or later, did Serrati minimize the loss of this group. He considered it far more serious than the defection of another group on the Right, that of Turati.

Turati, in the flush of the post-war Leninist euphoria, had joined his old enemies within the party, endorsing the party's adherence to the Third International and joining in the cry for "all power to the proletariat." Developments in Russia, however, soon eroded that wild enthusiasm, and when in 1920, an independent Socialist group returned from an inspection trip there and in its report suggested that the Socialist state left something to be desired, Turati's misgivings grew. For a while he continued to hesitate, but after failing in a brief sophistical attempt to persuade the Maximalists that the idea behind the Soviets was really only another version of some parts of his moderate Socialism, Turati burned his bridges. The return of Giolitti to power, furthermore, and the Liberal leader's radical reform measures, firmly fixed Turati in his new resolve. His position returned substantially to what it had been from 1892 to 1911. The October Revolution notwithstanding, Turati was still basically a man of order with a deep-rooted respect for law, and as such he soon found the wave of strikes, especially those of civil servants, intolerable, idiotic and self-defeating. Serrati had not encouraged the factory occupation movement, but he had sought to make capital of it, and that appalled Turati and his allies, the General Confederation of Labor. At the time of the threatened rail strike in 1920, indeed, Turati had become so incensed that he suggested that strike breakers keep the trains running if necessary. Socialist policy, he despairingly concluded by 1921, paralleled the disastrous condition of the country.

Accordingly, Turati applied all his skills to the impossible task of undoing the effects of the long Socialist abstentionist policy. Working with his old lieutenants and with some new followers, including Giacomo Matteotti, a Piedmontese socialist who had many of Giolitti's businesslike ways, Turati tried to pick up the thread of Socialist collaboration and offer whatever help he could muster to Giolitti, who was still for moderate Socialists the most enlightened and acceptable ally. The alternative, Turati was convinced, was the onset of a reaction such as the party had never experienced.

Under criticism from Turati, who denounced him for going too far to the Left, and from the Communists, who accused him of working too closely with Turati's Right, Serrati stood his ground, staunchly adhering to his abstentionist policy in Parliament while waiting for developments. Turati, the Maximalist leader judged, had his hands tied; and the Communists' revolutionary preaching was not likely to be more effective than his own. As a sign of his robust confidence, he even made a remarkable show of independence toward a Bolshevik order that year. When word came from Russia to excommunicate Turati, whom the Russian leaders held responsible for the failure of the factory occupations, Serrati refused. He did not consider the excommunication necessary. Out of practical considerations (he appreciated the power of the moderates in the cooperative movement in Central Italy and in the General Confederation of Labor), and out of sentimental reasons (he lacked completely the Turin Communists' iron sense of discipline), Serrati refused to read the old Milanese out of the party he had helped to found. Like Giolitti, Serrati was willing to gamble on the 1921 elections to vindicate his policy and to demonstrate that defectors on both the Right and the Left had completely misjudged the situation and that they were all extremist deviationists with a limited following.

When the results of that election were tallied, Giolitti and not Serrati appeared to have miscalculated badly. The majority won by the Prime Minister's national bloc was nowhere near the size required for a stable government. For the very last time, Giolitti stepped down—to the despair of Turati, who pleaded with him to try to form one more Cabinet—and the way appeared to be clear for Serrati's methodic, irresistible rise to power. True, the results showed that the schism had hurt the Maximalists, who dropped from the 153 seats they had won in 1919 to 138 (the Communists won eighteen seats), but in spite of that, and in spite of a slight Popular Party gain from one hundred to 107 seats, Serrati was confident. The election, he was certain, bore out his analysis of the situation, and though there was still a long piece of road to travel, tactically he had made no mistakes. The Popular Party was strong, no doubt, but it did not seem any more unsurmountable an obstacle than the wily Giolitti. They, in any case, were the enemy, they and a few Liberal-Radical factions, and not at all the admittedly troublesome Fascists, who had run on Giolitti's coalition ticket, winning some thirty-five seats.

It was true, however, that the Fascists had become a particular concern for the Socialists, and though Mussolini probably exaggerated in 1921 with his claim that his group, now constituted into a party, was 370,000 strong, the fact remained that the Fascists had made remarkable gains in two years. Defection from the Socialist Party had deprived Mussolini of a cause that would undoubtedly have been very much to his taste and skills—that of the October Revolution—but he had more than made up for that loss by fully exploiting the weakness of most Socialists (with the exception of Turati's group): their virulent, unbalanced, fanatic attacks on patriotism in any form. In the immediate aftermath of the war, when interventionists and neutralists were at each other's throats, Mussolini knew how to exploit the prevalent, many-faceted nationalism. Returning veterans and a new generation too young to have gone to war but impatient for action and violence were drawn in increasing numbers to the party's undisguised eagerness to use force against the Socialists, and so were members of the older generation, with Liberal or Popular Party sympathies, who saw a great deal of merit to the idea of "putting the Socialists in their place." As the issue of neutralism versus interventionism simmered down, Mussolini continued to capitalize on what had become a singular anti-Socialist crusade. Fascist squads of armed, uniformed men, each led by its "ras" (the tribal chieftain title suggests something of the ferocity of the African leaders who had fought against Italians in Abyssinia) made violent progress. Roberto Farinacci in Cremona and Italo Balbo in Tuscany were but two of those who were daily acquiring growing fame and notoriety with the systematic technique of their punitive expeditions against Socialist unions and strikes. The squads began humbly with an organized hooting down of Bissolati as he made a foreign policy speech at La Scala, but rapidly proceeded to more ambitious ventures such as burning down the *Avanti!* headquarters in Milan.

Mussolini's successes, however, were not confined to his *squadre*, or to support won from a number of industrialists persuaded that contributions to the party would be to their advantage. He was also making inroads among the great mass of the unpolitical, the great, vague middle class without party affiliations, almost hysterically calling for some stability, some protection from the unremitting strikes and unheavals, even long after any real danger had passed away, as in the case of the failure of the factory occupations. His success in this field, in fact, more than outweighed his failure to persuade workers at the time of the factory occupations that he was on their side, an attempt that went hand in hand with his efforts to win increasing support from industrialists.

In spite of the Fascists' advances, however, and even though Socialists bore the brunt of their attacks, the Maximalists and Serrati were, like the Popular Party and the Liberals, convinced that Mussolini's party was not a clear and present danger. Turati was more apprehensive than most Socialists, and for once more perceptive than Anna Kuliscioff, who did not consider the Fascists a threat, but even he had not the slightest inkling of the scope of Mussolini's ambitions or his skills, and in any case he would not have known what to do about it. Like many Italians, Turati was almost hypnotized by what he saw happening. The eyes were clear but the hand trembled. As a man grown old in the anti-violence persuasion, all he could do was to raise his voice in Cassandralike prophecy: the glorious limit of his moderate socialism. In the crisis that followed the resignation of Giolitti, there was nothing else to do. The decisions and responsibilities were not to be his, but those of the Maximalists and the Popular Party, heirs apparent to a broken, vacant throne.

VIII

MUSSOLINI'S TRASFORMISMO—
A NEW VARIANT

Of the post-war prime ministers, Giolitti was the only one who showed any of the vision and strength necessary for the crisis. He knew when to say yes and when to say no. He made a valiant effort to infuse spirit into a Parliament that no longer believed in itself.

He failed. In the 1920's, not even the most statesmanlike trasformismo could work. The first- and second-largest parties in the land would not allow Giolitti to carry off his time-tested technique of playing one group off against another. The Catholics and Socialists had their own programs and leaders and would not put them at Giolitti's disposal in order to have him take over most of their political program, leaving them with no option but to follow his lead.

For Don Sturzo, in particular, the *"pretuncolo,"* the insignificant little priest, as Giolitti had called him, Giolitti's defeat was a settling of accounts. Giolitti's last attempt to govern was, for the Sicilian priest, nothing more than a last desperate variation of the Gentiloni pact, a way of utilizing the Catholic vote for his own ends. The failure, the Popular Party leader hoped, would be instructive. A Catholic party of unprecedented strength, at least in terms of parliamentary power, had served notice for once and for all that it was no longer to be used for taking other parties' chestnuts out of the fire.

Although the defeat of Giolitti appeared to Sturzo as a giant stride forward, the Secretary of the Popular Party had no illusions as to the immediate gains for his party. Had any of its leaders, Meda, De Gasperi or Giovanni Gronchi (the latter two to the left of Meda's center), formed a new government, in all likelihood the combined opposition, from Salandra's Liberals to the Communists, would have closed ranks in an anti-Populist coalition that would have made that tenure short indeed; and the party, Sturzo was convinced, could not bear the strain of an early defeat in its first accession to power. One false step, moreover, he sensed, and the party would lose a following that it could not do without: those adherents whose nostalgia for the prewar social and economic order was the better part of their politics, and for whom the party was essentially a vehicle of anti-Socialism and anti-Communism. In need of this group, but equally in need of proving to the country that their party was not a tool of conservatives, the Populists had to give tangible signs of their progressiveness. For the time being, therefore, Sturzo preferred a policy of cooperation with moderate Socialists to collaboration with right-wing Liberals of Salandra's persuasion. He felt the party should support the reformist, Ivanoe Bonomi, who had already been suggested several times before to head a new government; it should accept positions in his Cabinet and study up to what point conservative Populist groups in Parliament would vote for moderate reforms now that Giolitti was out of the picture.

With the backing of the Catholics, then, and over the opposition of some Liberal groups, including Giolitti's, Bonomi took office in July 1921—the first Socialist of any denomination to become prime minister of Italy. Unforceful, peace-loving, with a weakness for D'Annunzio's patriotic rhetoric, the somewhat popular Bonomi did rather well in his short tenure, to the surprise of friends and enemies. He did not succeed where Giolitti had failed, and indeed he had to abandon completely Giolitti's proposal to tax stockholdings, but for seven months he adhered to reform policies and managed to win a following among diverse groups. He did not buckle under pressure from the extreme conservatives, and when in November 1921, the Banco di Sconto, on the verge of bankruptcy, called on the government for help, Bonomi authorized only reimbursement for depositors, and allowed the bank to go into bankruptcy rather than have the state assume the entire debt, as it had done previously in such circumstances. Eventually, however, the pace of his reforms

—too much for some, too little for others—undid him. When the last concerted attack was made upon his policies, Bonomi had no substantial support to fall back on, and in February 1922, after a vote of no confidence, he stepped down. Even more than to his reform program, however, the failure of Bonomi was due to the conjunction of two rapid developments: the unwillingness of many right-wing Populists to support him any longer, and, equally decisive, the whirlwind advance of the Fascists.

By February of 1922, the Fascists were unmistakably a power in the land. At the time of Giolitti's fall they were already strong in numbers, arms, and popular and clandestine support, and during the months of Bonomi's tenure they continued to batter their way ahead. Bonomi's inability to check their advance largely accounted for his loss of support among groups that he could not do without; for even moderate Socialists joined in the Parliamentary hue and cry against his weak pacificatory measures. Abruptly, the political situation was changing for all Socialists—Maximalists, Turatians and Communists—and it was taking an obvious plunge for the worse. Before Bonomi came to power, the primary concern of the Maximalists had been to determine how to outmaneuver the Populists and Giolitti in Parliament; six months later, their desperate need was to find ways and means to compel Parliament and the government to protect them from the methodic terrorism of Fascist squads. As Bonomi himself was among the first to recognize, the followers of Mussolini had made impressive gains in Romagna, where, after being called in by small landowners to defend them from Socialists and Communists, they had become for all intents and purposes the local and national police force. They had also made inroads in Tuscany, central Italy, parts of Lombardy and in the South, where their punitive squads wrought havoc reminiscent of the immediate chaotic aftermath of the war.

The Socialists and Communists fought back hard. In Rome in particular, where the Communists organized the *Arditi del popolo* (The People's Shock-Troops), resistance to the Fascists was vigorous. The fact remained, nonetheless, that in general the leftist parties had neither the arms nor the military organization of the Fascist squads—professional, technically competent units that were to be incorporated into the private Fascist army, the Fascist Militia, in October 1922; most important, they lacked the Fascists' wide popular support and the secret support Mussolini's group had won in high places.

Incapable of striking back effectively or for long, the Socialists were even less capable of understanding what the sudden rise of the Fascists meant. Even before Fascist violence reached its highest point, they had no other explanation for what was happening than the standard Marxist explanation: Bonomi, who closed his eyes to Fascist violence, was a contemptible *venduto* (sell-out) working hand in glove with vested interests who used the Fascists as marionettes. This interpretation of the upsurge of Fascist strength as confirmation of how the economic "powers that be" pull strings in the political arena (and there was no question but that industrial interests did aid and abet Mussolini) no doubt bolstered Socialist confidence in the truth of economic determinism. Unfortunately, however, it did little else. Oblivious to the truism that vested interests and anti-Socialist parties under attack by Socialists since 1919 were likely to fight back like the animal in La Fontaine's fable (". . . *un animal méchant, quand on l'attaque il se defend*"), and blind to the obvious explanation that Bonomi's weakness was due more to his almost timid temperament than to collusion and betrayal, the Socialists showed that they understood the nature of Fascism no better than most other parties in Italy, and nothing that Bonomi or the Popular Party did in these months could persuade them otherwise.

The Socialists were not impressed by the government's show of strength on July 21, 1921, near Sarzana, Tuscany, when police, at a cost of eighteen dead and thirty wounded, intercepted a column of Fascists on the way to free their *ras*, the fanatical Renato Ricci, from jail. They were not impressed when, toward the close of Bonomi's tenure, the Prime Minister made another show of firmness on the occasion of a threatened Fascist demonstration in Rome on the day commemorating the Unknown Soldier. They were infuriated when, alleging the threat of continued violence, Bonomi ordered the Communist People's Shock-Troops to disband. But the Socialists, caught in the mounting violence, did not act very differently from the Prime Minister in their own attempts to deal with the Fascists. On August 3, 1922, much to the fury of the Communists, the Maximalists signed a short-lived truce with Mussolini. In a very short time, a new wave of Fascist attacks spread throughout Tuscany, especially in Massa Carrara, a stronghold of the Maximalists, northwest Lombardy near Cremona, throughout the South, and, significantly, for the first time in industrial Turin. For Socialists and Communists, that violence was the last proof, if it were needed, of the collusion between Bonomi and the Fascists. More than once they urged Parliament to oust Bonomi on a vote of no confidence. When the Prime Minister was finally forced down, many Socialists of all persuasions felt they had been rescued just in time.

The danger was not over, however. Another threat of a totally different type, the Socialists were sure, would now come from the Popular Party: for if responsibility for Fascist strength was to be attributed to all bourgeois parties, the Popular Party, now the strongest, was obviously the most threatening.

The Socialists were not altogether wrong in their simplistic appraisal, for the policy of Don Sturzo was not void of uncertainties and ambiguities that could be easily misinterpreted. By 1920, Sturzo recognized in the scraps of ideology that passed as Fascist doctrine (the notion of the all-powerful state, the exaltation of brute force, the mystique of the nation) political ideals that were completely unacceptable to the Populists, and that justified the party's refusal to work with Giolitti, who was not ill-disposed to Mussolini's group. But after the defeat of Bonomi, Don Sturzo also realized that increasing numbers of Populists were casting admiring glances toward the Fascists, who were *doing* something to put Socialists and Communists in their place, even at the risk of their own lives, and who had even shown a promising appreciation of the papacy, as witnessed by Mussolini's respectful words for Pope Pius XI soon after his coronation in 1922. Moreover, Don Sturzo recognized that the appreciation of Liberals of all persuasions for their black-shirted allies was increasing. In consideration of all these factors, though he had no personal sympathies for the right wing of the party and was bitterly disappointed by their revolt against Bonomi, Sturzo toned down his misgivings and did not take an intransigent anti-Fascist stand. Instead, he concentrated all his efforts in Parliament on blocking the return to power of Orlando or Giolitti, and finding a more acceptable leader—a leader who was never to appear.

The policy of Sturzo was no doubt coherent and in keeping with the demands of his overall strategy. It put him, however, on a direct collision course with Turati's group, the one sizable anti-Fascist group of any conceivable help to him in solving the crisis of the power vacuum that followed Bonomi's resignation.

After the downfall of Giolitti, Turati, who had pleaded with him to try to form one more Cabinet, despaired of any solution to the crisis. Wearily and futilely he warned his own group, all other Socialists and Parliament that if parties would not here and now agree upon one strong prime minister respectful of Parliament, that body would cease to be; having warned them, Turati desultorily withdrew. The only forceful action to which the desperate moderate Socialist leader could bring himself was to veto the designation of any political man he was sure could not resolve the crisis—a negative policy that, as it turned out, was neither much different nor more successful than that of Sturzo.

Thus, with the reciprocal paralysis of the Socialist, Liberal and Popular Parties in Parliament, the growing defections to the Fascists from all groups, and the unwillingness or incapacity of any forceful representative of either the Populists or the Liberals to assume responsibility for a new government, the stage was set for the as yet untested parliamentarian skills of Mussolini.

An alliance of those Populists, like Sturzo, mistrustful of the Fascists, with Turati's Socialists might have made Mussolini's progress more difficult. But aside from the fundamental, enduring conflict over Giolitti that kept the two groups apart, there was an old animosity and partially justified mistrust of some thirty years' standing. Sturzo was willing to collaborate with Bonomi's Reformist Socialists, but because of Turati's reluctance to break completely with the Maximalists, he did not think seriously of approaching him; and Turati, willing to collaborate with Giolitti's program, balked at moving closer to Sturzo out of fear of pontifical pressure and because of the predominance of the conservative right-wing elements in the Catholic party.

Under such circumstances, consequently, the designation of a weak political leader to form a new government was tantamount to abdication by all parties. When Parliament, against the opposition of Don Sturzo and the Socialists, settled on the grey, hesitant Luigi Facta, a Giolittian Liberal whose ways made Bonomi look like a Renaissance despot, it was recognized by many that the legislative body had signed its own death warrant.

In every way Facta's tenure lived up to the expectations of those who dreaded the implications of his designation and those who, for the same reasons, applauded it. To the surprise of no one, the containment of Fascism became *the* problem of Facta's government. Throughout Italy bands of *camicie nere* (black-shirts) stepped up the tempo of their beatings, systematically attacking and mauling Socialists and Communists without any real interference by police or government troops. The question of whether Facta was in collusion with the Fascists or supinely acquiescing had by this time become irrelevant. In Emilia, in particular, the situation was completely in the hands of the Fascists; there were abundant signs that Fascist leaders and their squads were for all practical purposes recognized as *de facto* defenders of law and order. In fact, the Fascist campaign was so successful that in 1922, the May Day parades, which only a few years before had been joyous, confident heralds of the imminent triumph of the workers' state, were reduced to small bands of marching diehards, peered at furtively by passers-by.

Two months after the failure of the May Day parades, the battered and beleaguered Socialists, not knowing where to turn, yielded to the Communists' argument that there was still time for one last gesture, a united stand, a nationwide general strike. In this way, Serrati, Turati and Bordiga hoped, the defections from the leftist parties might be checked, Facta might be forced to some protective action, and the Fascists might grasp the limits of what they could accomplish with clubs and guns. On July 31, 1922, word was sent to all Socialists throughout the country to band together, to demonstrate to all that if the struggle in Italy was, as it seemed to be, a showdown between them and the Fascists, then Mussolini's followers still had an enemy to contend with.

Within a matter of days the general strike turned out to be a disastrous Socialist miscalculation. It had no sooner begun than Fascists informed Facta that anything less than a total suppression of the "attack upon the state" would be tantamount to treason and would be dealt with as such. Immediately, in Emilia, Parma, Ancona and Leghorn, Fascist squads attacked Socialist headquarters, newspaper offices, and anything that distantly resembled a gathering of Socialists. The fighting was not confined to central Italy. In Genoa, where the Maximalists were particularly strong, fighting lasted two days; in Milan, Fascists again attacked and burned down the offices

of *Avanti!* In a matter of days, the defiant gesture of the combined
Maximalist, Communist and moderate Socialist forces came to a
crumpled, gasping end. The mass following of those parties appeared to be totally destroyed and, the most ironic twist of all, they
had provided Mussolini with what seemed undeniable proof that in
Italy the true struggle was not in Parliament but in the country,
between his followers and the Socialists. He had "rescued" the nation from a last desperate Socialist attack.

As an almost immediate consequence of the swift suppression of
the general strike the number of sympathizers and followers of
Mussolini soared. Among Liberals, Populists and the great mass of
the unpolitical, the conviction hardened that when all was said and
done, the Fascists acted while other parties talked. The more politically sophisticated did not think much differently and waited for
developments, quite aware that a party generally looked upon as the
saviour of the country was not likely to moderate its ambitions,
especially with an irresolute and ineffectual leader as head of state.
There was very little else, of course, that the apprehensive among
such groups could do.

For their part, the Socialists considered themselves fortunate to
find some sort of refuge in the Parliament they had long covered
with abuse and helped to paralyze by their abstentionist policy. The
Communists, by contrast, plotted surreptitiously. In these months
Gramsci sought to make contact with D'Annunzio (who had given
ample evidence of his willingness to vie with Mussolini) in an attempt to work out some sort of an alliance with the aging poet and
with Captain Giulietti, the head of a left-wing maritime union, who
was particularly close to D'Annunzio. Nothing came of the scheme
—1922 was not the year for farfetched alliances, and the Fascists
were not a party to be done away with by even the most brilliant improvisations. D'Annunzio had a following, especially among
the military and the Nationalists, but he did not have the equivalent of the Fascist squads with their ruthless leaders, and since it
was not he who had crushed the Socialist general strike, his popular
support came nowhere near that of Mussolini. Neither D'Annunzio,
nor any political leader in Italy in 1922, for that matter, had the
growing consensus Mussolini enjoyed among all classes.

Mussolini enjoyed this consensus even among intellectuals, even
among those of the stature of Benedetto Croce. "As any fair-minded

observer must acknowledge," Croce declared in an interview in these times, "the Fascists have done a great deal of good." Although this statement, like most of Croce's, allowed for a fair amount of exegesis in spite of the apparent simplicity of thought and expression, it was not cryptic. The Fascists, in Croce's estimate (and here he voiced a conviction he held in common with his closest collaborator, Gentile, even more disenchanted with the Liberals than he), were defending a state that since the end of the war had barely survived repeated socialist assaults. Industrial strikes, parliamentary abstentionism, strikes of civil servants, attacks upon patriotism in all its various forms—all this Socialist-Communist agitated chaos infuriated Croce as it infuriated many in those months; he was therefore well disposed to the Fascist Party, which made of anti-Socialism and anti-Communism the be-all and end-all of its program. The Fascists were violent but Croce, who shook his head over Socialist violence, and deplored the vacillation of the prime minsters who followed Giolitti, did not consider that fact either outrageous or unjustifiable. The Fascists acted almost exclusively outside of and independently of Parliament, but Croce—who had reservations on a do-nothing Parliament and just as serious reservations on paralyzed parties—was not the man to defend inviolable party or parliamentary rights.

This was not to say that he was less of a Liberal, or less admiring of Giolitti. Croce had accepted Giolitti's invitation to join the Cabinet as minister of education principally because he saw it as the last chance to implement his program for educational reform; but he did admire the old political man, and his admiration grew with that experience. Like Giolitti he believed that once order was reestablished and the state was freed from the Socialist threat, the Fascists would then find it to their best interest to observe the law. Nothing about Mussolini himself or what was known of his political creed made Croce think differently.

It was not Croce's style to speak out on the contemporary political scene but certain inferences in his writings offer a basis for surmising his reactions to key issues. His attitude to some of Giolitti's pro-Fascist moves, for example, can be plausibly inferred from a reference, in the *Etica e Politica* (*Ethics and Politics*) of 1924, to a criticism commonly made of Mirabeau's dubious alliances for the cause of parliamentary liberalism. Mirabeau, Croce argued, had undoubtedly made some very compromising alliances, but they were to be judged in the light of the good ends he had in mind. In the same year, as in preceding years, Croce insisted (and we have no reason to believe that he had Mussolini in mind) not only that *ad hominem* charges had no place in politics, but that personal failings simply had no place in political judgments. The only criterion was technical political ability; so that if, for example, Croce suggested, a country had the mixed blessing of a gifted political leader with a dangerous appetite for the opposite sex, the only course for prudent fathers and beautiful daughters to follow was to take the necessary precautions and stay out of his way. The analogy was coy. Some readers just may have recognized that in terms of what was happening in political Italy the implications of the comparison were chilling. For political parties and for many non-political Italians, Mussolini was no threat as long as, analogously, he was raping somebody else's daughter.

In a similar way, Croce's attitude to the lack of any specific socio-economic Fascist doctrine can be inferred from a polemic he engaged in years later with Einaudi on the nature of political liberalism. Liberalism required, according to Croce, only one hard and fast position: a recognition that economic liberalism of the late nineteenth century was not of the essence, and an awareness of the need of a purely pragmatic judgment with respect to the degree of state intervention desirable in a private economy. On these grounds—his preference for a party that had no hard and fast political philosophy —Croce was drawn much more to the Fascists than to the Populists. He had many good friends among the members of the Catholic party, and Don Sturzo himself, according to the philosopher's own testimony, in considering a possible *Popolari* government had offered Croce a tentative place as minister of education. But the Catholic party, according to Croce, had an irredeemable flaw: its entire program and political philosophy was based on an impossible reconciliation of vague democratic aspirations with papal autocracy. A party burdened with an error of this magnitude could no more win Croce's firm support than could Socialists of any denomination.

This conclusion, if not the mode of arriving at it, was shared by many Liberals of Croce's generation with alert political interests, and by a greater number with only a sporadic interest in politics. Above all, these groups sought a solution to the parliamentary crisis, to the violence, to the confusion; for that end they were willing to give Mussolini a blank check.

Quick to sense the general mood of expectation after the failure of the general strike, Mussolini took a page from D'Annunzio's experience in Fiume. In autumn of 1922, he began to ready his forces for a *coup d'état*. The Socialists were no longer a power to contend with, and in that year, as a sign of surrender, the head of the powerful CGL (General Confederation of Labor) had declared its neutrality. The Popular Party continued to be badly split and to suffer increasing defections from its right wing. The Liberals showed little hostility. The only question marks left were the King and the army —and for some time, Mussolini had used threats and blandishments to bringing both into line. He alternated anti-monarchist comments with negotiations with the strongly pro-monarchist Nationalists, and in a similar way, while appealing to the traditional military man's appreciation of order, he made it clear that he did not intend to be blocked by the army.

By late October, all preparatory maneuvers had been completed and from Milan, where he directed the operation, Mussolini gave the word to some 26,000 Fascists, not very well armed or disciplined, to move from Naples and Perugia, where they had taken over the local governments, and to converge on Rome. On October 28, the black-shirted Fascists and the grey-shirted Nationalists arrived in the capital, ready to back Mussolini's months-old demand for the dissolution of Parliament and the calling of new elections. The rest was up to the King, commander in chief of a loyal army.

The King deliberated for twenty-four hours whether or not to declare a state of siege and call on the troops to disperse the Fascists. There were reasons why he did not need more time to deliberate. He, too, was grateful to the Fascists for having disposed of the Socialist threat. He, too, was weary of the instability of government (at the time of Bonomi's fall he had pointedly informed the ministers that that was the twentieth government crisis of his reign), the ineffectualness of Parliament and the increasing violence. He appreciated the judgment of the industrial interests that backed Mussolini. Of firm anti-clerical views, he had no particular use for the Populists and he particularly disliked Sturzo. He was also aware that there were members of the royal household, notably the Duke of Aosta, eager to capitalize on the enthusiasm for the Fascist cause. For all these reasons, the King refused to sign the declaration of a state of siege that Facta had prepared, and two days later, exercising his prerogative, personally designated Mussolini prime minister.

On October 30, consequently, with an insignificant number of elected Fascists in Parliament but with the support of many deputies there, the thirty-nine year old Mussolini became prime minister of Italy on his own terms. For in the feverish negotiations which took place while the Fascists were marching on Rome, Mussolini held firm to his conditions, refusing to share power with any other party. When he did concede places in his first Cabinet to representatives of most parties, he made it clear in each instance that the minister was chosen more on grounds of individual worth than as a representative of his party. The Liberal Italy of pre-World War I, and the Italy of the post-war period in which power seemed destined to go either to the Socialists or the Catholics, were no more. And to make that victory total, soon after, with the indispensable help of the representatives of most parties, Mussolini pushed through the Acerbo electoral reform law, without which the first Fascist elections of 1924 might have yielded far different results. That law, which won the support of Salandra and Giolitti, awarded disproportionate parliamentary strength to the party that could win the greatest number of votes; since the Fascist bloc could by then count on massive support, it made a Fascist victory absolutely certain. In the election of April 1924, the Fascists won with a popular vote of 4,305,000 (some 65 per cent of the total) and 356 seats in Parliament.

With legal sanction of their accession to power, one month after the election the Fascists completed mopping-up operations against the steadily dwindling opposition. Censorship of Socialist and Communist newspapers was tightened sharply as a preamble to eventual total suppression; a wartime defector then serving as a Communist deputy was expelled from Parliament; and in the exuberance of the moment the tougher elements among the Fascists relished the prospect of one last round of beatings of Socialists and Communists.

In all probability, had it not been for one sudden startling development, the takeover would have been completed in a curt, businesslike way. There were still remnants of the opposition to dispose of but none of them, certainly not the Socialists, were a threat. The Socialist Party, in fact, appeared to be doing its utmost to hasten its own disintegration. In October, the month of the march on Rome, a harried and panicky Serrati reconsidered his past attitude toward Turati and his group and concluded that nothing would better serve the Socialist cause than to accept the Communist notion that the Turatians were a contemptible petit-bourgeois party and that they were largely responsible for the triumph of Fascism. He accordingly expelled Turati and his group from the Socialist Party.

Consequently, when the Turatian, Giacomo Matteotti rose in Parliament to denounce the elections, no one present expected much to come of his attack, since he had only the weakest of parties to back him up. Matteotti had the courage to speak out in Parliament, but what he spelled out was already generally known. It was no secret that members of the Fascist militia had been posted at election booths to insure the desired returns, or that the more outspoken enemies of the regime (Amendola, for one, who had become the leader of the dissident Liberals) had been beaten; that threats of financial retaliation had been made to insure votes; that in one way or another all enemies of the regime had been harassed; and finally, that the Fascists had intended to remain in power regardless of the outcome of the election.

Matteotti's talk, unsurprisingly, was hooted down in parts, and there were the usual Fascist threats, not particularly noteworthy. What was worthy of note, however, was that on the afternoon of June 10, 1924, Matteotti failed to return to his home or to Parliament, and that for two months nothing was heard of his whereabouts. Then suddenly, on August 16, the newspapers carried the story of the discovery, in not altogether clear circumstances, of Matteotti's knifed body, half-buried in a wood some twenty-three kilometers north of Rome.

From the very first days of his disappearance, the *bien pensants*, all those who were well-disposed to the Fascists, were in a state of shock and incredulity. Matteotti was not a conspirational Communist or a firebrand enemy of the regime. A member of Turati's group, he was by no means a demagogic subversive threat to law and order. In horrified fear, consequently, many Fascist sympathizers turned away from the party; many who had but lately applauded Fascist brutality slipped into stunned silence. Whatever the actual extent of Mussolini's involvement (and at best, the murder implied that he was not in control of the tougher elements in the party), the entire country *knew* that the Duce was involved; and in this knowledge Italians waited in fear and horror for something to happen. Then and there it seemed impossible that life should go on as usual, that horror should be exorcised by a few sporadic demonstrations and protests. The murder demanded that Italians seriously reconsider their support of the Fascists and of Mussolini, and it cried out for an alliance of all opposition parties to hurl one last challenge at a regime which in terms of its own logic had been guilty of something worse than a crime—a gigantic blunder.

Indeed, the crime vindicated Don Sturzo's initial opposition to the Fascists and his insistence in 1924 that the Populists run on an independent ticket, a decision which resulted in the greatest number of votes won by any party except the Fascists, some 643,000 in all. It had taken all of Sturzo's prestige and power to persuade the party to do so, and the result, from the standpoint of party unity, was no doubt a Pyrrhic victory of sorts. For Mussolini soon after, by asking those Populists who had joined his Cabinet to hand in their resignations on grounds that the Catholic party at its last congress in 1923 had refused to give him a blank check, provoked a definitive break between the leaders of the Catholic right and Don Sturzo. The defection of the right wing, however, left the Popular Party still under Sturzo's leadership united and compact. Don Sturzo, with the unwavering support of De Gasperi, Gronchi and others of his persuasion, could now give a definitive rebuttal to the charge that the Catholic party was nothing more than a party of Fascist fellow travelers.

Similarly, the Matteotti murder led to a clear separation of one small group of Liberals from all the rest. That group, headed by Amendola, who had also run on an independent ticket, joined forces with De Gasperi and Gronchi (Sturzo had resigned as Party Secretary in July) and representatives from all Socialist parties to hurl one last challenge at Mussolini. Breaking off from Parliament, the group constituted itself as a rump parliament, the Aventino, so named after the Roman hill on which it met, and proceeded to ask for Mussolini's immediate resignation, the restitution of all political and civil liberties, and the abolition of the Fascist militia. These demands were made, in the name of the nation, to the King.

The King, however, in the celebrated phrase of Turati, "did not permit himself to be distracted from his philatelic studies," and the Aventino, as a consequence, busied itself with continued appeals to the country, further investigation into Fascist responsibility for and police collusion in the crime, and a search for a proper political form into which to channel popular indignation and the sudden loss of Fascist popularity.

Mussolini, in the meantime, had begun to reorganize his forces and face the crisis, as was his wont, with threats and blandishments. With each passing day his position grew stronger. Before long, he scored a remarkable success in the Senate. Blustering and uncertain, the Fascist leader had gone to that body, very soon after the murder, for a vote of confidence. He had conceded that he could not always hold back the extremists in his group, and defending the Fascists as the party of order and patriotism, he called upon the Senate to assume its responsibility in maintaining order and preventing further bloodshed. One senator present, Luigi Albertini, editor of the *Corriere della Sera*, protested that one speech could not undo twenty months of Fascist violence; Senator Croce, in particular, asked for very firm assurances from the Fascist leader that order and civil and political liberties would be reestablished and respected. When the final vote was taken, of the 253 senators, 225, including Croce, gave Mussolini the required vote of confidence; twenty-one refused and seven abstained.

No doubt Croce found the crime appalling and believed Mussolini implicated in it. He also concluded, apparently, that the involvement was not sufficient reason to deny Mussolini a vote of confidence; that as Mussolini had demonstrated authentic political gifts before that crime, so he would continue to demonstrate them after. It would have been more to Croce's liking, certainly, had the long violence and the murder never occurred; but Croce had long since come to terms with the dark side of politics. In the *Etica e Politica* (*Ethics and Politics*) of 1924, the philosopher approvingly quoted Sorel to the effect that "every time a man in politics acquires a reputation for decency and goodness, it is always necessary to get rid of him, because the invariable accompaniment of those political virtues is political ineptness;" and on his own, Croce had added that honest, decent men in politics were "usually like well-intentioned surgeons operating with insufficient knowledge and experience." Matteotti was unquestionably a more decent political man than Mussolini, but Mussolini had more knowledge and experience.

Against this first success of Mussolini, the Aventino countered some time later with sensational disclosures that documented in detail Fascist police collusion. It also continued to insist that the Fascist militia disband, and its newspapers and periodicals, in particular Amendola's *Il Mondo,* and *Il Popolo* of the Catholic editor Giuseppe Donati, did their utmost to keep alive the sense of skepticism and expectation that was gradually deteriorating into a state of head-shaking acquiescence.

Of all those who fought with the pen, though, none was so young, so dynamic, so strikingly confused and perceptive as twenty-three-year-old Piero Gobetti, the precocious editor of the *Rivoluzione Liberale,* a publication that gave the anti-Fascism of the Aventino a style and spirit that were to be remembered long after Gobetti himself ceased to fight. With an enthusiasm for ideas that outstripped his sense of discrimination, the attacks of the intense, puritanical Gobetti, even before the Aventino, had goaded Mussolini to write to the Prefect in Turin "to make life hard for Gobetti." Croce had personally intervened to free him from prison, but even when he was liberated, Gobetti showed none of the prudence or peculiar political wisdom of the philosopher, whom he admired and respected to the last. That admiration, however, in keeping with Gobetti's age, was rather confused. Initially (Gobetti had published his first magazine, *Energie Nove* [*New Energies*], in 1919 at the age of seventeen) the young publicist had argued that there was a common denominator between Salvemini, who was his political ideal, Croce, Gentile, Einaudi and a host of minor thinkers. As he had gradually realized that no such common denominator was very meaningful in a precise political context, he had gone to the other extreme of denying that the entire varied Liberal tradition was of much value. True liberalism, he was arguing by 1922, was the revolutionary Marxist liberalism of the Russian state; and in that discovery he had thrown himself heart and soul into a study of things Russian, and worked very closely with Gramsci and his followers on the newspaper *Ordine Nuovo* (*New Order*).

But his enthusiasm was not confined to Russia nor was it quite the same as the enthusiasm for Russia expressed by the Communist Party. An unsuccessful Gramsci-organized strike that had been for the Communist leader one incident among others, became a sustaining vision for Gobetti; even during the Aventino crisis, when the ideals of that strike seemed so distant and unattainable, Gobetti never quite lost sight of them.

On April 13, 1920, that strike, in brief, had been fought for the

rights of the *commissioni interne* in the Fiat works, factory committees that had a limited say in management and production, but that
in Gobetti's vision were to approximate the Russian soviets. By
assuming constantly increasing powers, by-passing do-nothing labor
unions and the acquiescent all-words-and-no-action Maximalist
Party, the factory committees, according to Gobetti, were ultimately to take over factories completely and erect the framework
of the new society, which was to rise out of a revolution not in the
political superstructure, but in the economic substructure. Once
firmly in power, the factory workers were to join forces with organized peasants, whose cause Salvemini had pleaded in vain, and the
work of both forces, acting in harmony, was to be the "Liberal
Revolution." Precisely which political party was to implement this
vision was not clear in Gobetti's mind, however; and there were
enough ambiguities in his position to make the charge of crypto-
Communism frequently levelled at him, implausible but not absurd.
In an obvious sense, no party, not even the Communists, could
implement this vision because of the very fact that it was a political
party acting in the political superstructure. But from another point
of view, Gobetti's Marxist-Leninist sympathies were strong enough
to make many Liberals to this day wonder just how his revolution
could be considered Liberal. The Liberals and Populists of this time
no doubt were hardly the soul of equanimity in their appraisal of
the Russian Revolution, but Gobetti was hardly *au dessus de la
mélée*. His willingness to believe the best of that Revolution at all
times, which made him stand staunchly by the Russian government
and its drastic suppression of the Kronstadt uprising, did not speak
well for his critical discernment; and his insistence, to quote one
example among many, that economic determinism demonstrated
that the great religious themes of the Russian nineteenth-century
novel were nothing more than reflections of unresolved economic
problems, was as crude and as heavy-handed as any of Labriola's
illustrations of the doctrine. It was also true that Gobetti's response
to the March on Rome, that this was "the hour of Marx, not Mazzini," did not particularly help to clarify matters, and at best
smacked of obscurantist dichotomy. Against all these inferences,
however, two equally relevant facts argue against easy classification
of Gobetti as a complicated fellow traveler. Gramsci, who knew
Gobetti very well, was quite probably voicing a completely sincere

conviction when he wrote that Gobetti was *not* a Communist.
Gobetti, in fact, had an ineradicable hostility to any party with
totalitarian claims and a highly centralized, highly disciplined political apparatus. Even more important, perhaps, at the heart of his
political creed there was a singular *avant la lettre* atheistic existen-
tialism that had nothing in common with Marxism of any kind—a
humanism without hope or despair, that called for sacrifice with or
without the presence of witnesses.

Whether or not Gobetti's *Rivoluzione Liberale* was Marxist, the
fact remained that his insights into the nature of Fascism and his plan
of action for the Aventino were extremely perceptive. Gobetti
understood Fascism, and the incisiveness of his analysis owed very
little to Marxist doctrine. The evil of Fascism, Gobetti argued, lay
precisely in its claim to be a supraparty, in its peremptory, arrogant
way of pushing aside all theoretical questions and labeling as ideology all political doctrine, in its claim to be a party of healthy,
robust, uncomplicated barbarians with the strength and will to cut
the Gordian knot of endless political discussion. There was nothing
new in this tendency to a supraparty in Italian politics, Gobetti
maintained, and trasformismo, whether that of Depretis or of Giolitti, was basically the triumph of that tendency; but at no time in
the past had the tendency assumed such monstrous, threatening
proportions. Fascism was a blasphemous alliance of irreconcilables, a
party supported by the viciously anti-clerical Futurist, F. T. Mari-
netti, the ex-revolutionary syndicalist Agostino Lanzillo, the ex-
Socialist Curzio Malaparte and the defrocked priest and Radical
deputy Don Murri. It promised all things to all men. It exulted in
incoherence, and for all of its boasts, its most solid support was not
in the more advanced industrial Italy (and here Gobetti's charge
had an obvious Marxist coloring), but in backward agricultural
Italy, and even there not in the great agricultural centers of the
country.

But after the murder of Matteotti, Gobetti believed, it was no
longer possible to believe that this "association of thugs" was the
party of law and order, or that Fascist trasformismo was basically
old-fashioned and harmless. It was no longer possible to believe in
Fascism in good faith. This was the time when the spearhead of the
opposition had to form its own *compagnia della morte* (suicide
squads), when anti-Fascism was to be recognized for what it was, "a

dignity to be won by renunciation and sacrifice, the right of minorities willing to be persecuted." In party terms, this was the time when those groups for whom party doctrine was not ideology—the Populists of Gronchi, De Gasperi and Jacini, the Liberals of Amendola, the Socialists, from Turati to Gramsci—were to give witness to the only alternative for the salvation of Italy. For the country, if it was to be saved, was to be saved through parties. The Aventino, therefore, regardless of its chances of success, had at least given an example of what the country had long needed, the want of which had helped to lead the country to its present crisis—a collaboration of parties that were deeply separated from one another but capable of a common "no"; a "no" that, had it been uttered at an earlier time, would have changed the course of Italian history.

But as the weeks turned into months, the country and Gobetti recognized that the Aventino was slipping into moralistic inaction. Nothing was happening, which was to say that Mussolini was regathering his forces, regaining lost prestige and power. If the Aventino was to have any effect at all, Gobetti urged, it had to act. It had to call new elections on its own authority, in keeping with its powers as the legal Parliament of the country. It had to take up arms against the Fascists if the King, as it appeared, had no intention of intervening in the crisis, much less disbanding the Fascist militia. In brief, the Aventino had to act like a government.

Gobetti demanded too much. The Aventino had come to the limit of its possibilities with its united "no." Without support from the King, ignored by the Fascist-dominated Parliament which rubber-stamped all of Mussolini's decrees in this period, confronted by the ever-present Fascist militia, after five months the Aventino began to crumble and the major parties in the anti-Fascist coalition began to revert to old positions. For the briefest time, Populist and Turatian Socialists had collaborated, and now they reconsidered their positions.

The Popular Party had ceased to be the party that Don Sturzo envisioned in 1919. Don Sturzo was well aware that his politics did not please the Pontiff, who considered the party an obstacle to the peace, and expendable. On October 24, 1924, soon after official Vatican sources voiced that displeasure, the leader of the party, ever obedient to implicit as well as explicit wishes of the Pope, left for exile in England. The group that succeeded him, led by De Gasperi, adhered to Sturzo's anti-Fascist policy, and defections from the party continued to accelerate. There were far more Populists in Mussolini's Parliament than in the Aventino, far more Catholics in politics who shared the Pontiff's fears of any kind of Socialist-Catholic collaboration than those who feared Mussolini.

The position of the Socialists had also changed. For a short time Turati was the dominant voice, but he did not speak for the majority of Socialists. Most Socialists had enthusiastically hailed the arrival of the Communists when, revising their abstentionist policy, they joined the Aventino; and these Socialists had as little interest in collaborating with anti-Fascist Populists as anti-Fascist Populists had in collaborating with Communists.

Thus, as the eight years from 1911–19 had marked the failure of any sustained Liberal-Socialist collaboration, and the years 1919–24 the failure of any Liberal-Populist-Socialist collaboration, so the five months of the Aventino brought to an end a very limited, ineffectual opposition to Fascism. In a speech in Parliament on January 3, 1925, Mussolini assumed responsibility for his party even if, in his own words, it were to be considered *"una organizzazzione a delinquere"* (a criminal organization). He carried the day.

Il Duce had passed the last shoals, vaulted the last obstacle. It was now up to him to try his hand at the unresolved problems that had largely accounted for the death of Liberal Italy—that of church-state relations, the South, decentralization, regionalism, the reformability of Italian capitalism, nationalism—and to see whether, with a monolithic party apparatus, he could post victories where pre-war and post-war parties had floundered and failed.

IX

FASCISM WITH THE CONSENT

OF THE GOVERNED

The final transition from the Italy of the Aventino to an "orderly" Italy, a short and relatively bloodless spasm, was welcomed by most Italians. Here and there a handful of die-hard opponents of the regime carried on some sort of underground resistance, but even when successful, they were neither admired nor emulated by their cautious sympathizers. In the mopping-up operation that followed the debacle, in the "normalization" of the country, these small, determined anti-Fascist groups were in no way a threat; the great mass of onlookers moved to the sidelines, seeking and finding an inconspicuous place in the new order, a "peace" that was based on fear, exhaustion and a mingled sense of apathy and relief.

In this tired climate, Mussolini swiftly leveled most remnants of the opposition. Liberal leaders of Giolitti's generation (with the exception of Count Carlo Sforza, who followed Nitti into exile) were no problem at all. In a state of shock following the recognition of Mussolini's skills and ambition, they withdrew in numbed silence. Like most other Liberal leaders, Giolitti, the spokesman of the liberalism of the past, left politics altogether and spent the remaining years until his death in 1928 in aloof silence, persuaded to the last that he had incurred little responsibility for the events that favored Mussolini from the march on Rome to the collapse of the Aventino (which the old Piedmontese statesman had disapproved of as illegal and ineffectual) and beyond. When the ex-Prime Minister finally brought himself to voice a strong criticism of the Fascist-manipulated elections of 1924 (to his credit he had refused to join the Fascist bloc), and Mussolini reminded him of his own reputation in the field, Giolitti's retort summed up the temper and limitations of his anti-Fascism: "Your Excellency," he replied, "I never even dreamed of going as far as you have gone."

The suppression of all anti-Fascist publications, ranging from *Avanti!* to the now Communist *Unità* and Gobetti's *Rivoluzione Liberale,* also proceeded smoothly, and the same could be said of the task of persuading Socialists, both Maximalists and Turatians, as well as leaders of labor unions and cooperatives, that to remain in Italy, they had to withdraw from all political activity. The leaders and spokesmen of the Aventino, however, were dealt with differently. Amendola was permitted to leave the country, but he died soon after in a Cannes hospital, partly as a result of a beating received from Fascist thugs before he left. Gobetti's send-off was a bit less brutal. Almost immediately after his arrival in Paris he began to make plans for a French edition of *Rivoluzione Liberale* and for an anti-Fascist publishing house to continue the work he had started in Italy with the publication of the anti-Fascist works of Luigi Salvatorelli (the editor of the important Liberal paper *La Stampa*), Nitti, Sturzo and a number of others. But some two months later, he died of exhaustion and pneumonia at the age of twenty-five. Salvemini, who held on until 1925 in Italy with his clandestine publication *Non Mollare (Don't Yield),* was more fortunate. He managed to escape to France, where he carried on a long career in cultural anti-Fascism, a fight that in spite of occasional excesses was one of the most telling of all the critiques by anti-Fascists in exile. Modigliani, who had infuriated Mussolini for his relentless work in gathering incriminating evidence of the Duce's role in the Matteotti murder, was for some reason allowed to emigrate to Switzerland, and Giuseppe Donati, the editor of *Il Popolo,* the Catholic newspaper in the forefront of the attack on Mussolini, was also allowed to leave for Paris.

Since most frontier guards between 1925 and 1927 were not yet imbued with Fascist zeal, and since the Fascist secret police had not yet earned their reputation for professional competence, a number of other Aventino anti-Fascists made their way clandestinely across the Alps in these years, though not all who tried were successful. No doubt Mussolini was irritated by the getaway of his ex-comrade Nenni and, though to a lesser degree, by the escape of Turati's old and trusted lieutenant, Claudio Treves. But Mussolini no longer feared political parties. His concern was rather with individual strong political personalities, and that was why, though he was annoyed at Nenni's escape, he was not ruffled at all by the formation of a Maximalist troika in Paris made up of Nenni, Angelica Balabanoff and young Ugo Coccia. Of all parties, the Maximalists bothered Mussolini least of all; in complete agreement with Turatians and Communists, he considered them the most inept of all Socialists, and with ostentatious tolerance, he allowed a broken Serrati relative freedom of movement in Italy until his death in 1928.

The Fascist leader thought differently, though of several moderate Socialist leaders, and of Turati in particular. In spite of its unmilitant temper, the party of Turati and Matteotti made a very good showing in the 1924 elections, and presumably still had a cowed but substantial following. It was that moderate wing that had given anti-Fascists a martyr, and the consequences of his martyrdom had given the regime its one really bad moment. This group, in Mussolini's estimate, could still be troublesome; and in spite of Turati's pleas on grounds of poor health for permission to emigrate, the old Socialist leader was repeatedly refused a passport and kept under virtual house arrest in his apartment near the *Galleria* in Milan.

The one hard Fascist crackdown in terms of parties, however, was not on the moderate Socialists but on the Communist Party. It was hardly to be expected, of course, that the Fascists, who had come to power with cries of "Rome or Moscow!" would show leniency to the defeated enemy. Mussolini had some very particular reasons for bearing down hard on them. The Communist Party was an indispensable whipping boy, but even more, it was a party that could point to Russia as a real alternative, and that had an excellent organization and fighting spirit. Moreover, Mussolini especially appreciated the political potential of the Turin Communist group, in particular that of its intellectual leader, Gramsci.

Since 1923, when he had returned from a year's stay in Russia, Gramsci had shown that his skills were not at all limited to political analysis. With curt efficiency he had taken the party leadership away from Amadeo Bordiga by persuading some of the latter's closest lieutenants, including Umberto Terracini, that the Neapolitan engineer had nothing to offer the party except wordy revolu-

tionary intransigence, and by convincing cadres of young, enthusiastic Communists determined to fight to the last that the party *had*
to follow a more elastic policy. Once in command, in charge of a
party virtually outlawed from its inception, Gramsci won over an
impressive number of Socialist Maximalists and almost succeeded in
forming a common front with Nenni, a not inconsiderable feat, in
view of the sulphurous denunciations the Communists under Bordiga's leadership had heaped on all other Socialists for not acting and
thinking in purely revolutionary terms, untainted by compromising
alliances. During the Aventino period, Gramsci vacillated, and perhaps he miscalculated badly in not joining the Aventino sooner, but
in all other respects, he gave singular proofs of leadership in his two
years in power. With Gramsci at its head, the Communist Party
attained what the Maximalists lacked completely—party unity and
real fighting spirit. They also had the financial and moral support of
the first Marxist state. Lastly, they had the advantage of Gramsci's
analytical speculative Leninist-Marxism, which at the last Congress
of the party, held at Lyons in 1926, laid down the guide lines that
the Communists, forced completely underground, were to follow.

Mussolini was not bothered by that Congress' condemnation of
Fascism as a coalition of conservative interests headed by a dema-
gogue—he had long been familiar with the accusation—but he did
take particular notice of the Communist plan, in keeping with
Leninist directives, to infiltrate Fascist-controlled labor unions. Because of this threat, as well as the party's past record, Mussolini took
no half-way measures against Communist leadership. The round-up
was not complete: Togliatti and Ignazio Silone, another young
Communist destined to have a large say in cultural anti-Fascism,
escaped, and Bordiga, after a period of imprisonment, was allowed
to remain in the country to serve, willingly or unwillingly, as a
decoy in the attempt to keep tabs on Communist sympathizers.
Most of the effective leadership, though, was arrested in 1926 and
brought to trial two years later in May 1928; all received lengthy
jail sentences. Gramsci was tubercular, but that was not considered
grounds for leniency, and he was sentenced to a twenty-year term,
which neither friends nor enemies, considering the state of his
health, expected him to survive.

Within two to three years after the collapse of the Aventino,
therefore, Mussolini had succeeded in suppressing all the old parties

of Liberal Italy and stripping the most militant opposition groups of assertive leadership. From the Extreme Right to the Extreme Left he had effectively neutralized the entire opposition, including the Aventino Populists: Gronchi and Jacini withdrew completely from politics and returned to private life, while De Gasperi found refuge in the Vatican, where as a librarian the only political activity possible was a more or less leisurely meditation on the implications for the future of what had happened.

"Normalization" made rapid progress. The great mass of the politically unaffiliated (for party membership in the post-war years was still an insignificant cipher compared to the population) that had moved about uncertainly during the Aventino crisis now swirled into channels artfully laid out by Mussolini. By 1928, the turbulence of 1925 was a thing of the past.

Yet the restoration of order did not altogether satisfy Mussolini. The *Popolari* had been largely absorbed into the Fascist Party, and the Pope himself, by making known his displeasure with Catholic-Socialist-Communist collaboration in the Aventino and giving no signs of displeasure with Populists who defected, had done his part to further the dissolution of the party. But the Fascist leader still had misgivings. Quite coherently, from his point of view, Catholics and the Pope constituted a potentially troublesome political force. As long as anti-Communism bound the Pontiff and most Catholics to the Fascist cause there was no reason for concern. But in case of an eventual substantial divergence, or the underscoring of radical differences inherent in their anti-Communism, there was a chance of serious conflict. Catholics had shown themselves to be more susceptible to the pull of nationalism, patriotism and their own class interests than to any pontifical moral-political teachings, and particularly ones such as were embodied in Leo XIII's *Rerum novarum*, but from Mussolini's point of view there were still real risks involved. The Pontiff was the head of a well-knit national organization that owed him ultimate absolute obedience (only this aspect, this exclusively political aspect of Catholicism mattered to Mussolini), and as such, he was a danger not quite done away with by the friendly relations that characterized those years. In some way, therefore, the Pontiff, like the leaders of other political forces, had to be neutralized. The fact that he was not the head of a political party in the usual sense made that need all the more imperative. A Pope who could expect and receive obedience from the hierarchy and from Catholic Action, a well-disciplined lay organization, was a power to contend with. At the same time, so soon after the Matteotti murder, which had frightened so many *bien pensants*, any farsighted preparations for eventual conflict had to be carefully camouflaged. In some way, that is, Mussolini needed, not to check political organization among Catholics, but to make sure that the overwhelming number of Catholics that supported him would continue to do so in spite of any possible future friction with the Vatican. Threats and blandishments would not suffice in pursuit of this end; what was needed was a lasting agreement that would bind the Pontiff to the regime or at least induce him to exercise caution in any future conflict. What was needed, in brief, was a concordat, a juridical settlement of the differences between church and state. The usefulness of such an agreement had grown immeasurably after the Matteotti murder, if only to pour oil on troubled waters. And so, not long after the collapse of the Aventino, the former revolutionary syndicalist and Sorelian socialist of sorts dedicated the greater part of his energies and skills to devising a settlement of church-state differences, differences that, by destroying the possibility of any real cooperation between the Popular Party and the ruling Liberals, had been among the central causes of the failure of post-war Italy to achieve any kind of political stability.

Any settlement, of course, required the agreement of both parties, and in this instance Mussolini could not have been more fortunate. As early as 1918, four years before the march on Rome, when Mussolini had had a secret exploratory talk with Benedict XV on the possibility of a juridical settlement of these differences, the Fascist leader had recognized the exploitability of the papal desire for some kind of settlement; and since 1919, with the rise of Maximalist power, such an agreement had seemed more desirable than ever to the Vatican. Pius XI, who succeeded Benedict XV in 1922, appreciated a man of action, a man who could get things done, especially after the long inaction in all fields since 1919. "A man sent by Providence," he called the Fascist leader in one of his unguarded moments; and whatever may be thought of this peculiar theological tautology, there was no mistaking the degree of papal gratitude involved.

And yet, though Pius XI did cooperate with the new head of the

Italian state and made no secret of his appreciation of the Duce's resolute ways, it was also true that the Pontiff, in shouldering his part of the responsibility for the Concordat, at no point had any illusions as to Mussolini's motivation. The Pope was well acquainted with the obvious, that Mussolini's notion of Catholicism did not go past an appreciation of the Church as *instrumentum regni*. He was aware that for years, Mussolini had alternated flattery and punitive expeditions in his dealings with the Populists, and especially with Catholic labor organizations. The appalling murder of Don Minzoni, a militantly anti-Fascist priest, was still fresh in the Pope's memory, and there was no dearth of counsel from some of his advisors that this was the worst possible time for a definitive juridical reconciliation with the Italian state. Against these counsels, however, Pius XI balanced other and (for him) more insistent considerations. The Pontiff's concern, contrary to what some embittered Catholics have alleged, was with something more than seeing that crucifixes were once again hung on the walls of classrooms and government offices, or maintaining the legal ban on divorce. Since the October Revolution, a juridical settlement of the Roman Question seemed to him indispensable; and he was willing in his negotiations with Mussolini to make use of the state, though in quite a different way than the church sought to make use of the church. The *dissidio*, the conflict between church and state, had been one thing in Liberal Italy, but in an Italy in which power had almost gone to the Maximalists, Pius XI was convinced that the church had to reinsert herself into the mainstream of Italian life, and as quickly as possible. A settlement, the Pope knew, had its risks (it was reported that he had doubts as late as the night before the signing), but a concordat that would help in bringing the Christian message to the people, in regaining lost rights in marriage legislation, and especially in defending Catholic rights to educate the young, was worth the risk.

Thus, after three years of negotiation, on February 11, 1929, the signed Concordat and Lateran Pacts replaced the old Law of Guarantees, Catholicism was recognized as the official religion of the Italian state, Vatican City was recognized as an independent, sovereign state, and a compromise was reached on the debated issues in education and marriage legislation. There was no doubt as to the immense popularity of the settlement. On an occasion when the Pope, the greater part of the clergy and countless men of unquestioned good faith and intelligence, both believers and unbelievers, spoke of the "statesmanship" of Mussolini, it seemed to be carping and picayune to dissent. Mussolini thus scored his first great, almost undisputed triumph.

There is no way, of course, of judging the extent to which the Pontiff succeeded in his ends, since those ends are not susceptible of statistical evaluation. There is abundant evidence, however, to show that Mussolini attained *his* ends and capitalized on them. What was accidental to the Pope was of the essence to Mussolini, and military honors paid to high ecclesiastical authorities, the omnipresence of state officials at public religious ceremonies, in a word, the constantly recurring public show of church-state unity, was precisely what the Fascist leader wanted. And those Italians (and they were many) for whom Catholicism was a *monumento nazionale* (a national monument), those who effortlessly reconciled practical atheism with baptism, first communion and burial in consecrated ground, redoubled their applause. Belligerently anti-clerical Fascists, of course, were at first unnerved by their leader's apparent concessions, but they sensed (and quite rightly, as it turned out) that regardless of what the Concordat stipulated, Mussolini would see to it that the church would never infringe on the rights of the Fascist state.

The day did come, of course (and sooner than anticipated), when the conflict between the church and Mussolini's notion of the absolute rights of the omnipotent state, including the right to control the education of the young, burst into the open. The conflict, however, only underscored the skillfulness of the Duce's maneuver. One year after the Concordat was signed, Mussolini made a frontal assault on Catholic Action, the lay association which Pius XI sought to protect from any kind of Fascist control. Charging the group with political ambitions that constituted a subtle threat to the state, the Duce did not let up in his attack until the Pope reduced the national organization to local groups, dismissed its lay leaders, and in general surrendered its freedom of movement. Mussolini did all this without provoking a national outrage among Catholics: he succeeded in passing off the conflict as a clash between two authoritarian temperaments over "political" issues. The Pope, faithful to his obligation to defend Christian teaching on faith and morals, in 1932 issued the encyclical *Non abbiamo bisogno*, an unequivocal condemnation of the Fascist theory of the state; but the encyclical was banned in Italy and the Pope's protest was only faintly heard. The Pontiff found himself effectively isolated. He could count on the aid and understanding of some Catholic university groups, in which the young Monsignor Giovanni Battista Montini was particularly active; but by replacing the monarch's traditional *placet* on the appointment of bishops with a Fascist *placet*, Mussolini had seen to it that most of the newly appointed bishops would manifest in proper measure the cardinal Christian virtues of patriotism and anti-Bolshevism. Not all of the high clergy were as enthusiastically pro-Fascist as Monsignor Agostino Gemelli, rector of the newly organized Catholic university in Milan, or Cardinal Ildefonso Schuster, Archbishop of Milan, but those who were not, were willing to let the Pope enunciate Catholic political doctrinal truths without feeling called upon to actively side with him in his disagreements with the regime. The laity, in general, was in this respect indistinguishable from its clergy. The few members of the laity and clergy who actively sided with the Pontiff did not find many eager to listen to them, and they were easily passed off as the perpetually discontented, fanatics of a sort. In the name of prudence, however, Fascist police kept those few under surveillance.

Nothing in Mussolini's long stay in power ever quite matched the feat of the Concordat, superbly timed, extremely adept in its concessions; nothing, perhaps, but his solution to the problems presented by the repercussions of the American economic crisis of the same year, the black year of 1929. In this instance, too, Mussolini showed an unrivaled skill—if not in far-seeing statesmanship, certainly in improvisation, not the least of all his ambiguous political skills.

In spite of the sound and fury of the post-war years, by 1922 Italian capitalism, like the main European economies, was demonstrating a capacity for general recovery. Thanks to government subsidies, shipbuilding and railroad construction were on the increase, and new industries that depended almost exclusively on export trade, like Snia Viscosa, a pioneer in artificial silk, were doing remarkably well. Export trade and government subsidies, however, continued to be the pillars of the Italian capitalist structure. The domestic market was sufficient for two industries whose vitality was impressive in these years—the electrical industry and the Montecatini chemical empire (the electrical industry was the most heavily invested of all private enterprises, and Montecatini rose from a capital of 451 million lire in 1921 to 733 million in 1929), but in general, the consumer limits of the domestic economy, still predominantly agricultural, were rather clearly delineated, and in this respect the post-war economy was indistinguishable from that which had preceded the war. In a still more essential respect, the economic structure had undergone no basic transformation. Although a few giant corporations, Fiat and Montecatini in particular, had succeeded in wrenching themselves free of bank control, in the 1920's, as before the war, most industries were dependent on banks; this remained true even though in Italy, as elsewhere, the heightened tempo of corporate mergers had led to a conspicuous concentration of economic power. Out of 107 corporations, it is estimated that fourteen accounted for almost half the industrial capital of Italy.

The effect of the 1929 crash on the gradual upswing of this economy was shattering. The major European economies bobbed up and down in the crisis; the Italian economy was engulfed. Prices plummeted; industrial stocks fell an average of 40 per cent, and commodities followed suit. Most telling of all, exports, on which the economy depended, dropped 25 per cent, and in a matter of months, an economy that had shown strong recuperative powers lost the gains it had slowly and painfully made.

The crisis caught Mussolini, like most other political leaders of the West, completely unprepared. In his first years in power, 1922–25, the Duce had made it a point to adopt a traditional Liberal economic policy, ostensibly to pay off political debts to industrial interests, whose help had not been niggardly. Under the direction of Alberto de Stefani, the Liberal-oriented Minister of Finance, the Fascist state had repealed taxes on stock dividends, shelved the proposal for compulsory declaration of holdings, maintained high iron and steel tariffs, and actively encouraged the *consorzi*, leagues of industrial and agricultural interests acting together to regulate prices and insure profits.

By 1925, however, Mussolini felt secure enough to consider the debt paid off. He had other plans in mind for improving the economy, and he wanted to show industrial interests that they needed him as much as or more than he needed them. Mussolini did not intend to let the banks and heavy industry call the tune indefinitely. Two years before the 1929 crash, therefore, Mussolini had made his first move to assert his power, defying the banks and heavy industry with his defense of the lira against their pressures for devaluation. The move—though its consequences are still a matter of debate— probably helped to weaken the vulnerable Italian economy, for it put the banks, which had invested heavily in expectation of devaluation, in a singularly exposed position. Unable to sustain the industries in which they had invested, which in turn were calling on them for survival loans, and equally unable to meet commitments to their creditors, the great banks of the country, the Banca Commerciale and the Banca d'Italia, like their counterparts in Germany and the United States, collapsed. In the crisis they were saved by government intervention, but having been rescued by the Fascist state their powers were radically curtailed. After the 1929 crash, banks no longer controlled heavy industry.

Mussolini now boasted that his defense of the lira in 1927 had been an act of clairvoyance and solicitous concern for the man in the street against gambling, reckless capitalists, and the economic policy initiated by the regime after 1925 under the direction of Mussolini's new Minister of Finance, Giuseppe Volpi, was presented as the foundation of an economic system that would be immune to the shocks and strains of capitalism. Because banks and heavy industry had depended completely on the state to rescue them, and because Fascist-controlled labor unions and workers in general approved the state takeover, Mussolini (very likely to his own surprise) came out not only relatively unscathed from the disastrous effects of 1929, but actually more popular and more powerful. Carrying out state rescuing operations that were not without precedent (as recently as 1922 a number of faltering banks had called for and received state aid), in a short period Mussolini's state assumed a degree of control over Italian capitalism such as no *classe dirigente* (governing class) had previously dreamed of.

Beginning with a few corporations like the *Navigazione Generale Italiana* (Italian General Navigation), the Fascist state in short order gained control of an astonishing segment of Italian industry. "If in addition to the industries controlled by the IRI [the Fascist Institute for Industrial Reconstruction, which directed the rescue operation]," Rosario Romeo, a contemporary historian has pointed out, "there are added others that the state was already administering in other forms, such as the railroads, it is evident that after 1936 the

Italian state controlled a part of industry proportionately greater than that controlled by any other European state with the exception of Soviet Russia." In 1937, when Mussolini declared the IRI no longer an emergency agency but a permanent organ of the state, he drew the last and most advantageous paradoxical conclusion from the crash of 1929. Under the most trying circumstances he had offered one more proof, were one more needed, that of all the problems that beset new regimes, economic problems are those least likely to bring them to their knees.

But Mussolini had not only wrenched power from banks and industry, dangerous allies; he had done it in such a way as to make those groups more than ever obligated to the regime. For the Duce, in spite of the increased power of his state, did not tamper with the traditional price-fixing system of the *consorzi*, and actually reinforced it with new legislation; and to the advantage of the established industries, he restricted still further the number of competing corporations. To further placate grateful yet smarting industrialists and bankers, Mussolini showed more deference to their counsel and requests than to those of labor, which was not allowed even the shreds of anything resembling an autonomous union movement; and considering that, by 1933, unemployment had risen to over a million, industrialists did not minimize that deference.

Although not all workers were enthusiastic over the fact that the rescue operation succeeded largely at their expense and caused substantial cuts in their earning power, the majority were willing to comply with the requirement of party membership to obtain employment, and were grateful for having gotten by in a disastrous worldwide crisis. The young without memories felt proud to belong to the worker class of Fascist Italy, the authentic socialist state. For this group in particular, unlike the majority of peasants, who were apathetic or hostile, the Fascist social legislation of these years—the *Carta del Lavoro* (Fascist Labor Charter), accident insurance, maternity benefits, camps for underprivileged children, leisure-time programs—was a magnificent program. That legislation, together with the IRI, proved that the old Socialist in Mussolini was very much alive, very much in command.

Thus by 1935, when the Italian economy, together with the others of the western world, gave tangible signs of recovery from the crash, Mussolini received the homage of two groups: that of the grateful and admiring workers, for having delivered them from (as Mussolini put it) the "crisis of capitalism," and that of the great corporations who, though cut in numbers and chastened in ambitions, continued to enjoy the same preferential treatment, though in a more restricted area, that had been accorded to them by previous strongly anti-Socialist governments.

Small wonder, then, that in retrospect Mussolini was to consider these his halcyon years. Things were going *very* smoothly. An indeterminate number of die-hards continued to nurse private resentment and contempt for the regime, but the success of the Concordat and of the Fascist survival measures after the 1929 financial crisis took the edge off their sarcastic jibes. "*Si campa*"—one gets by— and in the years immediately following 1929, that was a great deal to be thankful for. "*Si campa*"—and the teachers, journalists, catechism instructors and literary men with something to say about what mattered in life and in Italy showed a general sustained enthusiasm for the Fascist state, even though the Fascist monopoly of the press effectively sealed them off from the world of the "plutocratic democracies." Most teachers were overtly enthusiastic. Inclined by temperament and outlook to confuse docility and passivity, most elementary-school teachers working in Mussolini's Italy did not have to be coerced to show a spurious enthusiasm. Older teachers were sincerely grateful for the stability of these years, above all for the end of the fear of strikes and demonstrations, and younger ones, without any personal memories of pre-Fascist Italy, were proud, very proud. Most journalists (Emilio Cecchi was representative), the mentors of the secondary-school teachers, responded quite the same way, for all of their sophistication. The Fascist monopoly of the press was certainly inducement for a number of anti-Fascist journalists to reconsider their attitude; and those who refused to do an undignified about-face learned to either attenuate their anti-Fascism, to adopt a hermetic anti-Fascist style or, much more frequently, to avoid delicate areas. Those who remembered the days of a free press did feel occasional discomfort, but most learned to adapt. There were compensations: though the intellectual tone of the press dropped, yellow journalism in its many vicious varieties disappeared.

Several notches higher in the hierarchy of national pedagogy, up among the literary personalities, the general climate of approval was no different. There was a group of younger writers—Elio Vittorini, Umberto Saba, Eugenio Montale and others—with no enthusiasm for Mussolini's cultural-literary notions or his accomplishments, but since they remained in Italy, they expressed their disinterest or hostility discreetly. University professors by and large were not much different from literary men, and when in 1931 Mussolini requested an oath of allegiance from faculty members of the state-run universities under pain of removal from office, only twelve professors and one splendidly Quixotic instructor in the entire country chose not to take the oath. Not all those who complied, however, did so out of fear or servility. Some were convinced that only by taking the oath could they carry on some form of anti-Fascist activity, since they could not carry on even a minimum of academic warfare against the regime without a way of earning a living. As in the case of secondary-school teachers, though, approval was generally not the result of heavy-handed coercion. Long before Fascism became a political order, it had been a literary mood—the inflamed patriotism of D'Annunzio and the historian Alfredo Oriani, the Futurists' spirit of denial—and university professors were not unsusceptible to its pull. Furthermore, the Fascist *Accademia d'Italia*, which replaced the old and renowned *Accademia dei Lincei*, offered very tangible stipends, an inducement, especially for scholars and literary figures with no strong political feelings, to side openly with the regime. Most writers and scholars, however, needed no inducement. With or without the Academy, they would have come to terms with the political *status quo*. Thus, though few talented writers turned into vigorous champions of Fascist Italy, as did Giovanni Papini, many who earned a living with the pen did not long withhold their approval. This acquiescent mood, indeed, permeated the country; and though foreigners noticed that Italians had not lost their sense of humor, and treated Mussolini as they had treated all political leaders before him, their barbed jokes implied no activist discontent. Complaining and making fun of Mussolini's weaknesses and vanities, Italians stood staunchly by him.

It did not matter much to the Fascist leader, consequently, that in such a widespread consensus, a few Liberal, Catholic and Socialist voices uttered a faint "no." The anti-Fascism of the Liberal economist Luigi Einaudi and the more outspoken opposition of the conservative political philosopher Gaetano Mosca who, in spite of his known anti-Fascism was allowed to teach at the University of Rome until his death in 1933, were not troublesome. Indeed, the Fascist leader professed nothing but amused indifference even for the one anti-Fascist intellectual with a sizeable public who chose to remain in Italy and wage cultural warfare in the most open way possible— none other than Benedetto Croce. At the time of the Aventino, the philosopher had given Mussolini his vote of confidence in the Senate, but a few months later he made a clear public break with the regime. "A confusion of Liberalism and *democratismo*," he had labeled Fascism then; "an impure mixture of literature and politics"; "an arrogant suppression of democratic freedoms"; and later, "a sign of European illness."

Yet for all of the amused indifference he professed, the charges stung Mussolini. He permitted *La Critica* to continue publication, but teachers were urged not to renew their subscriptions, and even such politically innocuous works of Croce as his treatise on esthetics were ordered removed from the list of acceptable school texts. In the same spirit, a number of learned societies, including the *Archivio Storico Napoletano*, to which Croce had contributed since his youth, were ordered to remove the philosopher's name from their membership lists. As a last touch, a reminder to Croce of the conditions he was to work under, a plainclothes man was more often than not posted outside the philosopher's palatial residence in Naples, taking note of those entering and leaving. Police coverage, moreover, was not completely suspended when Croce, as he was wont to, made trips to Turin, his wife's city. The Fascist police were quite aware that Turin was a center of anti-Fascist intellectuals.

Having asserted his vigilance and control in this way, however, Mussolini went no further. *La Critica* continued publication and Croce was allowed to publish his books. Not one to minimize the importance of window dressing for the regime, Mussolini made the most of his toleration of Croce. That an internationally recognized anti-Fascist was allowed to live in peace and continue to publish was Fascist Italy's answer to those accusing it of despotic intolerance. The limits of that toleration, of course, were very precise, and Mussolini knew that he could count on a very effective Fascist rebuttal to Croce from none other than Croce's former collaborator on *La Critica* for twenty-five years, Senator Giovanni Gentile, since 1925 president of the Fascist Cultural Institute.

Uncertain of his liberalism after World War I, Gentile oscillated in his political preferences for some time; but by 1922, he whole-heartedly backed the Fascists, and by 1925, with the publication of the *Manifesto Fascista*, signed by a great number of intellectuals and artists, he had become the philosophical spokesman of the party. In contrast, that document had more of an effect on Croce than the Matteotti murder had had. It prompted him to an anti-Fascist coun-termanifesto, and provoked his irrevocable break with the regime. Indeed, the debate over Fascism brought into the open the total disagreement of two philosophers who for many years had been the embodiment of a Damon and Pythias friendship; and the charges of opportunism, fitting when directed against some Fascist theoreti-cians, simply did not hold against Gentile. The differences between the two philosophers long antedated the advent of Fascism. Even before World War I, Gentile had rejected Croce's distinction be-tween the economic and the moral moment, and as the ultimate conclusion of that divergent speculative point of departure, in polit-ical theory he had come to an idea of the state substantially indis-tinguishable from that of Mussolini: "Nothing outside of the state, everything in the state, everything for the state."

The differences, though, were speculative and intricate, and there was little chance that polemics could clarify them. And since thorny problems of Hegelian epistemology become more so when compli-cated by political arguments, it seemed to many unphilosophical observers that when all was said and done the abstruse disagreements were a cover-up for purely personal differences.

Toleration of Croce, consequently, involved no serious risks. Mussolini, though he had previously known Croce well enough to plagiarize one of his literary judgments, boasted in these years that he had never read a single line of the philosopher's works; and to judge from the evidence, Mussolini was speaking for the great majority of Italians.

And yet, unpredictably, the guarded toleration of Croce brought about a remarkable change in the philosopher himself, for out of these years a new Croce emerged, the third Croce, a rejuvenated sexagenarian with something to say to an older generation and to those few of the new generation who, though perhaps not disposed to a complete acceptance of his philosophy, were even less disposed to accept the Fascist versions of Italian history and the good life. As the first consequences of the revisions that Fascism forced upon him, Croce set about rectifying and repudiating the most glaringly anti-democratic aspect of his political philosophy—convictions that were in effect a residue of the Sorelian political ethos after the accompanying specific political forms had been rejected. Since around 1912, Croce, though continuing to admire the French publicist, had grown increasingly independent of him. Croce did not share either Sorel's apocalyptic view of World War I or the Frenchman's subsequent sulphurous denunciations of the "plutocratic democracies," France and England, or of the post-war period; and even though, like Sorel, Croce had seen some merit in Mussolini, their individual approvals were based on mutually exclusive estimates. Sorel had admired in Mussolini the mighty wind that would pull up and destroy the shell of a rotten liberalism; Croce had appreciated the political leader who had the strength to rescue the Liberal state from the Socialists and Communists; and who could eventually lead the way back to a defense of the Liberal state that he had saved. Croce was naïve in his assurance that a political leader who used power for selfish ends could not long remain in power, that a politician without a conscience was not capable of using the moral sentiments of others as instruments of his own selfish purposes, since not being able to understand the psychology of those morally superior to him he would be in no position to exploit them. But in so arguing, he revealed not only a logical weakness, but faith in a pre-established harmony between power and justice. This faith, if not altogether consistent with other parts of his political philosophy, was sincere.

The most striking indication of the differences between Sorel and Croce, however (differences that the Neapolitan philosopher, out of a sense of loyalty, preferred not to stress even in these years) was their estimate of Giolitti. In the year of Sorel's death, in 1920, Croce had accepted an invitation to become Minister of Education in the Cabinet of Giolitti, the political leader whom Sorel despised as the most corrupt and pragmatic of all corrupt, pragmatic Italian leaders.

At first glance, it would seem that Gentile was right in arguing that Croce was inconsistent in admiring Sorel and rejecting the Fascist notion of the state. It was also true, however, that there is some question as to which is the true Sorel—the Sorel who spoke well of Mussolini, or the admiring author of the *Plaidoyer pour Lenin*, or the austere moralist who had won Croce's loyalties. In any case, and regardless of the persuasiveness of the interpretation, there was no doubt that by the mid-1920's the particular Sorel that Croce admired would have opposed, not defended, the Fascist state.

Gentile and Fascist ideologists thus recognized fundamental ambiguities in Croce's political thought that left him open to attack, but there were many elements that required no clarification. With respect to his theory of the state, Croce was singularly consistent: from the 1890's to the Fascist era the philosopher consistently opposed the all-powerful, thought-controlling state. In his first political studies, he had rejected Labriola's Marxist state precisely because, he maintained, that state was legislating in an area in which it had no right to legislate—in the field of philosophy and ethics. Some twenty years later, in the post-World War I period, after witnessing years of intense struggle against the partisans of a Socialist-Communist state, Croce's opposition to the all-powerful state had stiffened.

Yet Croce could not but realize, in the light of Fascism's continuing success, that his idea of the state and his liberalism offered too little. Rather than a political philosophy, it was the residue left once the errors of Socialists, Communists, Fascists and Populists were recognized and discarded. It was a series of corrections, not a passionate cause. There were, moreover, some aspects of his liberalism, such as the way it minimized parties as basically no more than tools for the strong political leader, and derided moral indignation as an ineffective political tool, that, although not Fascist, were undeniably reminiscent of a Fascist mentality.

The break with Fascism itself, of course, was a resolution *in actu* of some of these ambiguities in Croce. That break made clear that when he had spoken of "effectual reality," of the virile acceptance of the hard facts of political life, he had never meant to justify the crushing of all political opposition in the name of political realism; nor had he meant his analysis of parties as the instruments of strong leaders to serve as a pretext for their suppression. Yet the fact remained—and Croce sensed it—that Fascist claims could not be refuted with a liberalism that was a set of piecemeal amplifications and clarifications. One totalitarianism had to be fought with another, different in kind and in quality. This was the challenge of Fascism, and after 1925 Croce met it. Against the total claims of Mussolini, the philosopher elaborated a new liberalism, liberalism as "religion" —in his own words, a view of the world with an attendant morality. Indeed, from 1925 on, in a wide sense the better part of Croce's work was no more or less than a study of comparative religions, with the recognizable end of demonstrating in numberless variations the superiority of his new version of liberalism over its Socialist, Communist, Fascist and Catholic counterparts.

The demonstrations assumed various forms—literary criticism, philosophical analysis, philosophy of history, history proper. Regardless of the medium, though, Croce had to comply with one Fascist *sine qua non*—he could not be forthright. In instances where he clearly had Fascism in mind, he could make no direct allusions. That one implicit and yet blunt condition, which would have disheartened a lesser man, sharpened Croce's wits; and in two historical works in particular, the *History of Italy from 1871 to 1915* and the *History of Europe in the Nineteenth Century*, he said all that he needed and wanted to say to readers who had ears to hear.

The outline of his new liberalism—with a state based on freedom of the press, of assembly, of political parties—was simple. It did not propose a golden age of the future any more than it claimed one in the past, not even in the pre-World War I Giolittian era. There were problems and tendencies in that period, such as the gap between southern and northern Italy, the unhealthy spiritual climate of D'Annunzio and the Futurists, and lack of experience in self-government, that contributed substantially to the collapse of liberal Italy.

Throughout nineteenth-century Europe, a similar condition had prevailed. A great liberal age in spirit and accomplishments, that century had also provided liberalism with its share of determined opponents in the fields of politics and ideas: the century of Guizot and Cavour was also the century of De Maistre, the author of *Du Pape*, a glorification of the political potential of an autocratic papacy, and the century of Marx, whose spirit of denial, Croce wrote, was imbued with Old Testament hate and fury. Nothing, therefore, could assure the uninterrupted sway or even the eventual victory of a liberalism that, with its cult of political-cultural freedom, represented the highest European "religion," the Religion of Liberty. The "religion" itself was capable of unlimited expansion and not confinable to any one political form, since liberty was a dialectic, not a fixed entity (the error of those insisting that their monarchism or republicanism or economic liberalism or socialist liberalism was the one true liberalism). Yet Liberals, as the custodians of that religion, could through no fault of the creed itself falter. Their faith and moral strength could wane, and then, as in the early days of World War I, they could succumb to

> a state of mind pitilessly avid for adventure and conquest, a frantic hunger for power, a restlessness, the coexistence of love and indifference, a state of mind proper to a person who no longer lives with a religious and ethical center.

The Religion of Liberty and its recognizable sign, the freedom-based state, could succumb, and had done so, but it could not die. *This* was the absolute newness of Croce's liberalism, the message he never wearied of repeating. An ideal that was inexhaustible and irreplaceable, liberty was the propulsive force in history as well as its end; for the course of history itself was determined not by moral-political forces and ideals of a lower order but by those demonstrably superior. Fascism in this light (and the implication was as clear as the situation permitted) was the furthest thing from a real religion. It was a phase, an interim of spiritual decadence; and those who remained faithful to the demands of rigorous thought and robust moral feeling were carrying on a positive work and practicing an active religion that was as indispensable and decisive as the anti-Fascism of Italian political activists abroad.

This point was made very sharply, but there is nothing to show that Mussolini followed the elaboration of this new liberalism with any interest, or that it gave him any misgivings. The ideologists of the party gave their rebuttal and he was content with it. That rebuttal, after all, had some merit: Croce, in defending liberal Italy against Fascist historians such as Gioacchino Volpe, had gone to extremes. His account of Giolitti verged on hagiography; few historians today are willing to attribute undeviating good intentions and works to the party that led Italy from 1871 to 1915. There are even historians today willing to agree with critics who argued that Croce, in postulating an end to history—the constant enrichment of the ideal of liberty—was, *mutatis mutandis,* doing precisely what he denounced the Marxists for doing.

But problems of history, at any rate, did not greatly interest

Mussolini. The Fascist leader publicly vilified Croce for one speech the Neapolitan made in the Senate against the Concordat, and was obviously more irritated by that speech than by all that Croce wrote during those years, including his transparent warning at the close of the *History of Europe in the Nineteenth Century* (published in 1932) against a policy Mussolini was then adopting—whipping up nationalistic sentiment in preparation for war.

A generally pro-English, pro-French foreign policy, Mussolini concluded by 1934, was not producing gratifying results. An attraction for Hitler's Germany as yet played little part in this change of feelings. (Indeed, in 1934, after the Dollfuss murder, fearing an Austrian *anschluss*, Mussolini had quickly sent troops to the Brenner Pass, a move that probably helped to make Hitler reconsider.) But the time had come, the Fascist leader decided, to disregard foreseeable British and French disapproval, and capitalize on the swelling consensus that followed the Concordat and the general economic recovery. Great powers had always demonstrated their strength by expansion and Italy, Mussolini felt, was ready for the test. Italians understood, Abyssinia beckoned, and the justification was the familiar pre-packaged one of a "place in the sun," to which was added that of the needs and rights of a "have-not" nation among the "haves." These arguments served as well as they had in the Libyan War of 1911, and though not all Italians rallied enthusiastically, the war *was* popular. Its popularity was increased by the opposition of England and the sanctions of the League of Nations; its members were all hypocritical moralists, most Italians were convinced, denouncing others for what they themselves had done time and again on a far greater scale.

The donation of wedding rings and precious metals for the Abyssinian War manifested the sturdy support of the war and the regime; and a less clamorous gesture, the return of a number of expatiate Socialists (including Arturo Labriola, who felt more patriotic than Socialist during the war) showed how superbly Mussolini had calculated and maneuvered. As a last crowning touch—for the only truly popular wars are short—the hostilities, which broke out in October 1935, came to a successful conclusion in May 1936.

Mussolini could well afford, then, considering this cumulative success, to have one anti-Fascist with an international reputation preach the Religion of Liberty and dismiss the cultural ambitions of the regime with urbane irony and exquisitely aristocratic common sense. For the Duce, it was no more than a mosquito bite on a tough bronzed skin. The almost seventy-year-old philosopher could continue to write and to "right" history; Mussolini, in the prime of his manhood, meant to go on making it—and with the consent of the governed. Fascism, too, was a "religion" and though the Duce perhaps did not put as much stock in his theoretical improvisations as did some of his followers, he did consider the notion of the Fascist totalitarian state, superseding outmoded democratic parliamentarianism and its independent unions and political parties (Mussolini officially abolished the old Chamber of Deputies in 1939), more than a match for the rival religions of Marxism, Catholicism, and liberalism. Fascist *corporatismo*, the fiction that the various groups that constituted society all had a voice in the Fascist state, and that that state was the impartial judge that passed on all conflicts between them, provided a firm dogmatic structure for that religion. And only that religion had the one attribute which the Fascist leader prized above all others—tangible, manifest, and up to this point, unlimited power.

PART TWO

THE PETRIFIED

SPIDER WEB

1925-1945

X

SOCIALISTS IN EXILE

The story of anti-Fascists in exile, from their exodus after the Matteotti murder to the end of the Abyssinian War, is at best unfelicitous. The successes of Mussolini served only to accentuate their mutual mistrust, and when it became ominously clear that Fascism would not pass away like a summer storm, that year by year it grew in power and consensus, the gelatinous bonds holding the opposition together quite liquified. The *Concentrazione Antifascista*, the union of most opposition parties with headquarters in Paris, dissolved some ten years after its formation, even before the outbreak of the Abyssinian War, and quite as much for reasons of internal dissent as for increasing Fascist successes. It could hardly have been otherwise. The very favor that Mussolini's regime found in and out of the country ruptured the fragile unity of the anti-Fascists; and when, after the Abyssinian War, exiles finally won some backing from the western democracies, it was altogether offset by proportionately increasing dissent as to what should be done and how.

The *Concentrazione Antifascista*, however, had at no point been a particularly sturdy structure. Neither the Communists nor the Populists (whose leader, Don Sturzo, conducted his cultural warfare from London and then from New York) joined it, and as a consequence, it functioned at best as a reputable information center, an occasional reminder to the world that there were exiled Italians who were not Communists and who opposed the regime out of no petty vindictive spirit. It could do little more. Beset on one side by the swelling prestige of Soviet Russia and all that that implied for the Italian Communist Party, and on the other by an assertive Italian nationalism that branded all enemies of the Fascist state as enemies of Italy, the *Concentrazione* had all it could do to survive for ten years. The groups it represented, furthermore, had no interest in constructing a solid common political platform. Marking time, uncertain of the number and quality of the followers left to them in Fascist Italy, the anti-Fascist groups strained to preserve their party physiognomy until the day when they might return to Italy and reacquire authentic political meaning. But this expectation was not a strong cohesive force, and the ranks of the federation thinned out noticeably before its final break-up. A substantial number of anti-Fascists, out of disgust for what seemed a hopelessly polarized political situation—successful totalitarian socialism of one kind or another on the one hand, and indifferent if not ill-disposed democracies on the other—withdrew from the struggle. On more than one occasion the decision was hastened by the skills of the OVRA, the Fascist counterintelligence organization, which unfortunately did not conform very closely to the comical caricature version popular among us.

Considering these roadblocks, it is remarkable that certain exiled political groups—the Liberals in particular—actually survived at all. Represented by the undynamic Nitti, the Chairman of the *Concentrazione*, this older group of Liberals was quite aware that it had not left any substantial following behind in Italy, and that it could expect only the most passive nostalgic loyalty from whatever following it still retained. Like other Liberals of his generation, in the first years of exile Nitti had expected Mussolini to be undone by the sheer weight of the consequences of the 1929 crash, but as the years passed he, too, was forced to revise this idea. He accordingly modified his principal aim of persuading the leaders of the West that Fascism was weak, illegal and immoral, and argued instead that the regime was strong, illegal and immoral; he had no more success in his last endeavor than in his first. By 1935, consequently, the Liberals were disposed to accept the realities and accomplishments of Fascist Italy and to resign themselves to carrying on the fight with book and pamphlet.

In spite of their freedom as an exiled group (a relative freedom, for Mussolini put constant pressure on the French government to limit the movement of the anti-Fascist exiles), the Liberals by 1935 were conducting an anti-Fascist policy not very different from that carried on, though less overtly, by Croce within the country; and they conducted it in such a way as to bother Mussolini hardly at all. Nothing done by this small group of articulate Liberals—Nitti in Paris, Salvemini at Harvard, the ex-foreign minister Count Carlo Sforza in Brussels, or Guglielmo Ferrero at the University of Geneva—affected the solidly entrenched regime. Their denunciations of the Concordat and of Fascist economic policies, though read and appreciated, brought about no changes in French or English policy toward Fascist Italy. Fascism was popular abroad, and even those who had misgivings frequently concluded cynically that "Fascism is good enough for Italians." Even the first great propaganda success of the *Concentrazione*, the condemnation of the Abyssinian War, proved to be double-edged. It was obvious to Italians that when France and England subscribed to the exiles' denunciations, they were merely objecting to the colonial ambitions of a rival power, not to the moral-political quality of Fascism. The Fascist press, in one of its rare acknowledgements of the existence of an opposition in exile, stressed this aspect and pointed out to Italians that the viciously partisan choral condemnation showed the extent to which exiled enemies of the regime would go to express their petty vindictiveness—in effect, offering aid and comfort to the enemies of Italy. That charge, in a country still fresh with the glow of a victorious colonial war, was tantamount to convicting the exiles of treason.

But if the Liberals and groups sympathetic to their cause were inconclusive in their cultural warfare, they were disastrously so when young Fernando de Rosa, seeking to *do something*, resorted to direct action. The scion of an affluent family, de Rosa could think of no more dramatic way to focus the attention of the world on the exiled anti-Fascists' cause than by a pretended attempt on the life of King Victor Emmanuel's son, Prince Umberto. De Rosa accordingly fired on the Prince, without intention to kill, on the occasion of Umberto's visit to his royal fiancée in Brussels in October 1929. At the much-publicized trial that followed, it took all the eloquence of Nitti and Salvemini to persuade the world that anti-Fascists in exile were not a conspiratorial, terroristic organization. Italians, who read of the attempt in the Fascist-controlled press, were shocked; but the rest of the world quickly forgot the shooting as it went on to read of others less political but just as shocking.

Ten years later there was a flurry of equally confused Liberal conspiracy within Italy, captained by young Mario Vinciguerra, who sought to win over high-ranking anti-Fascist elements among the higher clergy, the royal household and the army to his clandestine National Alliance. Jails were becoming a Communist monopoly, Vinciguerra rightfully observed, and something had to be done about it. Once the conspiracy was uncovered, Vinciguerra had the satisfaction of breaking the Communist monopoly by joining them in jail.

In contrast to the Liberals, at least, the Socialist Maximalists in exile were a political presence. They preserved the spirit of a militant political party. Nenni, Coccia, Angelica Balabanoff, Bruno Buozzi, leader of the powerful FIOM union, the Federation of Metallurgical Workers, and young Giuseppe Saragat, who had aided Treves in his escape, were political activists accustomed to some form or other of persecution. They had the moral certainty of a scattered loyal following in Italy. Once the Paris edition of *Avanti!* began to appear, they hoped to smuggle copies into Italy, and although their clandestine anti-Fascist press activity could not compare with that of the Communists, the risks involved kept them on the alert.

But the Socialists as a group had also some very exposed weaknesses. In 1932, the Socialist Maximalists and the previously expelled moderate Turatian *Unitari* Socialists merged to form the *Partito Socialista Italiano*, but the union was unsteady. A small number of key Maximalists, including Angelica Balabanoff, refused to recognize the merger and formed a group apart from both Socialists and Communists; and within the reunified party itself it was apparent that the new leaders, Nenni and the more moderate Saragat, had declared not peace but a truce. In exile during the 1930's, the dilemma of the Maximalists—torn between the Communists and the moderate Socialists—had become more acute yet. Against the Fascist "reaction," all Socialists felt called upon to band together in a phalanx; but in practice there was no way of truly uniting Socialists that would be acceptable both to those approving of substantially all developments in Russian Marxism-Leninism and to those insisting on a very independent attitude toward Russia and the Italian Communist Party. The resultant union, consequently, was rather unique. Nenni, who at this time tended to stress the bond that united Socialists and Communists in the battle against corrupt capitalism and its most corrupt form, the Fascist state, bent over backwards to reassure the more moderate elements that, for all his contempt for capitalism, he did not subscribe obediently to every move of the Soviet Union. Saragat, for his part, who was more wary of Soviet dictatorship and horrified by the tyranny of Leninist Communism, went out of his way to insist that he had not the slightest intention of letting his socialism degenerate into a weak state socialism. But in spite of their good intentions, the Socialist leaders had all they could do to cope with the centrifugal forces within the party and to maintain their independence from the Communists, who, depending on the circumstances, often looked on them either as superfluous fellow-travelers or as the spokesmen of a *petit-bourgeois* corruption of authentic Marxism.

The political-philosophical arguments that accompanied these quarrels, debates and reciprocal excommunications over the years were dismal as well as confusing; although open doctrinal warfare was prevented by the resolve not to let the polemics give aid and comfort to the Fascist enemy, socialism in exile was the poorer for it all. In general, Leninism did not raise the level or tone of Marxist polemics either outside or within Russia; but for Italian socialism in exile, it lowered the quality of disagreement several perceptible notches. Nenni was no Labriola or Gramsci, nor was Saragat a man of rare speculative temper. Arguing, as Saragat did, that class struggle in the Russian experience was not authentic, because authentic class struggle could not possibly lead to state tyranny, was confusion worse confounded. It also produced few practical results. Nenni and his Maximalist followers were still convinced that Saragat, like Turati before him, was a *petit-bourgeois* in disguise. On rare occasions, as at the time of the renewal of the Berlin-Moscow Pact in 1935, Nenni and Saragat stood shoulder to shoulder in their denunciation of Soviet Communism, "cravenly indifferent," as Nenni wrote, to the fate of the German Socialist Party, and willing to join forces with the Nazis, who had destroyed that party; but even at such moments unity was precarious. For when all was said and done the differences that separated Nenni and Saragat were more than differences of approach to the Communist problem. The two men were poles apart in their ideas of a proper Marxist party, but they were also rivals for party leadership.

In spite of the merger, then, Socialists were as divided in exile as they had been in pre-Fascist Italy, and Mussolini lost no occasion to sow discord among them. By the end of the Abyssinian War, however, the Fascist leader had no doubts: the Socialists in exile, for all of their activism, were in the last analysis not much more effectual than the Liberals.

But just as Mussolini showed marked respect for the Communists at home (to the last he refused to free the dying Gramsci, despite a widely publicized appeal by European intellectuals months before the death of the Communist leader in 1937), so he showed a particular appreciation of them as a force in exile: the group knew how to maneuver. Under the leadership of Palmiro Togliatti, Italian Communists managed to accomplish the remarkable feat of following a party line that at one and the same time approved of the Russian alliance with Nazi Germany and indignantly denounced the *Concentrazione* as the tool of *petit-bourgeois* parties; and Togliatti's adherence to this party line was inflexible. When Angelo Tasca and Ignazio Silone, the most outspoken and independent voices within the party, criticized the hard Stalinist line that banned collaboration with "deviationist" reformist Socialists, they were summarily expelled; and a similar tough stand was taken against the few Trotskyites within the party. To insure absolute doctrinal unity, Togliatti himself, heir to the Gramsci tradition that called for a high level of cultural preparation, directed the party's ideological warfare as well as its tactical political moves. He had extremely competent assistants in this work, foremost among them Luigi Longo, who had no cultural pretensions but who knew how to take orders and pass them on. In the all-important labor union field, the party had the good fortune, furthermore, to have Giuseppe di Vittorio, one of its most idealistic, personable and hard-working leaders, in firm command of the exiled *Confederazion Generale del Lavoro*.

Soon after 1930, Togliatti's party, the most unrelenting and daring of the exiled groups, sent some of its best men (Edoardo d'Onofrio, Guiseppe Amoretti, Girolamo Li Causi and others) back to Italy to establish cells in Fascist labor unions and to work from within. In so doing, the party served notice that it was not limiting its anti-Fascism to the printed word, even though its *Battaglie Sindacali* (*Union Battles*), the best Marxist publication of its kind, reached a considerable number of readers especially in northern Italian factories. On that occasion, virtually all of the clandestinely returning party members were intercepted and jailed. Six years later the party made another attempt. Once again, the Fascist police arrested the greater number of the Communist leadership (among them Pietro Secchia and one of the more intense women workers in the party, Camilla Ravera) as well as a few Communist intellectuals who had remained behind in Italy and had been tolerated up to that point, in particular the agrarian experts and historians, Manilo Rossi-Doria and Emilio Sereni. The clamp-down did not crush the fighting spirit of the party, but it did check its momentum and ambitions. The most combative group in exile, the Communists from time to time did win over an isolated intellectual or group of workers in Italy, but their clandestine following did not perceptibly increase, not even among the industrial workers of the North, where the party made its greatest effort. For all of their dynamism and superior organization, and in spite of sporadic demonstrations in Italy, the Communists, too, proved to be quite containable.

As a leader, Togliatti had one telling limitation. Unsurpassed in reconciling the demands of Soviet directives with those of Italian Communist policy, the steel-nerved, distant Togliatti had no strong appeal to those outside of the party. A politician's politician, he lacked the charisma of the great political leader; this limitation, added to the onus of heading a party that took its orders from Moscow, allowed Mussolini to sleep easier. Indeed, these two disadvantages so emboldened the Duce that he saw no particular reason why he should not fully exploit the anti-Communist mood of the country and lump the most disparate opponents of the regime all together as Communist conspirators. The strategy seemed perfectly safe.

Yet Mussolini, so genuinely Machiavellian in his appreciation of the strong man in politics, was aware of embers among the opposition. From 1926 on, one strong political personality in particular bothered him, sometimes more, sometimes less: Carlo Rosselli.

Rosselli, then twenty-seven years old, had first forced himself on Mussolini's attention in the notorious anti-Fascist event of 1926, the widely publicized escape of Turati. Confined to his apartment in Milan, the old and sick Socialist leader had lost all fighting spirit in 1925 after the death of Anna Kuliscioff, whose funeral became a pretext for Fascist demonstrations. But with the encouragement of Rosselli and a few other friends, he had gradually taken heart and by November 1926, agreed to a proposed escape plan. Following the instructions of Rosselli, Turati slipped out of his apartment, entered a waiting car, and made his way from Milan to a place near Savona, on the Ligurian shore. After a wild motorboat dash across choppy seas he reached Corsica, and from there left for Paris. Rosselli, however, not content with having brought off the daring escape, risked a return to the Italian mainland and was caught by the police soon after he landed on an isolated Tuscan beach.

At his ensuing trial, Rosselli acquitted himself superbly. The young Socialist made the most of his distant past—he was a descendant of a distinguished Risorgimento family that had sheltered Mazzini in his dying days—and of his immediate past—a student of Salvemini, he had continued the tradition of *Non Mollare*, publishing with Nenni a short-lived periodical, *Quarto Stato* (*The Fourth Estate*). He was eloquent. His defense rested on an appeal to true patriotism and a higher law, and it won for anti-Fascism its last popular representative. Mussolini took due notice. From then on, enemies of the regime were treated as enemies of the state, and were no longer tried by regular courts but by special courts in closed session. As for Rosselli, Mussolini did not expect to hear any more from him, once the court sentenced him to ten years of confinement on the island of Lipari, north of Sicily. Some two years later, however, Rosselli again forced himself on the Duce's attention. With the aid of his English wife and a few other conspirators, Rosselli, the Sardinian socialist Emilio Lussu, and Francesco Fausto Nitti (a relative of the former Prime Minister) escaped by motorboat from Lipari, sped to Tunisia, and from there, jubilantly hailed by Turati, joined the anti-Fascist groups in Paris.

One of Rosselli's first moves in the French capital was to publish *Socialismo Liberale*, a doctoral thesis he had written under Salvemini which he now used as a restrained though not unimpassioned political manifesto. The work received the compliment of being banned in Fascist Italy, but since the unoriginal ideas presented had won no appreciable following in pre-Fascist days, the ban was directed more at Rosselli the political activist than at Rosselli the author or competent theoretician. In general, *Socialismo Liberale* reechoed the "plague on both your houses" that Salvemini had hurled at both Italian Socialism and Italian Communism, and argued the case for a state socialism that purported to take the best of the Liberal and Marxist traditions.

Nothing in Rosselli's analysis gave Mussolini pause. The Duce had taken Salvemini's measure, both as theorist and political man, and he was not likely to take much notice of the book of a disciple, even a very activist disciple. And yet *Liberal Socialism* did say something: even though Rosselli's style was hardly reminiscent of Gobetti or Labriola, in years in which neither Liberals nor Socialists were saying much his work had merit. It had a moral timbre that was new and fresh among Italian Socialists in the 1930's, and a refreshing mistrust of certain brittle Marxist tenets. In effect, Rosselli took a stand that, though to the right of Gobetti's *Liberal Revolution*, captured much of Gobetti's moral fervor; a stand that, though quite different from Labriola's Marxist vision, was curiously reminiscent of it at points, in scale if not in spirit. If there was one country, Roselli wrote, where facile formulas, fixed and rigid, lose their shape in rubbing against the insurmountable varieties of climate, nature, cultural and economic forces, that country was Italy. The Marxist claim that economic determinism explained the root reality of political Italy was nonsense. Italy's politics and its problems were not deciphered by any one neat formula, certainly not by a Marxism that continued to insist in 1930 that the only choices for the country were *laissez-faire* capitalism (which had long since disappeared) or an Italian version of the Russian experience. Marxist alternatives of this type were inept. Moreover, Russian Marxists made a bad situation worse by their constant insistence that moral indignation, which had been indispensable for their victory, was to be minimized in political battles, and by their even more peculiar insistence that nationalism, which they had used to such good purpose in Russia in the establishment of the first Socialist state, was to be roundly denounced in other countries as a tool of the reaction.

With their defeat at the hands of the Fascists, however, Socialists and Communists had more than paid for these blunders, for the stress on crude economic determinism, and for their obtuse, righteous denunciations of nationalism. It was time, therefore, Rosselli urged, to discard those demonstrably false, outdated Marxist tenets, including that of the imminent catastrophic end of capitalism. This was not to say, though, that Italian Socialism was to return to its Turatian origins. Rosselli, who as a young man had contributed to *Critica Sociale*, and who had rescued Turati at the risk of his life, meant to save the man and bury the cause. Turati's socialism, he argued, was dead, and could not be revived. It deserved to pass away, for as Salvemini had fulminated for years and years, it was in no way distinguishable from the Giolittian liberalism that it professed to fight.

It *was* possible, though, to undo the blunders of socialism; it could be done if Socialists stood up to the hard truth that the political problem in Italy, in post- as in pre-Fascist Italy, was moral. Liberal Socialists were to live out their obligation, to act as new leaven. "It must be said for once and for all, for it is regrettably exact, that in Italy the education of man, the formation of the individual, the basic moral cell, is still for the most part non-existent." The political problem of the day, then, Socialists had to recognize, was that

> . . . . destitution and indifference, a resignation born of centuries, has brought about with respect to the majority of Italians a deplorable absence of a jealous and deep sense of autonomy and responsibility. A servitude which has lasted for centuries has made it possible for the average Italian to still hesitate between the resignation of the slave and anarchic revolt. The concept of life as struggle or mission, the notion of liberty as moral duty, the knowledge of the limits of their rights and those of others, are wanting in Italians.

A superficial people, the Italians

> . . . . more often than not . . . pride themselves on external relationships. . . . Their interior life, quite rich, is also rather unilateral: it is quite rich above all in sentiment, which often assumes instinctive and exasperated forms. Calm reflection on the great problems of existence, that fecund inner torment that slowly creates a whole world, that alone can confer a knowledge of oneself as a distinct autonomous whole, all this is lacking in Italians.

The cult of the state and the church, and the poverty of the country, Rosselli felt, contributed to this decadence:

> Catholic education, pagan in its cult and dogmatic in substance, together with a long series of tutelary governments, have prevented Italians for centuries from thinking for themselves. Destitution explains the rest. Even today the average Italian yields to the Church his own spiritual independence; and the

state conceived as an end takes from him the dignity of man and makes him no more than a simple instrument, the logical conclusion of a growing process of renunciation.

Fascism, born of "a factional spirit, a sense of adventure, a restless yearning for the new and untried," had made the most of this Italy. It was a divided nation: modern industrial Italy and old rural agricultural Italy, alien to Western civilization, where "still-enslaved masses obstinately cut themselves off from the conditions that are the indispensable premise for the birth and affirmation of a solid Marxist socialist movement." And this was the Italy that Liberal Socialists, Rosselli argued, had to transform root and branch.

In view of these last affirmations, what was and what was not Marxist in liberal socialism was certainly not always self-evident, and by approvingly quoting as his conclusion Kautsky's dictum that in socialism the movement is all, the end nothing, Rosselli no doubt ended on a stirring note but he also darkened the obscurantism. By the same token that ineradicable blurriness also marked the limitations of his peculiar liberal socialism. It was much too vague and indeterminate for either Socialists or Liberals; and it disturbed members of both groups by the way in which its initially austere Mazzinian political-moral passion was rapidly and very perceptibly transformed into something resembling a mood that had done its share to wreck Italian Socialism in the past: the peculiar indignation of Sorel.

Rosselli himself did not expect his book to accomplish much. The anti-Fascist who escaped from Lipari and made his way to Paris had not come to the French capital to publish a worked-over doctoral dissertation. He was impatient to return to political action. Together with his closest friends—including Salvemini, Lussu, Alberto Cianca and Alberto Tarchiani, a former editor of the *Corriere della Sera*—he founded his own political network, *Giustizia e Libertà*. The name, Justice and Liberty (taken from a poem of Carducci, the great nineteenth-century poet who felt the Risorgimento as a modern epic), fittingly expressed the spirit that Rosselli hoped would unite the group; for its unity was to be based above all on love of and dedication to these ideals. In terms of specific political outlook, however, the members of the group were startlingly far apart, ranging from Liberals and Republicans to revolutionary Socialists. Thus, though not strictly a party and with no past party following of any kind to fall back upon, Rosselli's group took its place in the *Concentrazione Antifascista* and quickly made its mark on organized anti-Fascism. In Milan and Turin as well as in Rome, in Trieste and in some smaller northern cities, clandestine subsidiary groups were rapidly organized, and the organization soon had an unusually wide following within Italy. There were differences among individual centers, though not as noticeable as those among members at the Paris headquarters (the Rome center was the most conservative, inclined to a moderate Republicanism; the Turin group, the furthest to the Left, to a revolutionary party of the industrial proletariat), but they were all active anti-Fascist centers, carrying on a dangerous propaganda war against the Fascist state.

At the outset, Rosselli's group in Paris carried on anti-Fascist activities virtually indistinguishable from those of other exiled groups. It carried on propaganda warfare, and in particular slipped letters past the Fascist censorship to the clergy, the military, peasants and workers. But the letters did not always reach their destinations, and even when they did, they brought about no perceptible change. Soon tiring of this form of epistolary sabotage, consequently, Rosselli made the first of his characteristic anti-Fascist gestures to win worldwide publicity. On July 11, 1930, a plane rented by the Giustizia and Libertà group swooped down low over the Piazza del Duomo in Milan, dropped leaflets exhorting Italians to sabotage the regime in any way possible, and informed them of the presence of a national underground network of armed Giustizia and Libertà centers. The gesture had some of that faint aura of absurdity that marked a number of Rosselli's initiatives—the leaflets, among other things, called on Italians to smoke less so as to cut the profits of the government tobacco monopoly. On its return trip to France the plane, in something resembling an anti-climax, crashed in Switzerland. The subsequent trial of the pilot, Giovanni Bassanesi, on charges of having violated Switzerland's neutrality, turned out to be an unforeseeable boon: Rosselli and his friends, testifying on behalf of Bassanesi, again won worldwide coverage for their anti-Fascist crusade.

Within a matter of months the OVRA retaliated by tracking down and arresting leaders of the Milan Giustizia and Libertà group, and Fascist courts imposed a twenty-year prison sentence on its head, Ferruccio Parri, and his close associate Riccardo Bauer, who had been the publisher of a short-lived anti-Fascist periodical in 1925. There were also arrests in the Giustizia and Libertà centers in Turin and in Rome. Though mindful of the need for good public relations with the international intellectual community, Mussolini did not in this instance allow himself to be dissuaded by a plea for clemency signed by thinkers and artists of the stature of Thomas Mann and Ortega y Gasset. Rosselli's flight, quixotic as it may have been, irked him.

After this exploit, though, for a number of years Rosselli's star declined. The accomplishments of Mussolini depressed him as they did the rest of the opposition in exile; indeed, the effect was greater on the impatient leader, determined to do more than firmly and ineffectually protest, together with the *Concentrazione*, in the style of the Aventino. In this respect, although aeronautical activism was an improvement over the usual propaganda warfare, or at least no less effective, Rosselli was aware that that too left much to be desired. The pressing threat of immobility called for a new style, a new political vision, and in January 1932, spurred by a dread of inaction and by a thorough reevaluation of the ideals of liberal socialism, Rosselli issued a manifesto directed to all Italians, a ringing declaration of what anti-Fascists had to do.

There was still a place for something approximating a Liberal outlook and Liberal values in the new vision. The state that would succeed Fascism, Rosselli announced, would be Liberal in the negative sense, that is, it would not be the omnipotent, completely centralized state. It would allow for a maximum of local autonomy and would be based on a mixed economy like that envisioned in *Liberal Socialism*. But the ethos of the new state Rosselli envisioned was no longer Liberal in the Salveminian sense, much less as Croce conceived the Liberal state. A revolutionary proletariat was to animate and forge that state (here Rosselli reflected the profound influence of the Turin Giustizia and Libertà group) and the class that would subvert the foundations of Fascism was to be the new *classe dirigente*. The new state would come to be, Rosselli proclaimed, because revolution was in the air. The duty of anti-Fascist groups, therefore, and their only rational policy, was to aid and abet the revolutionary industrial proletariat, to contribute to a counterattack initiated from within that would, under the leadership of the exiles, eventually overthrow the regime.

As a way out of the inaction in which Rosselli found himself, the shift to the left was coherent and to some extent in keeping with the general direction of his thought. But the manifesto, while failing to win over to the Giustizia and Libertà those revolutionary activists dissatisfied with both Socialist and Communist policy, actually did a great deal to worsen Rosselli's relations with the Socialist Party. It confirmed both Saragat and Nenni in their ever-growing mistrust of Rosselli's overtures. For them, as for most other exiled leaders, the notion of an imminent revolution in Italy and the idea of the existence of a militant revolutionary industrial proletariat was preposterous; and Rosselli's explicit catalogue of the programs that the new state would undertake—the expropriation (with indemnities) and collectivization of large land holdings, while leaving small private properties in the hands of their owners; the socialization of key industries but not all; the compulsory listing of stock assets; an active government-subsidized housing program—all this appeared no more or less than a mania for detailed implausibility. Moreover, from one point of view, in spite of his shift to the left, Rosselli's state appeared not very different from that he had envisioned in *Socialismo Liberale;* and from another, with its talk of local revolutionary committees, and particularly its notion of a special republican guard to defend the new state from the enemies within, it did not seem very different from Fascism, which Rosselli abhorred.

Not surprisingly, then, some two years after his manifesto, Rosselli was still without a substantial following. The Socialists, more and more irked by him, withdrew from the Giustizia and Libertà executive committee, on which they had collaborated for some time. Since the manifesto Rosselli had professed to continue his alliance with them but had actually been competing with them for the leadership of labor. Their example was soon followed by Liberals and Republicans, who withdrew from the *Concentrazione Antifascista.* Exasperated by an attempted maneuver of Rosselli to change the *Concentrazione* into a Socialist-Republican alliance favorable to his militant revolutionary ideas, the member groups preferred to disband rather than identify themselves with his cause. Among the last paradoxical consequences of Rosselli's militant activism, then, was the dissolution of the one tenuous symbol of anti-Fascist unity that had survived until the eve of the Abyssinian War.

The low point of Rosselli's fortunes, however, came with that war. The Giustizia and Libertà confidently asserted, as did other exiled groups, that this colonial war could be no more profitable than any similar venture in the past. But the Giustizia and Libertà did not stop there: in the period that immediately preceded the war, when the Fascists were drumming up a war mood, Rosselli repeatedly taunted Mussolini and accused him of bluffing, so that after the war the Liberal Socialist had to go to Canossa and acknowledge that he had miscalculated badly. Mussolini himself gloatingly took the occasion, in a short insert in the *Popolo d'Italia,* to congratulate Rosselli on his acknowledgement that Fascism was not all bluster, and that it did not lack sustained popular support. The Duce was right. The Abyssinian War was not, as Socialists and Communists insisted, a war forced upon the people, but one that had their backing.

Mockingly taken notice of by Mussolini, having permanently lost the support of the Socialist Party, support that was indispensable to his revolutionary anti-Fascism, Rosselli as a political presence seemed to be rapidly fading away in the year following the Abyssinian War. It had confirmed him in his frantic persuasion that Fascism had to be defeated on the field of battle rather than in that of ideas, that Socialists had to prepare themselves for an immediate confrontation and form the equivalent of Mazzini's *Giovane Italia* groups in Risorgimento days; but no one listened. Wary Socialists kept their distance from him and from his notion of a democratic "preventive war," and the Italians, to whom he directed another manifesto in 1935, paid no attention at all. "We appeal to the workers," he wrote, "to the young Italians who, though wearing the Fascist uniform, feel the stirrings of a higher life. We have faith in that unknown Italy taking shape in silence, rising out of the tyranny of dictatorship." As in the 1932 manifesto, Rosselli again gave a detailed picture of the eventual post-Fascist state—a republic that would abrogate the Lateran Pacts, decentralize political authority, and carry out radical educational and economic reforms, thus laying down the necessary basis for an authentically moral culture. Still no one listened, in or out of Italy. In the judgment of the best-disposed sympathizers, it seemed evident that, politically, Rosselli had come to a dead end. The likelihood of this prospect was reinforced by the obscure and obscurantist talk of an authentic socialism not disposed to make a fetish out of the will of the majority. That ominous notion, first alluded to in Rosselli's new publication, *Quaderni di Giustizia e Libertà,* isolated him altogether. In theory as in action the professor of economics turned conspirator was now definitely cut off from political Italy.

Rosselli's prospects, however, suddenly brightened in July 1936. The outbreak of the Spanish Civil War, which altered so much in Europe and in Italy, radically reoriented Rosselli's life and politics. It also accounted for a drastically revised estimate on the part of Mussolini: now the Duce saw Rosselli as an enemy who had to be done away with. In 1933, Rosselli had visited the newly established Spanish Republic, and though unsuccessful in obtaining permission to use it as a base for a propaganda flight over Italy, he remained on very friendly terms with the regime. With the outbreak of the Civil War, consequently, Rosselli sped to the defense of the republic. Italian volunteer legions were pouring into Spain, lending substantial support to Franco's cause, and now Rosselli's warnings on the war dynamism of Fascist Italy could no longer be dismissed. The Spanish Popular Front needed the help of all anti-Fascists, and needed it urgently.

Yet again Rosselli was rebuffed by the Socialists, cautiously following the lead of the Communists, when he appealed to them to take a stand, to send Socialist brigades to Spain immediately; but this time the rebuff did not sting him. The Socialists and Communists, Rosselli felt, could continue to press for French intervention, and consider support in terms of arms and equipment more important; he, Rosselli, was about to realize his dream of confronting the Fascists on the field of battle, of carrying the fight to the enemy. Exulting in this prospect, Rosselli with twenty followers left France and joined syndicalist-anarchist forces allied with the Loyalist cause in Catalonia, forces so close to him in general outlook that he expected to serve with them indefinitely. In the minor battle of Monte Pelato on August 28, 1936, Rosselli had his baptism of fire. He fought valiantly. *"Oggi in Spagna, domani in Italia!"* he broadcast exuberantly. "Today in Spain, tomorrow in Italy!" and the war cry was picked up and heard by those tuning in on the banned broadcast in Fascist Italy. Not long after, increasing numbers of Italian Socialists, and even more Italian Communist volunteers, joined the Loyalist cause. As Rosselli had anticipated, Spain became the testing ground for international anti-Fascism.

As the war progressed and the Loyalist forces continued to retreat, Rosselli made one last necessary shift. Because the Catalan syndicalist-anarchist group was wracked by internal dissension, and because the Italian Socialist-Communist group which had recently arrived in Madrid was better organized and more efficient, Rosselli left Catalonia and joined the main Loyalist forces in Madrid. His group was a cipher in the five-hundred strong Garibaldi batallion composed mostly of Italian Socialists and Communists.

In the context of this new alignment of forces, Rosselli could be seen in true perspective—a forceful, resilent leader, but a man without a substantial following. The Communists were in command, and it was not to be expected that they would be any more amenable to his suggestions than the Socialists had been. Disregarding the increasingly kind words that Rosselli had of late found for the Bolshevik Revolution, the Communists, who had been engaged in a bloody rivalry with Rosselli's ex-comrades, the Catalonian anarchists, were not disposed to delegate an important position of command to the leader of *Giustizia e Libertà*. Rosselli had realized his dream but he was again alone. In Italy, furthermore, the Giustizia and Libertà groups had been almost completely suppressed: in 1936, the police bore down hard once again, and virtually all those who staffed the major centers, including the key center in Turin, were arrested and given long-term sentences.

Presumably the almost total collapse of the centers in Italy and the restricted role Rosselli was assigned in the Popular Front should have been enough to mollify the exasperation and fears that nagged Mussolini after the outbreak of the Spanish Civil War. There was not the remotest chance that any meaningful number of Italians would answer the call to revolt. The massive Italian intervention in the Spanish struggle presented many problems for Mussolini, but none involving the basic loyalty of the overwhelming number of Italians. And yet precisely at this point, Mussolini decided that he could no longer wait, that the time had come to pay heed to the Machiavellian necessity to *"spegnere il nemico"* (to snuff out the enemy). In the midst of a grim, demanding war that threatened several times to expand into a world war, the continued presence of Rosselli had become unbearable to the Fascist leader. Accordingly, when the historian Nello Rosselli, Carlo's brother, a restrained anti-Fascist who had remained in Italy, requested a passport for France, his wish was granted. The Fascist police were certain that he intended to visit Carlo, then recuperating somewhere in France from ailments and slight war injuries. They trailed Nello, and at the appropriate moment informed the French right-wing extremists known as *cagoulards* of the precise whereabouts of the two brothers. On June 11, French newspapers carried the first account of the discovery of the beaten and knifed bodies of Carlo and Nello Rosselli in a field near Bagnoles sur l'Orne.

The Fascist press, in its brief notice of the murder, suggested that in all likelihood the crime was the work of Catalan anarchists striking back at Rosselli for his desertion of their faction. According to this version, Rosselli was not the first to pay the price in this struggle between the Communists and the anarchists. Sometime before, a well-known Italian anarchist and close friend of Rosselli, Camillo Berneri, had been murdered by the Communists. The suggested explanation chilled rather than convinced Italians with still vivid memories of the Matteotti assassination. Younger readers, though, saw no reason for doubting the plausibility of the account. Besides, for that youthful group, Italian and anti-Fascists in exile who fought against the *legionari* were either Communists, fellow travelers, or criminally stupid dupes.

Quite likely the slow pace of Franco's advance, a pace that exasperated an increasingly tense Mussolini, had something to do with Rosselli's abrupt end. It is even probable that the murder was also meant to be a lesson to underground groups such as the Socialist group uncovered in Milan some two months before the Rosselli murder. That group, which included among others Rodolfo Morandi, a former member of the Giustizia and Libertà movement who was to assume a key role in future Socialist policy, had been disposed of with ten-year prison sentences. Whatever the case, though, with the removal of Rosselli, anti-Fascists lost the one leader who, as Mussolini perceptively feared, might yet, given the proper political climate, have rallied a surging, supraparty following. Henceforth, anti-Fascists in exile were put on notice, the continuing successes of Mussolini at home did not preclude a sudden return to the brutal style of Fascist origins. It was an old style, no doubt, but one to which Mussolini's German partner on the battlefields of Spain took no exception: enemies of the state, whether at home or abroad, deserved no better treatment.

XI

THE DUCE'S MISCALCULATED RISK

The first contingent of Italian volunteer *legionari* sailed for Spain only two months after the end of the Abyssinian War. To become involved in a new conflict fast upon the heels of even a victorious one is risky policy for any regime, but if the Duce had qualms, they were not discernible. The stakes were high, and Mussolini was confident that the possible gains justified the risk, since intervention might open new possibilities for his foreign policy.

In Fascist Italy as in pre-Fascist times, foreign policy had one major goal—a more or less close alliance with the major power or power group that offered most; by 1936, Mussolini and his son-in-law, Galeazzo Ciano, a close confidant of the dictator and generally considered his heir apparent, had decided that France and England no longer offered most. The conclusion involved something of a reversal. As late as 1935, Mussolini had followed a generally pro-English, pro-French foreign policy. In January of that year, in fact, the dictator had signed a pact with Laval aimed at containing German expansion, and three months later he had been host at the Stresa Conference, which formulated a common Italian-French-English policy with respect to German rearmament. Even after French and English opposition to the Abyssinian War strained relations, resentment did not shape Fascist policy. German support during that war and Hitler's loud admiration for the Italian leader no doubt had something to do with the shift; but the change was due to something more than vociferous German approval. By 1936, the Duce was convinced, on grounds of Hitler's occupation of the Rhineland and the speed and quality of German rearmament, that Europe's future was in German hands, and Italian intervention in Spain was the first oblique sign of that new appraisal. An alliance with Germany entailed the risks common to all alliances in which one partner is far stronger than the other, and whether Mussolini remembered Machiavelli's admonitions on this score or not, he acted very much in their spirit. Intervention in Spain was in part a gamble that in the event of a rapid Falangist victory, Franco would offer due compensation in minerals that Italy needed badly to build up her war potential; but much more, it was designed to impress upon the potential German ally the mettle of Mussolini's forces, and establish Italy's mastery in the Mediterranean.

It was not long, however, before the Fascist leader was forced to admit that a rapid Franco victory was out of reach, and that Italian participation in the Spanish war was becoming a burden. Peremptory urgings did not hasten Franco's advance, nor did occasional direct interference in the conduct of the war, as in the case of the bombardment of Barcelona, carried out at the Duce's orders. Nonetheless, after a year of see-saw fighting in a war that had become a test of strength between international Communism and Fascism, Mussolini had few regrets. The superiority of German armaments and military techniques used in that war bore out his estimate of German war potential, and the European events that followed hard upon the close of the war confirmed his appraisal of the measure of German might and ambition.

Europe was no longer the Europe of post-World War I. The first sign of the disappearance of the old order was the eclipse of Austria, which Mussolini had made it a point of honor to defend against threatened German annexation four years before. The next stage in German expansion, the annexation of Czechoslovakia in 1938, was more impressive. With respect to the danger that increase in German power implied for Italy, it was also disturbing. German brinksmanship was paying off, and in retrospect, Italian intervention in Spain appeared all the more prescient. Though dwarfed by Hitler's subsequent bloodless conquest, the effort at least added some stature to an ally distressingly conscious of its limited power. Indeed, in the light of Mussolini's much acclaimed diplomatic victory at Munich, where he was credited with preserving the peace, Spanish intervention appeared to have accomplished an essential task if only in reorienting the country to a popular acceptance of the shift in alliances.

Mussolini had trouble in executing the tricky maneuver of acting as both the determined ally of an expanding Germany and the statesman whose chief aim was preservation of the peace. Foreign policy demanded a "split vision" that aimed in different directions at one and the same time, and the Fascist leader, who had come to power and strengthened his hold by proving satisfactory to the most diverse groups, was certainly not wanting in that type of vision. The political man who appeared now as the authentic Socialist, now as the defender of the Catholic Church and enlightened capitalism, was not the man to break under the strain of wearing many masks. And yet for the first time since the Matteotti murder—although not as yet conspicuously so—Mussolini felt a shortness of breath and a mounting fatigue and exasperation. The hard fact that he found so unmanageable was that the prestige he acquired by being credited with preserving the peace at Munich worked frustratingly at cross purposes with his militant pro-German policy. Most of those who fought with enthusiasm in Abyssinia and dutifully in Spain were conspicuously and shamelessly relieved at the prospect of escaping a second world war; and their sentiments were shared by key groups, starting with the military.

The professional army people, with a rather precise idea of the price of the African war and of Spanish intervention, privately expressed their relief to the Duce. In 1937, the Chief of Staff, General Alberto Pariani, threatened to resign if his request for an appropriation of some twenty billion lire for the army was not granted, and although the General acted as most military men would have under such circumstances in order to get the maximum possible, there was no question but that the Italian army was woefully ill-equipped. Pariani's claim that Italy in 1937 was even less prepared for a long war than it had been at the outbreak of World War I was based on facts. Industrial production, in spite of the self-sufficiency drive of the Fascist Institute for Industrial Reconstruction was not up to the requirements of a long conflict. Of the sixty-seven divisions, forty-three lacked indispensable equipment for general mobility. Most of the artillery and a good number of rifles were of World War I vintage, and anti-aircraft weapons were very slow in coming off the production line. The air corps, vaunted as the pride of Fascist Italy, was more impressive on paper than in fact. Individual Italian planes had made numerous contributions to the record books, but production was extremely limited, and the number of pilots ready for combat duty numbered at most thirty thousand. The navy by contrast was somewhat prepared, but certainly lacked the fire power to face the combined French and English Mediterranean fleets. In some areas—chemicals and synthetic rubber, for example—industrial Italy had made remarkable progress, but not enough to compensate for a long list of handicaps. The most pressing consideration, perhaps, was that in Fascist Italy the sinews of war—coal and steel—were tissue thin. The price of coal was still three times that of coal in England, and steel was also prohibitive. In case of war, Italy inescapably would have to rely completely on inland transportation of coal from Germany, a dependence with obvious dangers.

There were Fascists high in party councils who shared the military men's relief after the Munich Pact. The Italian ambassador to Germany, Count Bernardo Attolico, who mistrusted Hitler and repeatedly sought to dissuade Mussolini from a German alliance, was particularly pleased, as were Ciano (who vacillated on the advisability of a close alliance with Hitler), the outspokenly anti-German Cesare Balbo, the popular hero of transatlantic flights and one of the few Fascists whose popularity was not totally eclipsed by that of Mussolini, and Dino Grandi, ambassador to England, who did not conceal his strong pro-British sympathies.

The precarious peace won at Munich also improved relations with the King, who had made no secret of his hostility toward a German alliance. Since the Abyssinian War, when Mussolini in the euphoria of the moment had designated himself *Primo Maresciallo dell'Impero*, relations had been somewhat taut between the dictator and the monarch, and they worsened when the Fascist leader privately ridiculed the King's misgivings over his pro-German foreign policy. In acting as preserver of the peace, however, Mussolini once again persuaded the powerless King that he was, when all was said and done, a remarkably sane and sensible leader.

Munich also reassured an indeterminate but substantial number of Italians who, after the intervention in Spain, had become increasingly tired of war and war hysteria. The *battaglia del grano* (the wheat battle), part of the drive for economic self-sufficiency (Mussolini never forgot the political consequences of the 1898–1917 wheat shortage in Italy), was for patriotic reasons fairly popular, but a number of other policies were not. A people that had clung to its sense of humor for centuries could not lose it overnight and listen seriously to Mussolini's incitements to population explosion. It was impossible, too, for Italians not to shake their heads over the caliber of men with whom Mussolini surrounded himself, particularly Achille Starace, secretary of the party from 1932 on. Almost a caricature of Mussolini, Starace had the drive of an aging martinet, with none of the Duce's political skills or his genius for knowing how to sound martial and patriotic and at the same time genuinely concerned with the commonweal. In a country that has never spared its political leaders (Mussolini himself at the height of his popularity during the Abyssinian War was the subject of many disrespectful, thoroughly enjoyable jokes), the humorless, stupidly anti-bourgeois Starace very soon became the favorite butt of jokes about the Fascist hierarchy. Italians willingly went to war in Abyssinia and supported, though less enthusiastically, Spanish intervention; but they resented Starace's exhortations to spend Sunday mornings not at home but on a drilling field, and they made appropriate comments when the middle-aged black-shirted Starace jumped though blazing hoops and directed other middle-aged black-shirted men to follow suit.

Mussolini's role in the Munich Pact, then, did a great deal to attenuate the general misgivings of many Italians on the caliber of his closest aides, on the unconcealable increase in corruption within party ranks, the increasingly ostentatious military posturing of the regime, the ceaseless talk of a place in the sun, and the onmipresent photographs of a stern-faced Duce being awarded his wings, or standing stiffly at attention reviewing a military parade. Mussolini's role in the Munich Pact, moreover, in this widespread popular point of view, seemed to express the proper deference to German scientific skill and industrial might, with an equally firm commitment to a peace policy. All that martial gesturing and martial talk, the dictator's role at Munich seemed to indicate, was just that and nothing more. Those gestures, like others dating from the same period (the decree that the *Lei*, the traditional respectful form of "you" was to be replaced by the less class-conscious *voi*, or the introduction of the *passo romano*, a barely modified German goose-step, or the ubiquitous signs bombastically exhorting to some kind of nebulous heroism), had to be read in context.

The military, the Fascist hierarchy, the man in the street, and even the new Pope, Pius XII, with whom relations were not generally good, all applauded Mussolini's peace-making role at Munich; and the cumulative effect, consequently, was at painful odds with the dictator's obsessive desire to show the Germans that Fascist Italians were a new breed, not at all like the Italians of World War I; that they were united and strong, a warlike people—in a word, worthy allies of Nazi Germany.

For a while, consequently, the Duce embodied the peculiar wisdom that teaches that in times of doubt it is best to hesitate. One minute he confided to those close to him his many fears as to the wisdom of a very close alliance with Germany; another, he ferociously attacked those advisors who urged caution and restraint, and branded them the worst type of "peace mongers." The dilemma, the indecision, was a vise which held him more and more tightly; and it did not add to his clarity of judgment or consistency of will that just about this time his health began to fail. The Fascist leader had an ulcer condition and, it was rumored, syphillis.

Failing health, however, was probably more the effect than the cause of Mussolini's malaise. For an activist temperament such as his, the ultimate cause, the ultimate torment was indecision. He had rare skill in playing a political waiting game, but only when an imminent resolution was clearly in sight, and in 1938 no such end was in view. Still, though irresolute throughout this period, Mussolini continued to draw closer to Hitler and vied with him in his totalitarianism. Toward this end, to make Italians more fanatically exultant in their *italianità*, their "otherness," he followed Hitler's example and in the summer of 1938, instituted the first Italian anti-semitic legislation.

In general, it was acquiesced to rather than enthusiastically complied with. Anti-semitism can become an export item, but it cannot be suddenly legislated as a grass-roots, popular cause, and in Italy it failed to become anything like the perverted Nazi mystique. Anti-semitism played virtually no role in Italian political history. There were only some 47,000 Italian Jews and they were almost completely integrated into the middle and high bourgeoisie. Indistinguishable from most Liberals of agnostic persuasion, a number of them who had gone into politics had become household names. Luigi Luzzatti, for example, several times prime minister in the Giolittian era, was Jewish, and so were some of the outstanding anti-

Fascist leaders—Treves, Modigliani, Rosselli. Italians, however, did not think of them as Jewish and by and large saw no ominous significance in the fact stressed by the Fascists, that there were many Jewish members in the Giustizia and Libertà groups (especially the Turin group, captained by Leone Ginzburg). Because of this background, the enaction of anti-semitic legislation in Italy met with only partial success, and in justice to Mussolini, the legislation there bore little resemblance to its German prototype. Intellectual life, it is true, was impoverished by the expulsion of a number of Jewish intellectuals and scholars, but the laws were often attenuated in their enforcement and on occasion bypassed altogether. German Jewish scholars, indeed, sought and actually found asylum in Italy. This "permissive" attitude did not mean, of course, that intellectual Italians openly opposed the new policy of anti-semitism. In 1938, a long manifesto appeared, signed by a number of distinguished professors (but bearing traces of Mussolini's style) that proclaimed the scientific basis of anti-semitism. But in spite of the edict, many Italians remembered that Mussolini himself had not long before ridiculed the notion of pure race; and those who took their Catholicism seriously had Pius XII's condemnation of racism (in the encyclical *Mit brennender Sorge*) to sustain them.

Another measure that Mussolini passed in imitation of German totalitarianism, the establishment of the Ministry of Popular Culture, met with even less success. Minculpop, as the ministry was cacophonically called, tried to lower all cultural activities to several levels below what Italians would tolerate, and the attempt boomeranged. Instead of turning virtually all Italians into egg-faced legions saluting a stern Duce, it drove many well-disposed if not enthusiastic Italians to increasingly open dissatisfaction. In literature this growing dissent was unmistakeably expressed in a number of works, of which Elio Vittorini's *Conversazione in Sicilia (Conversation in Sicily)* is perhaps the most daring and outspoken.

The relative failures of the anti-semitic campaign and of Minculpop added to Mussolini's mounting exasperation. In a burst of resolution and impatience with an allegedly weak, undisciplined, pusillanimous Italy, in May 1939, to the shock of many of his closest associates, including Ciano and Attolico, Mussolini announced the signing of the Rome-Berlin pact, which clearly stipulated that Italians would be required to join their allies should Germany go to war. The alliance proclaimed a firm commitment, but in secret session Mussolini reassured his aides that Hitler had been informed that Italy could not be ready for war for at least four years, and the Fascist leader let it be understood that the advantages of the pact all accrued to Italy. Hitler would work closely with the Fascist government, Mussolini was confident, without making excessive demands on it. In this peculiar interpretation of the pact there is nothing to indicate that the Duce remotely suspected that Axis or no Axis, Hitler meant to keep his counsel, that he considered Mussolini an ally to be consulted only on minor matters.

The first unequivocal revelation of Hitler's interpretation of the Rome-Berlin alliance was not long in coming. When German forces invaded Poland in September 1939, Mussolini was informed only at the last minute, and then Hitler made it clear that a well-disposed Italian neutrality would suit his plans admirably. The German willingness to "go it alone" should have reassured and pleased Mussolini; instead, it completely consternated him, by now more and more subject to brusque changes in moods and ideas. For a while, with wounded pride, he reverted to the role of the mediator, keeping all channels open and remaining in close contact with the Allies—with Churchill, Reynaud, and Roosevelt as well. Conceivably (for in these months it became virtually impossible to distinguish labyrinthian Machiavellian moves from abrupt and often pathological improvisations), he may have had second thoughts and seriously considered accepting Hitler's invitation to remain neutral. The Duce could not mistake the joyous gratitude of Italians for their non-belligerent status, or fail to recognize that his recently intensified anti-French campaign, which demanded Tunis, Bizerte and Nice, was more vocal than popular. His anti-English campaign found a more enthusiastic response, but even there Fascist-encouraged denunciations of English control of the Mediterranean through Suez and Gibraltar were anything but a grass-roots agitation for intervention. In 1939, it was clear that the Abyssinian War (largely because of its brevity) was Mussolini's only popular war, and that since the Spanish intervention, popular feeling had become increasingly resentful of the continued war policy. There were soldiers in Italy who by 1943 had served in the army for nine continuous years. And because the Italian dictator was aware of this sullen mood he allowed the anti-German Ambassador Attolico to remain in Berlin and made no move to rebuke Ciano for his "wait and see" approach to the war in a speech before the *Gran Consiglio*, the Fascist Council, in December, 1939. Indeed, he not only tolerated approval of Italy's non-belligerent status: he had second thoughts himself. In a secret report to Hitler he compiled such an endless list of demands for the raw materials and machinery Italy would need for a successful military action that refusal was a foregone conclusion.

Still, Mussolini did not relish the prospect of going down in history as a peacemaker, and he viewed the swift course of the war with growing apprehension. The *drôle de guerre*, the uneventful first period of the war, did not last for long. By April, German armored divisions were roaring through Belgium and Holland, and not long after they had left the Maginot Line behind. The electrifying tempo of German successes stunned Mussolini. Reproaching himself for his doubts and indecisiveness, and persuading advisors that Italy could not afford to let a golden opportunity slip by, he hurled the country into war. Attolico was recalled and replaced with the more docile and less perceptive Dino Alfieri. The military were told to do their utmost in a war that was presumably drawing rapidly to a close, and once more, as in World War I, the anti-war feelings of the overwhelming number of Italians were brushed aside. They might not fight with enthusiasm, Mussolini expected, but in a short war they would fight.

Having issued his orders, the Duce found his old strength again. The dissident voices in the party became murmurs, the military set about its preparations, and Italians, frightened and awed by the pace of the German offensive and hopeful for a short war, took up arms again. Hitler did not seem particularly pleased, but that did not disturb Mussolini. An ally entering a war at the last minute—and Italy entered it on June 10, 1940, three days before the fall of Paris—could not expect a cordial reception. Mussolini's Italy received only a curt nod of recognition as it took its place at the conference table to help settle France's partition and fate. Indeed Hitler, citing the need to maintain a minimum of good relations with occupied France, persuaded Mussolini to abandon temporarily most Italian claims, including those to French territory in north Africa. In a war that seemed to be approaching its climax, Mussolini did not find a request for patience unreasonable; and considering how little and how late the Italian contribution had been, a brief skirmishing on Italy's northwestern front, the Duce was hardly in a position to protest.

In other areas, however, and notably in eastern Africa, Italian troops won meaningful victories. Kassala in the Sudan capitulated by July 1940, and soon after, Italian forces occupied all of British Somaliland. In northern Africa, Italian troops met with similar success and in September, forces under the command of General Rodolfo Graziani pushed to the Egyptian border.

These successes made up in part for the general disappointment over Hitler's failure to pound England into submission—a failure generally acknowledged by Italian military men by September 1940. The war, evidently, was to be longer than anticipated, but softening this blow was the comforting knowledge that the German leader had made an impregnable fortress of Europe. Even when Italian advances in north Africa stalled, Mussolini expected them to push ahead again shortly.

In the European theatre of war, at any rate, Mussolini, together with Ciano, had decided on a swift move to be executed without any previous notification to their ally: an invasion of Greece through Albania. Tactical considerations played only a minor role in the plan. A successful invasion would have secured supply lines between Africa and Italy that were steadily hammered by attacks from Greek-based British ships; but the point of the invasion was to show Hitler and the German General Staff, not impressed with the Italian military contribution, that they seriously underestimated their Mediterranean ally; that Italy on its own initiative could mark off the Adriatic area as its own sphere of influence. Italy's conquest of Albania in April 1939, before the outbreak of the war, was a first clumsily executed step in that direction; considering the extent of the German victories, Fascist Italy now had to take a giant step.

To the amazement of the country and even of General Pietro Badoglio, the Chief of Staff, who had opposed the invasion, and of bureaucrats and war profiteers well aware of the discrepancy between the paper figures of Italian military strength and the hard facts, after two weeks of cautious advance the Italian forces pushing their way down just past the Greek frontier were utterly routed by hammering Greek counterattacks. Fighting heroically but with inadequate weapons and with no depth of reserves, crack Alpine troops retreated all along the line. The Greek invasion turned into a defensive Albanian War and the expected victory turned into a desperate rear-guard action to keep the waves of Greek counterattacks from hurling the Italians off the Albanian shore and into the Adriatic.

Begun soon after the collapse of France, when many troops had been prematurely released from military service in the overoptimistic conviction that the war was almost over, the Greek campaign was a massive indictment of the military improvisations of the Duce and the acquiescence of the military to his *diktat*. Just as important, that defeat was responsible for the first manifest major break in the web of consent that the dictator had been weaving for almost nineteen years, a web that had now become hardened, petrified. For the first time since he had assumed power, a miscalculation of Mussolini turned into a catastrophe. After seven months of fighting, the dead numbered 24,000; the wounded and missing in action, 87,000. As was the case after Caporetto (the shame of its memory explained in part Mussolini's obsession with turning Italians into a warlike people), recriminations flew. Generals accused officers and enlisted men of lack of fighting spirit; officers and enlisted men in turn accused the General Staff; the *gerarchi*, the Fascist leaders, denounced the "traitors" and war profiteers; and relations between the regular army and the Fascist militia, never good, flared into murderous rage. Unlike Caporetto, however, there was an upper limit beyond which accusations could not go. But even though Mussolini's hold was still not perceptively weakened, and the military continued to fight and obey numbly, the Duce's popularity, erratically decreasing since the high point of Munich, took a downward plunge. In war Italians, as Croce had said in speaking of World War I, acted as if "the only thing to do was to win it"; and they carried on in this spirit. But they were appalled at the contrast of continued German successes with the gigantic failure of Mussolini's attempt to carry out one full-scale military operation on his own. Increasing numbers of military men were outraged at Mussolini's scapegoat removal of General Badoglio as Chief of Staff (he was replaced by the more pro-German General Ugo Cavallero), and a number of Fascist *gerarchi* began to feel more than a smouldering resentment for the way in which the Duce's shake-up sought to pass on to them the responsibility for the debacle.

In all probability, had the war been going badly elsewhere in

Europe at this point the resentment and loss of faith might have assumed a more threatening form. Yet the very continuing success of the German war effort, while protecting Mussolini, was not completely to his advantage. It also accelerated the decline of his fortunes. It has been argued that because of the Greek debacle Franco, whose limited aid to Italy was a bitter disappointment for Mussolini, refused to enter the war; but far more telling, the Greek catastrophe, which Hitler considered "stupid" and transparent in its political intent, led the German dictator to express openly his opinion of his ally's intent to stake out a sphere of influence. By March 1941, German forces came to the rescue of the Italians in Albania, and Mussolini never survived the rescue. From this time on, for all practical purposes, Italy ceased to be an independent ally. The daring impulsiveness of the Greek invasion, with which Mussolini had hoped to bolster Italian claims in the region, plunged Italy into the state of complete dependence that Mussolini from the very beginning of the alliance had desperately sought to avoid. The stronger of the two partners now began to totally assimilate the weaker, and in a quiet, firm manner Hitler took Fascist Italy in tow. In the same month that the Germans rescued Italian forces pinned down in southern Albania, Hitler dealt Mussolini another hard blow. German troops, helping in the rapid suppression of the Yugoslav revolt led by Peter II, blitzkrieged into that country; and Yugoslavia too, on which Italy had long had her eye, became one more territory to be shared with Hitler. Italy had to content herself with control of parts of Dalmatia and Slovena. In Italy proper, meanwhile, the Germans had already virtually taken over the Alto Adige region, much to the satisfaction of inhabitants, who had long resented Mussolini's attempts to italianize the region by encouraging Italian immigration to the newly industrialized area, banning German from the schools, and pressuring the Vatican to appoint to that zone only ecclesiastics persuaded that the Italian language and Italian culture were among the greatest legacies that Christ bequeathed to the world. But German infiltration did not stop in the Alto Adige and the Trentino: General Kesselring located his headquarters on the outskirts of Rome. And in north Africa, after the last Italian reverses, General Rommel assumed command of all Italian troops.

The debacle in Greece showed Italians that the emperor wore no clothes, and although Mussolini sought to pass it off as the work of traitors and saboteurs and "incompetent idiots," indeed he had only himself to blame. But he could not be blamed for the *coup de grace* in the precipitating situation, Hitler's invasion of Russia in June 1941. The Greek fiasco had taught the Duce some lessons, and he dreaded the implications of a war on two fronts. German military and technical assistance was proving to be both too much and too little—too much direct German control in the country, too little military and technical aid. In his letters to Hitler and his meeting with the Fuehrer, Mussolini expressed cautious reservations on the projected Russian campaign, and after the American entry into the war in December 1941, his fears swelled. But at this point, there was nothing that the Duce could do. What little influence he may ever have had on the German dictator had long since evaporated, and once the Russians assumed the offensive after the Battle of the Don, there was nothing for Italy to do but bear the consequences of diminished German aid and increased Allied bombings.

Italy had few searchlights, no anti-aircraft guns to speak of, virtually no air corps; and all through 1942, the principal northern cities were subjected to intense aerial bombing. In a war that had the dogged backing of the people, the pounding would not have crippled morale; but in Italy, especially after the failure of the Greek invasion, the unremittant bombing pulverized the will to fight. Rationing, mounting casualties, war profiteering and the total absence of defenses totally demoralized Italians. Aldo Vidussoni, a second-generation Fascist who became secretary of the party after Starace's dismissal, was an absolute nonentity, and could do nothing to bolster morale or the regime's crumbling support. Rommel's drive up to one hundred kilometers from Alexandria had been a glimmer of light, but by October 1942, that light too had been snuffed out.

This was the moment. Ciano, Dino Grandi and other *gerarchi* who had seen the handwriting on the wall in the Greek invasion drew close together; and when Mussolini relieved his son-in-law of his position and sent him to the Vatican as ambassador, and let a number of other Fascist leaders learn from the newspapers that they had been relieved of their posts, the panicky resolve grew stronger. In the General Staff, which clearly recognized that the only question now was where and when the Allies would invade Italy, similar conspiratorial moves were taking shape, and General Badoglio, certain that Italian and German forces could not repulse an Allied attack, was taking secret steps to see what could be done after that invasion.

And yet even at this moment, when self-preservation demanded speed, the conspiracy moved very slowly. Not until after the surrender to the Allies of the island fortress of Pantelleria, which was to guard Sicily against invasion, and not until the invasion of Sicily itself on July 9, 1943, did the Ciano-Grandi group move against Mussolini. The quality of the Sicilian defense—not a glorious page in Italian military annals—was probably the decisive factor for the conspirators. Here and there, and particularly when fighting alongside German divisions on the eastern coast near Catania, Italian forces put up stiff resistance, but in general, theirs was the rote resistance of combatants who had long since lost faith in the cause. In a matter of weeks, the entire island was in Allied hands.

Even at this point, though, a broken Mussolini found loyal and outspoken Fascists (notably Carlo Scorza, the last Secretary of the party) to tell him what spartan measures were necessary to salvage anything from the oncoming holocaust. But for months Mussolini had been moving about in a sort of desultory sleep-walking; he would suddenly come to, act with feverish impulsiveness, and then fall fack into a torpor. Very probably he was aware that the time had come for Ciano and Grandi, and others he had long suspected of conspiring against him, to make their move; and yet when they called for a meeting of the *Gran Consiglio*, which had not met since the beginning of the war, he offered no resistance. He may have had some spectacular move in mind, he may have trusted in some unforeseeable turn of fortune, or he may have seen the hopelessness of it all. At any rate, at the meeting of the Grand Council on July 25, the twenty-year regime of Mussolini came to a formal end, overturned by a handful among the party, who charged him with having led the country to ruin. According to their own testimony, until the very last moment the conspirators expected Mussolini to turn on them and have them summarily executed.

A handful of his close associates had toppled the gaunt Fascist leader from power—but quite understandably they were not alone. Insurgent Fascists were not in a position to command loyalties from indispensable elements—the army, the navy, civil servants. Those groups, essential to any successful break-away from the dictator, were loyal only to King Victor Emmanuel III; and on him fell the responsibility of participating in the revolt and seeking to cautiously disentangle Italy from the war and from the Nazi alliance—ends which, as it turned out, were completely beyond his reach.

It was an unexpected assignment, certainly, for a monarch who, in spite of occasional friction, had collaborated for twenty-odd years with Mussolini and his regime, a monarch who would almost certainly have maintained excellent relations with the Fascist regime had Italy won the war. But with the Allies already in southern Italy and a hysterical anti-war exhaustion sweeping the country, the King no longer hesitated. Earlier, when approached by Bonomi (who had remained in Italy throughout the Fascist years, and since 1942 had been organizing an anti-Fascist group made up of his own followers and Liberals such as Einaudi and Orlando), the King had refused the ex-Prime Minister's urgings to take the initiative and depose Mussolini. He had refused again when insurgent Fascists came to him and appealed to him to intervene directly. But knowing that in Fascist Italy, where the suppression of non-Fascist parties had been total, he was the only force to whom any opposition could turn, the King agreed to cooperate on his own terms. His conditions demanded that the Fascists themselves depose their leader; he would then guarantee that the army would carry out orders, that Mussolini would be taken into protective custody, and that he, the King, would work toward a secret armistice with the Allies and do his utmost to prevent the explosion of a civil war.

In so doing the King, in spite of the tardiness of his anti-Fascism, acted coherently, in keeping with the instinct of self-preservation and with a patriotism of sorts. At the moment, the problem of his motivation did not matter; Italians asked only that something be done to put an end to a war for which they had neither weapons nor heart. It was asking too much, of course, and the King was not to be blamed altogether for failing in the attempt. There was bungling on the side of the Allies as well as on the Italian side, and it cannot be forgotten that the attempt to work out a peace was being made under the shadow of German armored divisions roaring into northern and central Italy, down to Rome. With the help of his new Prime Minister, General Badoglio, the King had all he could do to keep the Germans at bay and not be taken prisoner by them. For forty-five days the new government carried out a policy of desperate duplicity, with Badoglio assuring the Germans that the war (as the King announced in a radio broadcast) would "go on as usual," and at the same time negotiating for a secret armistice. On September 3, with the signing of a short armistice, the King, the Prime Minister and a few trusted aides, without previous notification and leaving no instructions for military or civilian government units, fled from Rome and made their way south to Allied-occupied territory in Brindisi, Calabria. From there, after signing a second and more complete armistice document, the King, sovereign of a minuscule territory, declared war on Germany and on Fascist Italy, once again led by Mussolini after a daring rescue by German paratroopers in September.

But though he occasionally showed signs of life in spasms of activity, Mussolini, the *gauleiter* of Italy, generally let his fanatic hard-core followers, Farinacci and Alessandro Pavolini, whip up enthusiasm for his new Republic of Salò. All confidence and political insight appeared to have been drained from him. At most, he clung to the will to live. Though he came to life with the Trial of Verona in January 1944, and the subsequent execution of those captured Fascists who had turned on him (including his son-in-law Ciano), he never regained his old forcefulness.

With his glazed vision, looking backward taught the haggard Duce nothing: he understood everything that had happened, and he understood nothing of what had happened. The King, Badoglio, and a people who had refused his call to greatness—all were traitors, as were the war profiteers, and a treacherous party leadership that was as corrupt and as effeminately peace-loving as the Italian people. The Nazis, too, in this look, had their share of the blame; they were bluffers, incompetents, utterly unworthy of the miscalculated risk he had taken. In all this shuttling from one "responsible" party to the other, however, Mussolini was completely unable to perceive the varying degrees of truth and falsehood in each of these explanations, and utterly incapable of recognizing that his enormous gamble in foreign policy was completely in keeping with his character, not a break with previous, sensible policies; and when, occasionally, he had an inkling of that truth he gloried in it. The Duce, glancing backward, had learned nothing. Nor did he learn more by looking about him. The loyalties of Italians in German-controlled Italy were obviously in direct proportion to the number of German divisions on hand, to German *savoir faire*, and to the slowness of the

Allied advance up the peninsula. Those Italian army units that, stranded and without leadership, had taken their place at the side of the Germans, were moved by no enthusiasm (although there were individual fanatics), but rather by fear or a stoic sense of loyalty. Already the number of defections was noticeably on the rise among young draftees; more and more were taking to the hills to join partisan bands.

Indeed, the only bitter-sweet satisfaction that Mussolini had in these months was news of the problems of the Kingdom of the South. The struggle there between the King and the representatives of political parties, again moving about with relative freedom on the political scene after long years of Fascist dictatorship, gave him his one palpable satisfaction. In that conflict between a King determined to hold on to Allied recognition of his sovereignty, and the returning parties, adamant in their refusal to join the government of a monarch whose anti-Fascism was so belated, Mussolini saw a vindication of his estimate of all past political parties. He could then admit that he had made his blunders, that he had taken a miscalculated risk. The fact remained that the new Italy, in the throes of civil war, and in the midst of the chaos and confusion of Allied occupation, was already steeped in a government crisis, an impasse distantly reminiscent of the crisis of 1922. And even when, after several months, that impasse was resolved, Mussolini took comfort in the vicious expectation that in post-Fascist Italy a rule of parties would fail once again. Italy, the *gauleiter* was convinced, with a characteristic mingling of cynicism and the perverted will to believe in his own political mythology, was Fascist because it deserved to be Fascist, because it could be nothing better. Against that craggy reality of the Italian character and political mentality, he was positive, the returning parties would be no more than dashing foam.

XII

OGGI IN ITALIA!

From the beginning of the struggle that pitted the anti-Fascist parties against the King and Badoglio, each and every group, in marking its return to political freedom with political intransigence, was conscious of the anomaly of its position. But each concluded that there was no alternative: no party could tolerate that the new nation, at war with Fascist Italy, be represented by a King who had been compromised by twenty years of collaboration with the Duce. The new anti-Fascist parties had no control over the course of the war, but in politics, in that small area in which they did have a say, they did not mean to start with a major concession. The Allies, they protested, were making a bad blunder in insisting that their obligation was to the King, the signatory of the armistice, and that under no circumstances would they ask for his abdication. Victor Emmanuel could insure that a token force of a few divisions under the flag of the new Italy would fight with the Allies, and fight gallantly; he might lessen Churchill's misgivings as to the danger of a Communist-Socialist takeover; but he did not embody the spirit or the cause of Italians in Allied-occupied territory or in Fascist-Nazi Italy willing to lay down their lives in the fight against the Fascist dictator.

All parties in liberated Italy—from Bonomi's Reformist Socialists, now the *Democrazia del Lavoro*, to the old Liberals (represented by Enrico De Nicola and Vittorio Emanuele Orlando) and Populists (renamed the Christian Democratic Party) to the Socialists and Communists—opposed the King. Representing them all in an eloquent supraparty spirit was the seventy-eight year old Croce, whose anti-Fascism had an international reputation, and whose counsel and judgment were much sought after by the officers of Allied intelligence and psychological warfare. Croce became a center for the concerted opposition to Victor Emmanuel III, in the philosopher's terse appraisal *"un re tutto prosa"* (an utterly prosaic king). To bolster the case of the defiant parties and to reassure the British in particular (more apprehensive than the Americans over the anti-monarchism of the new parties), Croce again and again stressed that there was nothing dangerous or revolutionary in their hostility; that most of the parties, like the southern Liberals he represented, sought not the abolition of the monarchy, but only the removal of Victor Emmanuel III.

The Italian people, Croce maintained, had never been wholeheartedly Fascist, and now that the dictatorship was overthrown and they were free again, the Allies had everything to gain by cooperating with the request of the great majority. In holding that their first obligation was to the King, the Allies were indulging in reasoning that was excessively legalistic and juridical, as well as particularly dangerous for their own cause. Their fear of communism could boomerang; if they persisted in misreading the situation and interpreting anti-monarchism as a Communist-Socialist maneuver they would be giving those left-wing parties the chance to pose as the only intransigent opponents of Fascism.

Just what effect these arguments had on the Allied Military Government is hard to assess. There is no question, however, that the opposition of all parties had its effect on the King and Badoglio and on their government of technicians. As a result of the continued pressure, after a few months the King yielded and gave his word to De Nicola, who was largely responsible for the compromise solution, that on the Allies' entry into Rome, he would return to the capital and formally abdicate in favor of the regency of his son Umberto, and let an eventual national referendum decide the fate of the monarchy.

The government crisis had been resolved. But from the point of view of the Liberals and the Christian Democrats, the King's concession came none too soon: Togliatti, unaware of the agreement, on his arrival in the Kingdom of the South very soon after announced that the Communist Party, in keeping with Russia's recognition of the Kingdom, would be willing to put an end to the crisis and form a government with the King. The offer indicated that the Communists preferred to make, not follow policy, and in keeping with a *politica spregiudicata*—a *realpolitik* willing to disregard temporarily the towering political differences—would not have hesitated to participate in the government of a king denounced by all other parties for his Fascist past.

The impasse, consequently, came to an end with a new Badoglio Cabinet in which all parties were represented, assisted by a great many ministers without portfolio, among whom was Benedetto Croce. The government could not do much to control the run-away inflation that followed the printing of Allied money, nor could it expedite the production of urgently needed medicines, particularly quinine. It failed, too, in tackling the delicate and tangled problem of epuration, and the appointment of Tito Zaniboni (a Socialist whose one distinction was that he had once made an attempt on Mussolini's life) as Minister of Epuration was no doubt one of the government's less felicitous moves. Yet in its brief three months in office this government, considering its very limited powers, did a workmanlike job. It kept administrative wheels turning, brought some order out of the chaos in transportation and communications, and in Naples, which had revolted against the Germans a day or two before the Allied entry, helped substantially in setting up a new city administration. It also won Allied approval for the first post-Fascist independent newspapers.

The situation appeared somewhat steadied. But once the Allies entered Rome in June 1944, and the King stepped down in favor of Prince Umberto (the parties, however, reneged on their promise to let the King go to Rome to abdicate) and Badoglio handed in his resignation, new problems arose. Even before Victor Emmanuel's flight to the South, groups of partisan bands in central and northern Italy had taken up the fight against the Fascists and Nazis. At first without any particular political orientation, these bands had rapidly acquired a party coloration and in the North were soon well-differentiated into groups representing the Communists, Socialists, Christian Democrats, the new Action Party and—fewer in numbers—the Liberals and monarchists.

Partisan bands of the CLNAI, the northern Italian branch of the Committee of National Liberation, were principally under the control of the Communist, Socialist and Action Parties, all parties of the left; and with the resignation of Badoglio's last government, this group, together with the more moderate national CLN in Rome (in which Liberals and Christian Democrats had a stronger voice) dictated the selection of the new government and its new head.

The compromise choice of these two groups was Bonomi, the head of the national CLN, who had on his own initiative sought unsuccessfully to have the King depose Mussolini. In 1945, as in 1921, Bonomi was barely acceptable to the far left. The Liberals and Christian Democrats backed him but the CLNAI, while agreeing to the compromise, from the very beginning actively mistrusted and opposed him. Two parties in particular, the Socialists and the Action Party, made things very difficult for the new Prime Minister. Bonomi was responsible to them, not to Prince Umberto, they insisted. *They* represented the true anti-Fascist Italy, the *lotta di popolo*, that redeeming popular revolutionary anti-Fascism that would not be a tool of Bonomi or the monarchy.

Principle and political reasons both played a role in the belligerent intransigence of these parties, making them far more difficult to deal with than the Communists. In war-torn Italy, as in exile, the Socialists had numerous problems. When Nenni finally reached Rome after being liberated from Ponza where he was held prisoner by the Fascists, he was depressed and astounded to find how little of the party apparatus and leadership had survived Fascism. "*Siam tutti qui?!*" he asked incredulously, "Are we all here?!" To make matters worse, the surviving Socialist leaders were not only few but they were divided among themselves. In this sense, the Socialist Party that was reconstituted in 1943 was somewhat reminiscent of the Socialist Party immediately before the advent of Fascism, and later, in exile. There was a left wing, captained by Morandi and Lelio Basso, a center-right wing, best represented by a Piedmontese of Turatian tradition, Giuseppe Romita, and seeking to hold them all together, Nenni's center-left. After his release from a Fascist jail, Morandi played a leading role in the resistance. Romita's group, meanwhile, began to work with Saragat (who narrowly escaped execution at the hands of the Germans on his return to Rome). The following the divided party might have retained was a matter of conjecture. Socialists hoped that their traditional strongholds in Lombardy and Piedmont would not have completely disintegrated, but Nenni, and all other Socialist leaders, knew in 1943 that they and not the Communists were struggling for survival: in post-Fascist Italy, the Socialists were moving in the long shadow of the Communists.

The Communists, who had no serious divisions among themselves, capitalized to the hilt on their political activism during the years of exile, in which, though they had not "monopolized the Fascist jails," they had been disproportionately represented there. They made the most of Russian prestige and Russian heroism (the epic defense of Stalingrad drew more converts to the cause than any tract of Lenin or Marx), and their success throughout the Fascist era in keeping in some contact with workers and labor unions in Italy assured them of a position of strength in the unions of the northern industrial proletariat. In the space of one year, from 1943 to 1944, the number of card-carrying Communists soared from five thousand to one hundred thousand, many of whom were simply rapidly exchanging one totalitarianism for another.

In the Resistance, the party made deft use of lessons learned in the Spanish Civil War. Communist bands accounted for more than 50 per cent of partisan strength, as compared with a much smaller Socialist representation, and differences in mode of leadership were striking as well. The Communists in the CLNAI were led by one man, Luigi Longo, and Longo took orders from one leader, Togliatti.

In view of these disadvantages in comparison with the Communist Party, Nenni and the Morandi-Basso leadership resorted to a daring maneuver—a plan to outflank their rivals. To turn the tables on the Communists and denounce them for their compromising ways, their scandalous pragmatism, though it would still further alienate moderate adherents would, if successful, get the party out of an impossible "me too" situation. It would establish the Socialists, not the Communists, as the truly revolutionary party.

This bold maneuver, however, required allies, and the Socialists found them in the very small Action Party, which in number of partisan bands was second only to the Communists. In military skill and spirit, the Socialists could not have had a better ally; but in political terms, the Action Party left much to be desired. Its shortcomings, in effect, were those of the Socialist Party itself. Its leader, Ugo La Malfa, was but one leader among many. Its following consisted of a large number of intellectuals, professors, journalists, lawyers; and though they brought to politics an earnestness and freshness that had long been wanting, they were rather impatient with the need for party discipline and were often as intransigent toward one another as they were toward the opposition. Included in the party were members of Guido Calogero's *Liberalsocialismo* group (a clandestine political organization dating back to the time of the Abyssinian War whose creed was virtually indistinguishable from Rosselli's *Socialismo Liberale*); but most of the members were ex-Communists (such as Leo Valiani, who was to become the historian of the Action Party) or ex-Socialists, or former members of the *Giustizia e Libertà* network (Lussu, Tarchiani) or the *Rivoluzione Liberale* group (Gobetti's widow, in fact, actively participated in partisan warfare). It was not surprising, consequently, that that party rapidly ran into problems very reminiscent of the supraparty Giustizia and Libertà. Rosselli's group had never at one and the same time satisfied both rightist and leftist elements; similarly, the Action Party's acceptance of a place in Badoglio's last Cabinet was condemned by Lussu as a shameful betrayal, and lauded by Tarchiani as an act of political courage.

At the first congress of the party, held at Cosenza, very speculative polemics as to the nature of the party kept all wings of the party poles apart. There were long discussions as to whether or not the party represented a notion of "socialism conceived as a timeless function of the Spirit," and passionate debates as to whether justice or freedom was the primary goal of the party; in conclusion, delegates found it necessary to adopt a sixteen-point platform to distinguish the party from all others. The spirit of that document was aptly characterized by its assertions at one point that the party was unequivocally in favor of a mixed economy, and at another that it did not oppose but advocated the sweeping nationalization of major industries. With good reason the Roman branch of the party, appalled by the divisions and unnerved by Lussu's revolutionary fervor, moved that the party simply return to its original function of representing a coalition of anti-Fascist groups.

Despite this vagueness and the ominous absence of a common denominator, the Action Party had enough vitality to survive its lack of inner coherence. There was a war to be fought and won. The party's members wanted to keep faith with the prophets of old, Gobetti and Rosselli; they felt the obligation to demonstrate to Italians and to the world that this was the hour of fulfillment for Rosselli's dream—the cry was no longer *Domani in Italia,* but *Oggi in Italia.* Rosselli's "tomorrow" had now become "today." Italians would now atone for the past, take up arms and with their blood answer Mussolini's taunt that it was not his political enemies but Allied arms and the treachery of a few that had brought about the collapse of his regime.

This spirit pervaded much of the partisan resistance, which grew prodigiously, numbering ten thousand in the winter of 1943, seventy thousand by the following May, and in January 1944, according to the military intelligence estimates of Mussolini's forces, eighty thousand. In a very particular way, however, this was the spirit of the intense Action Party, which held in check so many centrifugal forces, and left an indelible mark of the history of the Italian liberation.

But just as the Socialists had an end in mind in working closely with the Action Party, so that party had its private ends. The Action Party appreciated the very visible rivalry between Socialists and Communists, and under the direction of Rosselli's close friend Ferruccio Parri (the same Parri who had helped in Turati's escape and Treves' flight, and who had been released not long before from a Fascist jail) worked to make the most of it. The chances for the success of the outflanking maneuver (which seemed crypto-Communist to the Allies and a nuisance to the Communists) were slim, but if any man could carry it off, it would have been Parri, the partisan leader known by the code name of Zio Maurizio. As head of the CLNAI, Parri was in a good position to further Action Party ends.

This understanding between the Socialists and the Action Party, this plan to outdo the Communists in revolutionary fervor, could not but worsen already bad relations with the national CLN and the Bonomi government. Had the Allied entry into Rome sparked an all-out campaign in the North, as many Italians frantically hoped, the plan would have curled up in smoke. But once in Rome the Allied advance slowed, and with every day that the CLNAI was left to fight on its own, the impatience and chafing of the Socialists and the Action Party became increasingly assertive. They were doing enough (partisan troops, it was estimated, were holding down eight of the twenty-six enemy divisions on Italian soil) to deserve greater recognition and authority from the government.

In March 1944, the partisans showed that they had not only the spirit and means to fight Mussolini, but the support of labor as well.

In that month, for the first time in Nazi-occupied Europe, workers in the principal industrial cities of northern and central Italy—in Milan, Turin, Genoa, Padua—organized a general strike. It lasted some eight days, and though it was not equally successful everywhere and ended with the deportation of some two thousand workers to German labor camps, it showed that the partisans had driven a wedge between the industrial workers and the Republic of Salò, and that they could count on martyrs among them as among their own fighting forces.

In partisan warfare, the CLNAI bands met with equal success, taking an increasing toll of German and Fascist forces. But these very successes, by leading to an expansion of operations, created a greater need of Allied help than at any time in the past, and partisan requests at this point came into open conflict with Allied objectives. From an Allied point of view, Italy was not the principle theatre of the war, and despite the partisans' substantial contribution, the Allied military command was cautious in offering help. There were also obvious purely political reasons for Allied caution. The Americans and English had no intention of cutting the ground under Bonomi, and accordingly, while not refusing Parri's request for increased help, scaled it down. As the first of a series of precautionary measures, they suggested that General Raffaele Cadorna, the popular son of the World War I commander, personally acceptable to many CLN leaders, and "safe" from an Allied point of view, be assigned a top-level position in the CLNAI.

The intent behind the request was not lost on the Action Party or the Socialists, and both balked at the designation of Cadorna. The General, they recognized, would be responsible not to the CLN but to Bonomi's government, and under the guise of acting as high-level liaison and technical military advisor, would gradually assume leadership of the CLNAI and in due time foreseeably wrest control of partisan bands from the parties. For a while, consequently, the Action Party and the Socialists held firm. The Communists, though, as impatient at this crisis within the CLNAI as they were of the first crisis in the Kingdom of the South, and more realistic in their appraisal of the indispensability of Allied help, know exactly when to tone down revolutionary ardor and speak with the voice of sensible compromise. They suggested (and in effect, as the majority group, directed) that Cadorna be accepted as commandant of the partisans, that Longo and Parri be appointed vice-presidents, and that subordinate positions be assigned to Socialists, Liberal and Catholic partisan leaders. With this deft settlement, the Communists reminded the excessively independent Action Party who the dominant power in the CLNAI was.

Champing at the bit, the Action Party and the Socialists concentrated on their common fight against the Germans, and by August, when Allied troops once more assumed the initiative, the CLNAI had scored a spectacular victory, liberating Florence weeks before the entry of Allied forces. Florence, like most of Tuscany, was a center of hard-core Fascists, and in bitter hand-to-hand fighting there, the partisans gave Mussolini, Bonomi's government and the Allies bloody proof of their spirit and means. They also solved the frustrating problem of wresting from Bonomi a greater degree of recognition for the CLNAI in the administration of liberated territories: for in Florence the partisans simply assumed power and presented the Allies and Bonomi's representatives with a *fait accompli*. The CLNAI, moreover, governed well. The Allies saw little need, when they came to set up a military government, to remove many partisans from office or to reverse many of their decrees.

But June 1944 was the month of the Normandy invasion, and the precedence of that campaign over any other had disastrous consequences for all the CLNAI parties. Hopes had leaped high with the Allied arrival in Florence, but it soon appeared evident that their advance would be halted there for some time. Mussolini, who had in the meantime been alternating carrot and stick with no appreciable success, promising now socialization of factories, now the discovery of secret weapons that would suddenly change the entire course of the war, ordered an all-out assault, a last massive attack to wipe out the entire partisan operation. Crack German-trained *Bande Nere* (Black Bands) of last-ditch Fascists ripped into action, and their grim successes cut sharply into partisan strength and morale. In Foscoli, sixty-eight partisans held in custody were executed; in Milan, in Piazza Loreto, fifteen; in the region around Verbano, forty-three; in the province of Marzabotto, near Bologna, Germans wiped out a town of about eighteen hundred. And in the most demoralizing partisan defeat of all, royalist and Catholic partisans who had overextended themselves in the occupation of the strategic Ossola Valley in northwest Italy, and because of strong rivalry refused the assistance of Communist partisan bands, were routed completely in October by a combined German-Fascist counter-attack. In November of that year the low point in the reeling parti-san fortunes, Marshal Alexander urged that for the moment, given the scant aid Allied forces could offer, partisan forces withdraw from all positions, cease all attacks, and go into hiding. When Parri made one last frantic bid for aid, he was informed that General Eisenhower, and not he, was running the war, and that the partisan leader should take care not to alienate friends.

Yet the dark had not fallen on the partisans alone. In November of 1944, Bonomi, buckling under the strain of submitting to Allied pressures, maintaining some kind of harmony in the national CLN, and defending himself from the attacks of the Action Party and the Socialists vociferously demanding more of a say for the CLNAI in liberated territories, precipitated a crisis by submitting his resigna-tion. The ensuing ministerial crisis, lasting for about a month, ended in a victory for Bonomi, but both the Socialists and the Action Party seized the opportunity to make an open break with the Prime Minister. On grounds that they could not accept Churchill's red-penciling of Count Carlo Sforza from the new Cabinet (Sforza had made frequent embarrassing public estimates of Churchill's political skills), the Socialists and the Action Party refused to join Bonomi's new government or to have any further dealings with him. The Communists, as had now become their custom, were amenable.

Having burned all bridges, the Action Party, exasperated and em-bittered beyond all measure, absolutely convinced that the Allies, Prince Umberto, Bonomi and the parties of the right would not yield an iota of their power, issued a manifesto in answer to Marshal Alexander's injunction to the partisans to go into hiding. Upon the liberation of northern Italy, the manifesto decreed, the Action Party, in collaboration with the CLNAI, would move to set up regional and provincial governments, pass all necessary laws, pro-vide housing and food for those in need, accelerate epuration, bring all Fascist war criminals to trial, and confiscate all industries (par-ticularly heavy industries) that had compromised to the last with Mussolini's regime. The Allied reply was instant and firm: with the conclusion of hostilities, General Maitland Wilson announced, Ital-ian partisans, like their French and Belgian counterparts, were to hand over their arms and disband.

Thus the dream of a fresh new start, sweeping away all the compromising ways of the new Italy from the Kingdom of the South to Bonomi's second government, was reduced to a last, defiant manifesto. The differences between the Allies and the Socialist and Action Parties—differences which had grown steadily since the appointment of Cadorna—were now insurmountable, and it was a foregone conclusion that as the last shots were fired, the Allies would keep close watch on any sudden moves those two parties, or the Communists, might make.

By the spring of 1945, as the war was coming to a close, the offensive in Italy began to roll past the Gothic line and the signal was given to partisan units, increasingly battered in these last months, to gird themselves for one more effort. With disciplined jubilation and a thirst for vengeance, the partisans came down from the hills and into the valleys and cities. All through Emilia—in Forlì, Ravenna, Modena and Ferrara—partisan bands assumed power, as they had in Florence, before the arrival of the Allies; and they did so also in the industrial triangle, occupying Genoa, Turin and Milan. The fighting in Genoa, where the partisans dramatically saved the port from a German plan to blow it up, was particularly bloody. It was less so in Turin, and even less so in Milan, where a general strike had preceded the takeover by the CLNAI.

Near Milan the partisans achieved another of their objectives. Mussolini, the leadership had decreed, was not to be handed over to the English or Americans. The partisan dead and wounded (seventy-two thousand dead and forty thousand wounded) were not to lie unavenged. The Duce had not recognized partisans as lawful combatants and had refused to apply the Geneva accords to partisan prisoners, and he was to be repaid in kind. Thus, a few days after the CLNAI intercepted a German column in which a cringing, terrified Mussolini sought to escape to Switzerland, the corpse of the dictator and that of his mistress Clara Petacci dangled upside-down in the very piazza where months before the Fascists had executed fifteen partisans. As the corpses swung in the air, passers-by spat on them. Soon after, and with similar dispatch, partisan firing squads disposed of Farinacci, Starace, Pavolini and a number of other Fascists. Had it not been for the arrival of Allied troops, the reckoning would in all probability have gone on in public for some time.

But the execution of Mussolini—who had long since ceased to be of any real account—and of his closest, most fanatic followers, was hardly the main objective of the CLNAI. On assuming power in the liberated territories, the principal parties within the CLNAI moved swiftly to put aside their differences. In the exaltation of the moment, the Action Party called on the CLNAI to constitute itself as a provisional government until the calling of a Constituent Assembly that would give the country its proper new legal form, and even the practical, cautious Communists now joined the Action Party and the Socialists in implementing a common program before the Allied Military Government would take over completely. CLNAI personnel assumed key positions in local governments and Fascist sympathizers were rapidly epurated. It was to the credit of the partisans, and in particular of the *Sappisti* and *Gappisti*, Communist units specially trained in the defense of industrial installations against sabotage by the retreating Germans, that the better part of Italian industry was not in ruins. But the partisans did not mean to save those plants in order to return them to the *status quo ante*. In its most striking innovation, the CLNAI promoted, in a number of versions, the *consigli di gestione*, management councils that assigned an unprecedented role to workers in factory administration. In a short time, factory councils were operating in over one hundred and forty factories, including the great Pirelli plant, throughout Piedmont and Lombardy.

Despite the certain knowledge that after the elation of their sudden triumph there would have to be a confrontation with the "other" Italy, and that the strength of that "other" would not suddenly ebb, all the parties of the CLNAI—the cautious Communists included—believed in the miracle of an enduring transformation. "The wind from the North," Nenni cried out, would sweep down over all of Italy, uprooting, transforming; and for a few tingling weeks, thousands joined him in his exultation. "It would be a fatal error," Morandi had urged, "not to enter into the very heart of the crisis, the situation that will coincide with the fall of Fascism. At that particular moment we Socialists will have to assure ourselves of places of command, defend ourselves, lay our hands on levers of the machinery of state, influence the course of events, and rally to our side the proletariat and all other groups in society." But even as the shouts of exultation went up, and as Bonomi, unwilling to contend any further with the CLNAI, definitively resigned, the Allied Military Government was taking over the administration of all Italy north of Bologna, and with this one businesslike gesture, checking the elation, the soaring hopes. Nenni and his group, sobered, now waited for further developments, and for the leaders of the embittered Action Party the only consolation was that their moral-political ideals were unsullied by compromise.

When Parri, consequently, succeeded Bonomi as prime minister in 1945, he took office with much stoicism and only a few illusions. All the coalition governments since Mussolini's fall had failed to agree on urgent, thorough reforms. There was no reason, he believed, to feel that under his leadership they would suddenly reach an understanding. All the evidence argued against that possibility.

The partisans, too, complicated the government's task. Though their struggle had without a doubt been a *lotta di popolo* (a people's war), that had witnessed some of the most heroic moments of any Italian war, not all of them were heroes fighting for a high moral-political cause. In the months that Parri held office, again and again partisans took machine-gun justice into their own hands, and throughout Italy personal vendettas were carried out under a thin veil of settling political accounts. On May Day, 1945, partisan bands paraded through the streets of Milan in a massive show of strength before representatives of the Allied Military Government and leaders of the CLN (Prime Umberto was conspicuously missing) and then officially laid down their arms; but not all weapons were handed in. In this continuing climate of violence, there was little Parri could do but appeal to the country and to partisans to lay down their arms, and be patient with the government's gradual rooting out of the Fascist sympathizers. As one of the two vice-presidents (the Liberal Manlio Brosio was the other), Nenni was in charge of epuration policy, but he moved slowly and cautiously. Civil servants who had taken an oath of allegiance to the Republic of Salò and members of the Fascist militia were epurated, but there the matter rested; and though far-seeing caution of this type steadied the situation and prevented blood baths, at the same time it failed to satisfy many partisans or persuade them to hand in their weapons.

Inflation, the black market and the problems of the South completed the picture. The leader of the Action Party found no way to stop spiraling prices, and according to Parri himself, a project of monetary reform had to be abandoned because there were simply not enough shoes to distribute to the *carabinieri* needed to stand guard over the stations where the money would have to be exchanged. With every passing day, inflation goaded all parties and groups to insist that something be done immediately, or else. In Sicily the unrest and turmoil went so far as to become the pretext for demands for completely autonomy, but Parri dealt with that threat firmly.

In a country still occupied in large part by the Allied Military Government, all this mounting chaos made Parri (and he knew as much) a figurehead, not a real power, and he was finally forced down in November, after four months in office. No doubt vested interests that fought his every proposal for reform, including an income tax and increased taxes on heavy industry, had a great deal to do with forcing his resignation; when Parri sought to give legal recognition to the management councils set up by the CLNAI, and acted to revise the traditional Fascist policy of preferred treatment for monopoly groups in heavy industry, favoring small firms instead in the allocation of raw materials, those interests formed alliances wherever they could find them—particularly among the Liberals—to unseat the Prime Minister. But Parri's downfall was ultimately occasioned by more than the opposition of moderate and conservative interests; it was more than a *coup d'état* of the Right. The truth of the matter was that Parri's allies of sorts, the Communists and Socialists, were unwilling to defend him to the last; though his resignation was triggered by the withdrawal from his Cabinet of the Liberals and then the Catholics, it was also traceable to a change in Socialist-Communist policy.

For the Communists, in particular, Parri was expendable. There was no way of definitely knowing as yet whether his party did or did not have a notable following, but from a Communist point of view it seemed too divided among itself and too inconsistent to make a good ally. To the Communists, Parri himself, when all was said and done, was a moderate (to the left of the last left-wing Giolitti, certainly, but not much more) with a very small following. In the coming struggle for power between the Communists and the Christian Democrats, consequently, he would not count for much. In that imminent confrontation, Togliatti, like his opponent De Gasperi, wanted to pick the time and the occasion to make pivotal moves; and a last-ditch defense of Parri was not in those plans.

The majority of Socialists also saw the wisdom and necessity of abandoning Parri. During the war, and especially in its closing months, they had been one with the Action Party; but now, in the light of an inevitable polarized confrontation between Communists and Christian Democrats, they left their old insurgent allies and moved over to the side of the Communists.

Parri had nowhere to turn, and the party which he had headed with La Malfa fell apart. It was hopelessly divided on basic issues, and that weakness was documented by a three-fold split at its Congress in January 1946, at which Parri's faction won only 3,000 out of 190,000 votes. In a sense the party deserved to fall, but Parri himself did not. He had been naïve, no doubt, in originally underestimating the difficulties of implementing radical social reforms with only Communists and Socialists as allies. He was even more naïve, no doubt, in believing that there was a following for an anti-Fascism as thorough as his. (Only a few short months after the close of the war, the *Uomo Qualunque* movement, the first party with unmistakable neo-Fascist sympathies and longings for "order," made its appearance in southern Italy.) But certainly naïveté of this type is not among the worst or the most frequent of political sins, and it also accounted for some of his finest accomplishments. Before stepping down, he fixed a date for a referendum on the question of the monarchy, over the delaying tactics of royalists, Liberals and some Christian Democrats; he also set up machinery for a Constituent Assembly that, although called for by all parties, was in danger of being postponed indefinitely.

With these two accomplishments, the stage was set for free elections, a test of whether the first real post-war Italian government would be Socialist-Communist or Christian Democratic. As in the aftermath of World War I, the opposition between Catholics and Socialists appeared absolute—but the analogy could be carried only so far. After twenty years of Fascism, a great deal had changed among political Catholics, Communists and Socialists that was to account for the slow emergence of a peculiar "anti-Fascism" in no way as extreme as the precocious, unpopular, but admirable anti-Fascism of the isolated Parri.

PART THREE

THE NEW DIRECTION

1945-1963

XIII

NEW WINE AND OLD WINESKINS

The mode and speed of Parri's fall, in the minds of many Italians, was but one more sign that the new Italy would be either Communist or Christian Democrat, and that in the interim before the first national elections, the contenders were merely marking time.

At first glance, there appears to be something perplexing in the sudden, phoenixlike rise of the Christian Democrats, the new version of the Populists of post-World War I. Although there was conflict between Mussolini and Popes Pius XI and Pius XII on matters of principle, the overwhelming number of Catholics, lay and clerical, found Mussolini's regime acceptable. On that basis alone, it would seem that they had hopelessly compromised themselves with the Fascist regime and that they could hardly meet with any success in forming a popular authentically anti-Fascist party. Many Catholics who turned into Christian Democrats did so simply because Fascism had been defeated and because they lived in terror of the Communists. They were undoubtedly more Fascist than Catholic.

But there was another Catholic political group, equally important, with genuine anti-Fascist credentials. Although many among the clergy had smugly applauded Fascist order in the halcyon days of the regime, there were others who gave sanctuary to Jews and helped Italians in the fight against Germans, even offering themselves as hostages to Fascist anti-partisan bands rounding up groups for execution. After the Fascist intervention in Spain, anti-Fascism grew among the laity as well, culminating in the organization of Catholic partisan bands. Together these elements were able to revive swiftly a Catholic party as a major political force.

The party had little trouble in finding followers or leaders. Catholic Action and the parochial structure in 1943, as in the post-World War I period, assured a numerous following; and there were sufficient numbers of Catholic political men, in particular the Catholic college students of FUCI (the Federation of Catholic University students), to staff key political positions. Most impressive, the acknowledged leader of the group was the same De Gasperi who had found refuge in the Vatican after being liberated from a Fascist jail in 1939, continuing from there to work underground for the reorganization of the Catholic party.

De Gasperi was well aware of how similar and yet how totally different the political situation of 1943 was from the years immediately following World War I, in which it seemed that either the Populists or the Socialists would come to power—and from the very beginnings he acted with a mixture of political boldness and prudence that marked him as the equal of Don Sturzo in political skills, if not his superior.

Like Togliatti, De Gasperi did not make much of the municipal elections of the spring following Parri's downfall. Togliatti went out of his way to deny that they were in effect a Christian-Democrat–Communist confrontation, but in spite of the declarations of both leaders, it was clear that a showdown was imminent. Communists and Socialists ran on a coalition ticket; the Christian Democrats, like their forerunners, the Populists, ran independently, refusing to form a bloc with potential allies. The revealing aspect of the 1946 municipal elections, however, was not so much their confirmation of the simplification of the political struggle, but rather the precise idea they gave of the geographical distribution of the two major parties' strength, the political conformation of the new state.

That conformation reflected the struggle between the national CLN and the CLNAI, the contrast between North-Central Italy, and Italy from Rome south. In those regions where partisans had been most active, the vote was more or less clearly Socialist or Communist. In agricultural central Italy—Tuscany, Umbria and the Marches—the victory was overwhelmingly theirs. In Emilia, where Communist bands had distinguished themselves for their heroic tenacity, the Left also gave clear proof that twenty years of Fascism had not wiped out the traditional orientation of the region.

But in northern Italy the victory was far from total. Indeed, the

Left made no inroads at all in the traditionally Catholic Trentino, which remained a stronghold of the Christian Democrats, or in Venetia, and it did not make as strong a showing as expected in Lombardy and Piedmont. In Piedmont, the scene of the exploits of the Action Party's Giustizia and Libertà bands, the Left won six thousand municipal elections to the four thousand won by the Christian Democrats, and in Lombardy the race was still closer, with 11,000 municipalities won by the Left and 10,000 won by the Christian Democrats.

By contrast, the South, which had not experienced partisan warfare or the last-ditch struggle with the Nazis and Fascists, was much more solidly Christian Democrat. Yet, as in the case of the predominantly leftist North, the vote was not all of one piece. There were Leftist gains in Puglie, Basilicata, Calabria and Sicily, and the parties of the Far Right, especially the *Uomo Qualunque*, made impressive gains: out of 2,243 municipal councils won by parties to the right of the Christian Democrats, more than two thousand were south of Rome.

Parri's fall, consequently, merely documented and underscored the speed with which Communists and Catholics were heading for a major confrontation; this feeling persisted even when, after the formation of a De Gasperi coalition government in December 1945, both parties joined in the common work of the Constituent Assembly that was to give political-legal form to the new Italy. The debates on foreign policy alone were a forceful reminder of how utterly polarized the situation had become, for all parties were forced to take sides for or against American foreign policy.

The choice was not as much to Togliatti's disadvantage as it might seem today in retrospect. It would be better for Italy to lose the war, Croce had jotted down in his diary in the darkest days of 1944, than to win it at the side of an ally like Germany; and allowing for differences, Togliatti could count on a substantial number of leftist-oriented Italians to react similarly to the United States. America, from their perspective, was the embodiment of the reaction that had crushed the possibility of any radical, thorough anti-Fascist reform. It was the corrosive force that had kept the King in power and that, with the end of the conflict and the beginning of the cold war, preferred to deal with the most thoroughgoing Fascist than with any leftist leader. De Gasperi's staunchest supporter, according to these charges, was the Allied Military Government. The Americans, who had fought in Italy and whose bombs had leveled Italian cities, were only interested in maintaining their economic grip on a battered "colony." The defeat of Parri (whom Togliatti obviously considered expendable), in this view, illustrated the growing power of the coalition of the Christian Democrats, American interests, and the neo-Fascists.

There was obviously some truth to these charges, but they won no great number of new adherents to the Communist Party, for De Gasperi too knew how to draw political advantages from the situation. Without American economic assistance, Italians appreciated, the way was open for a repetition of the disastrous consequences of the 1918 victory. Then, too, De Gasperi had established himself as a strongly anti-Fascist patriot who had rendered the country meritorious services. As Foreign Minister in Parri's Cabinet, he had won Allied approval for an Italian declaration of war on Japan, giving the country some standing as a co-belligerent, and further ground for softening the terms of a peace treaty based on unconditional surrender. It was also to his credit that the Alto Adige problem, which threatened to culminate in secession, took a turn for the better and the ground was cleared for substantial regional autonomy. De Gasperi also capitalized on the Yugoslav invasion of Trieste in May 1945, and rode the wave of anti-Communist feelings that move aroused.

Both Togliatti and De Gasperi, then, held strong cards, and the struggle between them was watched closely at every turn for clues as to which party was gaining ground. It was generally agreed, in this respect, that the referendum on the monarchy, held in conjunction with the first national elections in June 1946, for the selection of delegates to the Constituent Assembly offered no real indication. The vote was too difficult to interpret, even as a gauge of the strength of Fascist and anti-Fascist feelings. There were naturally very strong anti-Fascist convictions behind the republican cause, but they were not all of one color; and there were also, though they were not prevalent, some very strong anti-Fascist convictions behind certain groups that championed the monarchist cause.

Soon after the establishment of the Kingdom of the South, when the Action Party and the Socialists had peremptorily called for the immediate abdication of the King and the abolition of the monarchy, their mood was shared by a great many frantic, war-weary Italians. The only debatable aspect of the King's action, it seemed obvious at that time, was the degree of dignity with which the fleeing monarch had managed to save his own hide. But the climate of opinion in June 1946 was no longer that of 1943, and the change was all to the advantage of the monarchy. After the conflict between the CLN in Rome and the CLNAI, after the threatening increase in CLNAI strength and the revolutionary changes they brought about where they held power before the arrival of the Allies, ideas on Victor Emmanuel III and the monarchy had changed.

The fate of the monarchy was no longer being judged on what were ultimately the only valid grounds—whether it could represent the cause of the commonweal of Italy above all parties; whether it would be able, if necessary, to find the courage to oppose a cause to which the country and the majority of the people more or less willingly acquiesced. Instead, many Italians saw the King as custodian and defender of traditional values against Communist values, or as the defender of the lay Risorgimento against the threat of clerical domination, or, more simply, as the one stable point that would not be subject to intense and divisive party warfare. The King had become a power in the cold war, a power in the eventual showdown between the Christian Democrats and the Communist Party; judgments and feelings were revised accordingly. Indeed, the mood of the country had changed so radically, that had the King definitively abdicated as promised in 1943, instead of simply delegating his powers to Prince Umberto and postponing abdication until one month before the referendum, the results of the vote might well have been different.

Both De Gasperi and Togliatti sensed this very perceptible change in the political climate and both trimmed their sails. Communists, of course, would not vote for the monarchy, but Togliatti saw no point to matching the vigor and intensity of the Socialists' and the Action Party's anti-monarchist campaigns; the Communist Party, after all, had collaborated with the King once, and could do so again if necessary.

De Gasperi acted with equal prudence and insight. The Christian Democratic leader, personally inclined to see advantages in preserving the monarchy, maintained public neutrality. There was no need for the party to take a united stand, he declared, on a matter that did not involve fundamentals. The choice was a matter of individual judgment, and one in which party unity or discipline had no place. De Gasperi meant what he said—but he also knew that neutrality might actually help to preserve party unity, for the North was expected to go republican, the South monarchist; and the Christian Democrats had already been hurt enough in the South by the formation of the *Partito Nazionale Monarchico* whose political program was based almost totally on the monarchist issue.

The results of the referendum justified the prudence of both party leaders. The national vote was some 10,700,000 for the monarchy, 12,700,000 against—a difference of only 8.5 per cent. Had the monarchy made a stronger showing in traditionally monarchist Piedmont, or had the republicans won by a less overwhelming margin in Venetia (85 per cent of the vote), the results would have been closer yet.

The closeness of the referendum prompted an appeal to the highest court of the land on charges of fraud and improper returns, but the results were upheld, and soon after, the royal family and members of the House of Savoy went into exile. On June 28, 1946, the distinguished Liberal, Enrico De Nicola took office as the first president of the Italian Republic.

The margin between right and left was even closer in the election of members of the Constituent Assembly than in the referendum on the monarchy. The Christian Democrats received some eight million votes and elected 207 delegates, while the Communists and Socialists each won approximately four million votes. (Actually the Socialists, in a surprise show of strength, edged out the Communists, electing 115 delegates to their allies' 104.) Again the vote was reminiscent of the local elections two months earlier, in limiting power to the three major parties: out of 556 delegates elected, 426 represented the Christian Democrats, Communists and Socialists. The South remained in the Christian Democrat column, but the *Uomo Qualunque* won some thirty seats. Central Italy—Tuscany, Umbria and parts of Romagna—remained firmly Communist, and in the North, the Communists and Socialists again bested the Catholic party in Lombardy and Piedmont. The Liberals, with one and a half million votes and 41 seats, were the only other meaningful force. The Action Party, which had fought so gallantly for the Constituent Assembly, barely survived, electing only nine delegates.

For all practical purposes, then, the Constituent Assembly would be the work of Communists, Socialists and Christian Democrats. Politically the situation was still as polarized as it had been in the spring elections; but on this occasion, and especially in the early days of the Assembly, there was a remarkable harmony and convergence of views. The new Italy, the rival parties concurred, was to be a pluralistic party democracy; all past impediments were to be removed and the way cleared for the new structure. The Fascist Party was banned (although already diehards were actively organizing the neo-Fascist *Movimento Socialista Italiano*, the MSI); and guarantees of free speech, freedom of assembly and the press became the basis of the new government.

To balance stability and change in the legislative branch, it was decreed that elections would be held every five years. The real legislative power resided in the Chamber of Deputies even more than in pre-Fascist Italy. Each deputy was to represent some eighty thousand constituents, to serve for a five-year term, and to enjoy full parliamentary immunity. The Senate, by comparison, was drastically revised. Under Fascism, the office of senator was appointive, and open to all those past the age of forty who had not been niggardly in their financial endorsement of the party. In the post-war years, consequently, the Senate became a prime target for sustained epuration. By the end of 1945, 218 of 420 members were expelled, and other cases were still awaiting trial. In the new Senate, members were to be elected to a six-year term. The President of the Republic was the ceremonial head of state, elected to a seven-year term by members of the Chamber of Deputies and the Senate. His primary duty was to defend the Constitution, and to that end he was given power to appoint one-third of the members of the Constitutional Court (the remaining two-thirds to be appointed respectively by the houses of Parliament and lower courts). He also had the power to nominate a limited number of senators and to join their ranks as a *de jure* member of the Senate on his retirement from the presidency.

The real executive power, the equivalent of prime minister, was to be the President of the Council of Ministers. He was to be a member of the party in power, chosen by that party, and removable by a vote of no confidence.

The judiciary was also subjected to a thorough overhaul. The

Constitutional Court was constituted the highest court of the land, with functions analogous to those of our Supreme Court. All special Fascist courts were abolished, secret trials were declared illegal, and judges were made more independent of the executive branch. Once in office they could not be removed.

From many points of view, the new political mechanism was a good one, and certainly an acceptable compromise between the various parties. Inter-party harmony continued as the Constituent Assembly went on to other essential government reforms, principally the problem of decentralization or regional autonomy. Since 1890, while virtually all parties with the exception of the Liberals continued to insist that decentralization was no longer postponable, centralization had methodically grown at a gradually accelerating pace. Such differing political personalities as Salvemini, Gobetti, Rosselli and Sturzo had seen eye to eye in the struggle for increased regional autonomy, and none of them had met with any degree of success. Under Fascism, the national government stripped municipal administrations of every shred of local autonomy, and the *podestà* of the most insignificant village (the Fascists had replaced the title of mayor with the much more Roman-sounding *podestà*) was appointed by Rome to insure complete party control.

In 1945, however, regional autonomy in certain areas was a *de facto* situation. Even before the end of the war in Sicily a certain amount had been granted. In northeast Italy, too, in the Alto Adige, and in the northwest, in the Aosta Valley where during the partisan war the Action Party had made wise, far-seeing concessions, some action had been taken. The question before the Constituent Assembly, consequently, was whether regional autonomy should be recognized and amplified in public works, agricultural policies and education, and extended also to other regions in the peninsula clamoring for similar rights.

Originally, the Communists had had some misgivings as to the desirability of regional autonomy, considering that a centralized state was easier to take over eventually; but on this issue, as on so many others in the past, they quickly concluded that they could afford to be reasonable. The Communists and Christian Democrats thus made the first substantial post-war political change in the country and they made it much against the will of the Liberals. The party that had blocked regional autonomy during its long rule up to the Fascist era was convinced that in a pluralistic party system, only a strong centralized state could maintain order. Regionalism, its leaders charged, would be ineffective, expensive and self-defeating, replacing one bureaucracy with another; but worse, they were convinced, it would eventually permit the Red sections of Italy, particularly Emilia, to assume complete independence, in effect, to set up small Communist enclaves within the country.

The Communists and Christian Democrats decided to extend regional autonomy, however, and Italy was accordingly divided into nineteen regions to be granted in time a certain degree of autonomy. Four—Silicy, Sardinia, Alto Adige, and the Aosta Valley—were granted immediate recognition. In cooperating in this achievement, the Christian Democrats took a first resolute step in the creation of the new Italy. They showed that they, unlike the Liberals, would not let the fear of communism determine policy at all points. To this extent, the right wing of the Catholic party did not have a decisive voice in the Constituent Assembly.

But De Gasperi did not lead the Christian Democrats to a similar breakthrough with respect to suggested reforms of the capitalist structure as it had developed under Fascism. The Prime Minister appreciated that under Mussolini, in the words of the Liberal Senator Ettore Conti, "for all the Fascist party's incessant claims that it went towards the people, it had favored a financial oligarchy reminiscent of medieval feudalism." Production, in fact, was controlled by very few groups, and in each major group, power was concentrated in one man, industrialists such as Agnelli, Cini, Volpi, Pirelli, Donegani, Falck and others, who literally dominated the various branches of industry. Under Fascism, capitalism was hardly the enlightened brand of Adriano Olivetti that was to leave its stamp on post-Fascist Italy, but rather the unenlightened variety of his father Gino, the founder of *Confindustria*, the very pro-Fascist alliance of industrial interests. De Gasperi was quite aware of the compromised status of those interests. The fact remained, though, that he needed their help and in any case, quite independent of that consideration, he had no intention of presiding over the liquidation of the entire private enterprise system.

For the time being, consequently, modifications in the Constituent Assembly proceeded principally along two lines: counterbalancing the capitalist structure by the reinstatement of the rights of labor to form unions and to strike and a continuation and radical reinterpretation of the IRI. There was no possibility, of course, of a return to *laissez-faire* capitalism. The question was how far the new spirit could go, and there De Gasperi exercised caution. The outstanding success of the Christian Democrat Left (as represented by Amintore Fanfani, Professor of Economics at the University of the Sacred Heart, and the jurist Giorgio La Pira) was the insertion into the constitution of the rights of labor to fight even for such ends as an increased say in management and profit sharing; but the Christian Democrats did not go beyond a declaration of principles.

On the entire issue of the reform of the capitalist structure, the Communists, whose *raison d'etre* was the destruction of the private enterprise system, quite naturally broke with the Christian Democrats. But with respect to the IRI the situation was quite different. Mussolini had made excessive demands on the agency, which it had been unable to satisfy, but the IRI was not really a failure. Contrary to Mussolini's charges, it had not squandered the public patrimony, been grossly incompetent, or lagged behind private enterprise in technological progress. The problem, therefore, was whether an IRI directed to different ends could be consonant with a degree of state socialism acceptable both to the Communists and the Christian Democrats, and the answer was yes.

For De Gasperi, the retention of the IRI was a pledge that the Christian Democrats would not turn back the clock, that the party intended to hasten the reform of capitalism, and with its own brand of state socialism, pursue the common good in a way superior to that of the Fascists and Communists. For the Communist Party, the decision was an act of confidence that even with an IRI controlled by the Christian Democrats, the way was cleared for the easier attainment of Communist ends. An official Leninist-inspired explanation gave an authoritative ring to this decision. The IRI, according to this analysis, had grown out of a crumbling capitalist economy following a worldwide crisis of overproduction, in which the great trusts had been saved only by state intervention. Those trusts, however, enmeshed in the contradictions of capitalism, had been rescued by the most undemocratic of states, the Fascist state, and once rescued, had lost all chance of regaining their autonomy. To return lost power to those groups at this point would have been absurd; even in a Christian Democratic state, a far cry from a

workers' state, the Communists had everything to gain by support-
ing state socialism. The Communist Party could take the measure of
a rival Christian Democratic reform, and do so by remaining within
the law, avoiding all revolutionary tendencies.

As a result of this collaboration between the Christian Democrats
and Communists, the Italy that emerged after World War II and
the fall of Fascism could be considered a capitalist economy only in
the most fundamental sense. The Italian economy, De Gasperi informed Molotov at one point during the peace conference in 1947,
was a capitalist economy in which the state owned 60 per cent of
the metallurgical industry, 90 per cent of the shipyards, 100 per
cent of passenger shipping, 70 per cent of the telephone networks,
and 30 per cent of electric power.

Thus, collaboration between the Christian Democrats and the
Communists gave an economic dimension to the political reforms
of the Constituent Assembly. The last consequence of this collaboration, however, was in many ways the most striking—and with
respect to a not distant future, the most ominous—agreement of all.
Before coming to a close the Constituent Assembly voted for the
renewal of the Concordat and the Lateran Pacts and for their inclusion as part of the new constitution.

In the jubilation of the war's close, Red flags had dipped in
homage to Pius XII in St. Peter's Square, and all of Italy had been
aglow with pride and a sense of comradeship with the Pontiff who
had saved Rome from bombardment and had given a lofty example
of Christian justice and charity by throwing open the doors of the
Vatican to all refugees. Few popes in recent history were more
popular than Pius XII was in those years. But that general gratitude
and admiration had waned as the time came closer for a final choice
between the Communists and the Christian Democrats. Concurrently, a few Catholics expressed doubts as to whether the renewal
of the Concordat would be to the best interests of the papacy or of
Italian Catholicism. The Lateran Pacts, these small groups believed,
may or may not have facilitated Pius XI's work of giving testimony to Christ; but it could not be denied that in that testimony one
element was conspicuously missing: a political education, an awareness of the implications of a Christian approach to politics. Given
the terms of the Concordat it could hardly have been otherwise,
however.

Under Fascism the overwhelming number of Catholics had effortlessly reconciled their religion with their allegiance to the regime—
not only those Catholics for whom Catholicism was merely a national patrimony, a badge of *italianità*, but a good number of those
who professed to meditate at some length on the problems of state,
church, Christ, and Fascist ideas on the meaning of life and love of
country. When the differences between Pius XI and the Duce had
flared out into the open—differences on the rights of the state in
education, the freedom of Catholic Action, and the possibility of
coherently reconciling Fascist totalitarian claims with Catholicism
—the Pope had fulfilled his obligation as the custodian of Christian
truths; but the great majority of the faithful had taken little notice
of his action. Indeed, under Fascism the Pontiff's protests did not
always find a warm reception even among the clergy, not even
among the higher clergy, who felt that the good Pope was taking all
too seriously some of Mussolini's rasher statements, and that once
some judicious concessions were made, particularly with respect to
Catholic Action, everything would be smoothed over. Not until the
introduction of anti-semitic legislation, in fact, did noticeable seg-
ments of the clergy reconsider their sympathies. Only then did
members of the hierarchy with intense Fascist sympathies (Cardinal
Schuster, for instance, who had graced the Institute of Fascist
Mysticism with an inaugural lecture) moderate their approval. The
war, perhaps, had further weakened those loyalties; and even before
the war broke out the Pope was gaining a wider following among
Italians for his open anti-war stand.

The point stressed by the small groups of Catholics and non-
Catholics who opposed renewal of the Concordat was that this increase in respect and affection for the Pope did not have much to
do with the Concordat; and because of that there was reason to
hope that the Pope might seriously reconsider the desirability of
renewing it. If he had outmaneuvered Mussolini and gained enduring advantages it was not because of, but in spite of, the Concordat.
The disadvantages of any such agreement, the necessary *do ut des*
aspects, were no less manifest in 1946 than before, of course; but
there were some conspicuous advantages in not renewing it. In the
exhausting work of strengthening a political conscience made flac-
cid and uncertain by the long experience of Fascism, the Pontiff
would have far greater freedom of action if he were not closely

associated with the new Italian state. There was even something to be said for the advantages accruing to the Christian Democratic Party. Unburdened by a concordat, it could make a more convincing case for its being a basically non-confessional party, not dependent on the hierarchy or the Pontiff. And lastly, a not insignificant advantage, the very daring gesture of renouncing the official understanding with the state would add a bold new dimension to the very nature of the Pontiff's anti-communism and that of Catholics in general: a willingness to oppose communism without the aid of those forces that lent plausibility to the Communist charge that the Vatican consistently allied itself with the most reactionary elements.

Pope Pius XII undoubtedly considered this alternative, but for reasons that can only be conjectured he rejected it. He may well have concluded that regardless of the inherent disadvantages of a concordat, the hierarchy, faced with the first strong Communist party in a "Catholic" country, needed the continuing support of the state in the administration of the sacraments and in its defense of Christian education. He may well have also considered the task of undoing the damage of Fascism too lengthy and difficult for the hierarchy to face without a modicum of state support. Possibly, in spite of his admiration and kind words for American democracy as a political ideal, he may have thought that conditions in Italy simply were not ripe for a radical revision of policy, for the separation of church and state, particularly when the country was faced with the Communist threat on home grounds.

Be that as it may, there can be little doubt that De Gasperi knew of the Pontiff's preference, whatever its reason. Regardless of De Gasperi's own convictions, politically he had no choice but to fight for renewal; the Pope had too many supporters among the Christian Democrats. A few scattered members of the Left (particularly La Pira and Giuseppe Dossetti, a brilliant young canon lawyer, in his intensity reminiscent of Gobetti) had some initial objections; but they too very soon closed ranks with De Gasperi. The overwhelming number of Christian Democrats, needless to say, rushed to comply—some out of a sense of absolute loyalty and trust in Pius XII's political acumen; some out of the conviction that the closer the ties between party, hierarchy, and Pope, the greater the victory in the coming elections; and others (perhaps the majority) for both reasons, and out of a willingness to obey that was very reminiscent of long training in the halcyon years of the Duce. And on this occasion (unlike 1929, when many Liberals fought the Concordat tooth and nail) the greater number of Liberals, ranging from Nitti to Count Sforza, vigorously applauded the measure as a bulwark against communism.

Opposition, accordingly, was initially concentrated among Socialists and Communists; and for a short while both parties remained recalcitrant. But it was not long before the Communist style reasserted itself. Togliatti to date had deftly pushed aside nearly every practical difficulty that seemed to categorize the Communist Party as a dangerous revolutionary party or an obstructionist party. He had been willing to form a government with the King in the Kingdom of the South, to join Bonomi's government without the Socialists, to join De Gasperi's Cabinet, to cooperate in the main work of the Constituent Assembly. He was not going to be burdened, at this late date, with the onus of representing the anti-God, anti-Christ party. There were many Italians who reconciled their Catholicism with their Leninist Marxism as effortlessly as Catholics had previously harmonized their faith with Fascism, and Togliatti was not disposed to lose this following. Mussolini had made good use of Catholicism, and Togliatti expected to do likewise. After some initial skirmishing he directed the party to vote accordingly.

The Socialists, for their part, did not hold out long in their opposition after the Communist shift. Their revolutionary ardor had cooled. The least of agrarian reforms, Nenni announced, interested Socialists much more than any aspect of the Concordat; and with hearty and hollow political pragmatism the party soon after voted its approval of re-ratification. One party alone, the Action Party, fought the Concordat to the last, arguing that it was to the advantage of both the church and the state to maintain their independence of one another. For this they were roundly derided by Catholics as well as Communists, and for his impractical approach their leader, Piero Calamandrei, was hailed by Togliatti as "the last of the Mohicans."

The approval was substantial, but there was still scattered opposition bent on delaying tactics. At one point, therefore, De Gasperi acted quickly to bring the debate to a close. There was no need to fear that the Lateran Pacts would fix church-state relations permanently, he argued; modification by mutual agreement required only a simple parliamentary majority, not the involved procedure of a constitutional amendment. The real question, he insisted, was whether the republic was willing to accept the religious peace offered by the Concordat. When the final vote was taken, the measure passed, with 350 votes in favor, 149 against.

This peculiar deference to the Pope's political wisdom, a deference which assumed many forms—from a martinet loyalty, to an unenthusiastic adherence, to an old Machiavellian determination to make the most of *religio instrumentum regni*—was the first setback for the Christian Democrats' moral idealist élan. But all parties, not the Christian Democrats alone, stumbled with that inauspicious first step. Liberals, Communists and Socialists—all acted on the cynical persuasion that, new Catholic party and new Italy or no, for all practical purposes, the Fascist solution to the problem of church and state was difficult to improve upon. Of all the aspects of church-state relations, the least important, it seemed from this point of view, was how the renewal of the Concordat would affect the revival of a Christian political conscience. Even less thought was given to the potential damage that renewal might do in one of the most important areas of Italian politics (barely recognizable in years when the situation was dominated by the Communist-Christian Democrat confrontation)—the need for Socialist-Christian Democrat collaboration. An embittered Catholic of the Left saw in the renewal of the pacts, with their unchanged provisions on non-Catholic sects, a complete triumph of the spirit of Alfredo Rocco, the founder of Fascist jurisprudence. The judgment was excessively bitter, but the fact remained, as the future would eventually demonstrate, that that renewal was the first ominous failure of the post-Fascist era, and in it virtually all political parties bore some responsibility.

At the time, however, other problems seemed more pressing. A great deal was going on in Italy besides the work of the Constituent Assembly. For the Christian Democrats and De Gasperi, the most substantial achievement was the final ratification of the peace treaty in 1947, especially in the light of its effects on the Communist Party.

The treaty's restrictions on armed forces caused no real hurt or disappointment. The Fascist experience had put an end to all expansionist desires, and the Italian people, in any case, had read the atomic handwriting on the wall. By comparison, the articles stipulating the loss of all colonies, including those won in pre-Fascist times, did cause resentment—it did not escape notice that the wealthier and more powerful countries who liberated Italian colonies retained control of their own. The French annexation of Briga Tenda, a small town in northwest Italy whose important electrical works were of substantial use to Turin industry, was also recognized for the insolent *realpolitik* act that it was; and the outrage for the loss was only partially assuaged by Italy's retention of the Alto Adige with the important hydroelectric works built there under Fascism. But in general, the resentment and apprehension felt for the treaty were directed principally against the Russians, who occupied Vienna, rather than the Allies, and the one vital issue that remained unsettled, the fate of Trieste, continued to be to the advantage of De Gasperi and his party. True, the Allies' temporary expedient of making the city a free territory divided into an Italian and a Yugoslav zone presided over by a neutral governor, made them particularly unpopular at the time; but Togliatti, in acting to exploit the situation, made one of the few blunders of his entire career. Acting as a peace broker, probably to stress the independence of the Italian Communist Party from foreign directives, he transmitted to the Italian government Tito's proposal that the problem of Trieste could be solved if Italy would in exchange yield all of Gorizia. The move occasioned a wave of outraged protests even among some Communists. In the bluntest way Togliatti appeared to be using the strong-arm methods of international communism, pushing aside duly constituted national representatives to let Yugoslav and Italian Communists resolve the differences; and he appeared willing to dispose of a territory that most Italians, including Nenni and many Socialists, considered as Italian as Trieste. It did not add to Togliatti's popularity, either, when the Allies waived their reparation rights and Russia instead insisted that Italy pay due compensation to Yugoslavia, Albania and Greece.

But in general, the effects of the peace treaty that followed World War II were quite different from those after World War I. In a world dominated by Russia and the United States, Italians realized, there was little place for the spirit of revenge. There was only the hope that in the inevitable inflation that followed the war, the American and English economies would prove stronger than they had in 1918–19, that American aid would be substantial, and that there would be no eventual recurrence of 1929. Toward this end, with the assistance of the Liberal Einaudi, Minister of Finance, and Cesare Merzagora, another Liberal who was Minister of Foreign Trade, De Gasperi acted to stem the rising tide of inflation that accounted for a frightening increase of currency in circulation, from 395 billion lire in May 1946, to 577 billion in September 1947. Under Einaudi's very firm hand the spiraling rise was gradually arrested. Bank credits were severely restricted and it was not necessary to devaluate the currency. As a result, goods that had been hoarded in anticipation of devaluation were put back on the market, and prices steadied. A similar effect followed the action of Merzagora in encouraging a policy of substantial imports of foodstuffs to check the booming black market.

But throughout the country the rising number of unemployed, especially in central and southern Italy, rioted again and again, and strikes zigzagged from one end of the peninsula to the other. While the Constituent Assembly was drawing a blueprint for the future, and De Gasperi was acting to check inflation, labor unrest appeared to be swelling rapidly to post-World War I dimensions. This was not the least of the reasons why Togliatti and his Socialist allies expected to make an extremely strong showing, and possibly even come to power—in a law-abiding way—in the elections of 1948.

XIV

MARXISTS AND CHRISTIAN DEMOCRATS

The three years from the end of the war until the first parliamentary elections in April of 1948 attested that the Communists had learned more than any other party from their defeat at the hands of the Fascists. From the day that Togliatti set foot again in Italy to the eve of the elections, the party avoided virtually every pitfall that had led to the Maximalist-Communist defeat of some twenty years before.

In the aftermath of the war, the Communist Party maneuvered freely, no longer burdened by the post-World War I anti-nationalism that had made it so vulnerable to Fascist attacks. Relations with left-wing Socialists were particularly good and Togliatti meant to keep them that way—since the Communists did not believe that the capitalist structure was about to crumble they were not likely to make the Maximalist mistake of counting all alliances of only trivial importance. Togliatti's Communists also went to particular pains to improve their relations with the Catholic party, or at least to avoid provocation. To the extent that he could control the situation, Togliatti discouraged the recurrence of the cheap anti-clerical, anti-religious propaganda of earlier days.

For a very short time, in the closing days of the war, the party almost succumbed to a revival of Maximalism, but obedience to Togliatti's clear-eyed directives enabled the leadership to keep a violent following in line. Togliatti himself, as Minister of Justice in De Gasperi's Cabinet, urged partisans to surrender their weapons. In his relations with the Christian Democrat leader, he was above all intent on showing that a coalition government with the Communists was feasible. Though he did not succeed in this key objective (in

January 1947, De Gasperi dissolved his Cabinet and formed a new one without Communist representation), it was through no fault of his. Aside from this failure, over which he had little control, Togliatti achieved all other principal objectives.

The party apparatus was compact, hard-working and dedicated. Its disciplined following was growing day by day. Toward the end of the war, in a spirit reminiscent of Fascism, the Communists began to organize their own leagues of young men, young women, professional people, etc., and down to 1948, they met with increasing success in gaining control of labor unions. The party's gains in propaganda warfare were equally impressive. The circulation of *Unità* was one of the highest in the country, and the vast network of Communist centers was run very efficiently.

Another respect in which post-war Communists differed from the Maximalists of the early 1920's was in their full appreciation of the support of intellectuals. Indeed, the party was strikingly successful in winning converts among this group. Enthusiastic and talented Communist-oriented novelists like Vasco Pratolini took pride in a harmony of views which bound them indissolubly to party and people. They were earnestly convinced that the Communist Party alone could redeem the Fascist past, that it was the only authentic political humanism; they did not need Marxist or Leninist tracts to buttress a conviction that grew out of the stifling Fascist tyranny and the blood of the Communist heroes of the Resistance. Togliatti's work as editor of the official political-cultural publication of the party, *Rinascita*, and defender of Marxist-Leninist orthodoxy, was therefore not very demanding, even though intellectuals could not, like most party members, be kept in line by Leninist pamphlets. Occasionally Togliatti ran into problems, as in the case of Elio Vittorini and his *Politecnico*, the Marxist-Leninist publication that styled itself an example of "open" communism willing to carry on a dialogue with all living currents of art and thought in Europe or America. From one angle, the publication was a feather in the party's cap, especially for a leader so concerned with cultural warfare as Togliatti. But literary men and intellectuals had to learn that they were as subject to the demands of unity and discipline as all other party members, that they had no special privileges or freedoms. Togliatti accordingly voiced strong objections against the *Politecnico's* "open" Marxism, which ultimately substituted its editor's convictions for those of the party leadership. By 1947, after a brief polemic, Vittorini discontinued publication. Then and there however the Vittorini case, the first Italian variant of an experience that was to become familiar among Communist intellectuals, had no lasting repercussions. The intellectual following of the party was not very concerned with what appeared to be a personal problem of Vittorini; more exciting Italian Marxist cultural developments held their attention. They were awed and spellbound by the publication of the letters and works Gramsci had written during his imprisonment. The prison writings, amounting to some three thousand closely packed handwritten pages, gave impressive testimony of an intense, uneven intelligence that, despite tuberculosis, the almost total lack of any but the most banal government-approved reading matter, and the absence of the kind of human contacts his intelligence and sensibility cried out for, survived, in his own words, "the molecular disintegration of the organism," and carried the fight to the enemy on the only terrain possible.

Smuggled out of prison by a friend, Gramsci's notebooks, including notes for many studies, covered an enormous range of interests. There were essays and notes on the meaning and role of dialect and popular literature, with a special place for the dialect theatre of Pirandello (eventually published as *Letteratura e vita nazionale*); on the role of the intellectual (*Gli intellettuali e l'organizzazione della cultura*); on the problems of Italian political unity (*Il Risorgimento*); on political philosophy (*Note sul Machiavelli, sulla politica, e sullo stato moderno*). There was also, as a compendium of all the other works, a study of the philosophy and politics of Croce (*Il materialismo storico e la filosofia di Benedetto Croce*). There was one central truth that gave form to all his meditations: history and all values were determined by the class conflict, and the Italian understanding of the development of that doctrine from Marx to Lenin was a contribution equal and in some respects superior to that of some Russian theorists. Italian communism, in a word, was not simply an import item. Indeed, Gramsci argued, Italian Marxism had in Antonio Labriola a thinker who, despite some pre-Leninist shortcomings (a touch of colonial imperialism and a relative unconcern for the peasantry), was superior to the Leninist-Marxist theorists of later times.

Gramsci maintained that Labriola was the theorist who, without error or confusion, had singled out the totalitarian self-sufficiency of Marxism and defended it from those confused theorists who sought to pollute it with Darwinian evolutionary thought, Kantian morality, or metaphysics of some other kind. He had left a heritage for Italian communism—an authoritative, indispensable core of doctrine that revealed the uniqueness of the party and marked off the limits of Communist collaboration and intransigence. Labriola had his limitations—those of Marx with respect to Lenin—but now that Italians appreciated the revolutionary importance of the peasantry, there was no mistaking the implications of his thought on the goals of Italian Communist policy: the party spoke for both the northern industrial proletariat and the southern peasant, and the party alone, because history was on its side, could unite those two forces to create the new Italy.

This mission, which Gramsci stressed repeatedly in his brief leadership of the party before his imprisonment, was the most insistent point made throughout the notebooks; and it was this message that made all intellectual Communists anxious to be one with the party. This was the vision that Togliatti held up for all to see, and it more than compensated for unpleasant disagreements such as the Vittorini case. But Gramsci not only offered tactics and a vision; he also offered a detailed Magna Carta of the Italian Marxist-Leninist intellectual, who was to replace the bourgeois intellectual, and who was to be as different from him as a scientific Socialist was from a Utopian Socialist. In constant contact with the masses (for unlike other parties, the Communists, according to Gramsci, overcame the tensions and distance between a political elite and the masses), the Communist intellectual or *dirigente* assimilated, utilized and transformed all bourgeois cultures.

Croce, for Italian Communist intellectuals, was a case in point. No intellectuals, Gramsci wrote, were in a better position than they to understand and "surpass" the philosopher, for they alone understood his limitations. Like any thinker who did not grasp the primary, decisive fact of the class conflict, Croce had an unavoidable blind spot. He was, in the most derogatory sense, an Italian intellectual: in Gramsci's estimate, one who, in a backward society, enjoyed a prestige that was utterly disproportionate to his value. More decisive yet, as a member of the southern intelligentsia, he incurred special responsibilities; for with his cosmopolitan, allegedly supra-class outlook, he consciously or unconsciously played into the hands of the southern conservative class. He preserved the huge distance that separated the peasantry from his class, helped keep the peasantry in its place, and perpetuated for members of his class the academic ideal of a culture olympically indifferent to the social-economic problems of the South. As much as any member of his class, therefore, Croce had done his part in suppressing any political initiative on the part of the peasantry, and maintaining that class in a state of supine acquiescence. In addition, he had personal failings that were common to humanists. Like Erasmus, he lacked the stuff of martyrs: he did not follow his premises to their logical conclusions but, like the Renaissance humanist, condemned those who did.

The Marxist intellectuals could therefore not learn much from Croce's approach to Marxism or to the basic problems of the Italian economy or the Italian state. The philosopher had not understood pre-Fascist Italy; he did not understand Fascism. He had, in fact, participated in a conspiracy of silence toward the Leninism-Marxism of his time, and the anti-Fascism of the *History of Italy* was nothing more than special pleading for a basically nineteenth-century Restoration Liberalism, just as the Religion of Liberty in the *History of Europe in the Nineteenth Century* was a vague eclectic notion, not at all a "religion." The Communists knew that one of the marks of a true religion was its ability to unite intellectuals and masses, and on that score the Crocean Religion of Liberty was a resounding failure.

Yet, despite these errors, there was something of use in the Neapolitan philosopher's work, Gramsci argued. Now that the urgent Communist need was no longer that of a simple ideology to counteract the equally simple ideology of the bourgeoisie, the *dirigente* could filter out the errors in Croce and use what remained. In Lenin's time, philosophical idealism was part and parcel of the intellectual arsenal of the reaction, and that explained Lenin's vigorous espousal of philosophical realism. But now the situation had changed, the crudities of philosophical realism or materialism were no longer necessary, and therefore this was the time for the Marxist intellectual to reexamine Lenin's realism and decide if it should be retained, or whether an idealist approach, revised and Marxist, might not be of use in the analysis of problems of epistemology and of the laws of nature.

Gramsci's suggestions to Italian Marxist intellectuals were no doubt in general intended for the most speculatively inclined. But in his stress on the Communist Party as the party of both the industrial workers and the peasants, in his view of the *dirigente* as a different breed from the bourgeois intellectual, he buttressed all the arguments of Togliatti and facilitated party discipline; and whatever vagueness and lack of clarity there was in his approach was compensated for in the splendor of his final vision of the heavenly city of the Marxist philosophers, as stirring to intellectual Communists as to the unintellectual. In that state of the future (already operative in Russia) all conflict between ideology and truth would cease, and therefore one government newspaper would suffice. Intellectuals and masses would be one, the pillars of a free democratic society. Marx had stressed that "man knew all that he needed to know"; the ideal state would see that man had all that he needed to have. It would embody Communist social justice in a cultural climate of the greatest freedom and variety. Philosophy and science, art, and that amorphous necessity, literature—pursuits that in a capitalist society were a luxury, a furtive, not quite legitimate pause in the ever-pressing class struggle—would be able to flower. The Communist state was not the enemy of culture: it appreciated the fruits of the spirit, and asked only, as had Labriola, that those fruits not be enjoyed by the few at the expense of the exploited masses.

In the construction of the heavenly city, the Communists could learn from Croce, Gramsci held, but more from his failures than from his accomplishments. In the same negative sense, the political-religious structure of Catholicism could serve, even better than any individual philosopher, as a case study. According to Gramsci, it was the genius of communism that it could learn from the Catholic religious-political structure as from Crocean Liberalism; and having made full use of them, at the proper time it would be able to cast them aside as superfluous.

The Communist Party, then, presented a formidable challenge in the 1948 elections, with its compact organization, its highly competent leader, and its wide following, awed by the theories and vision of Gramsci. And all these advantages were further heightened by a unity pact with the Socialist Party.

The Socialist Party, however, was no carbon copy of the Communist Party. It had few regrets for the revolutionary élan of 1945, when Morandi had urged that Socialists lay hands on the levers of the machinery of state. Nenni, in fact, was dismissed as foreign minister in De Gasperi's Cabinet because he insisted to the last that a minister's first loyalty was to his party. Morandi, as minister of industry in the same cabinet from July 1946 to May 1947, pressed for legal recognition and retention of the *consigli di gestione;* and though he failed in that attempt, he did manage at least to sponsor a government agency that was to plan, with private enterprise, the first steps in bringing industrialization to the South. In 1946 as in 1935, Morandi's ends, like those of Nenni and Basso, were the ends of the *Centro Socialista Interno,* the clandestine Socialist group of late Fascist days—including the nationalization, without indemnities, of all monopolies; the expropriation of all large land holdings and their transformation into cooperatives; the complete nationalization of banks and insurance companies; very heavy taxation of the middle class; and a large-scale program of government-owned and operated housing.

Morandi was the leading theoretician of the group. For him, practical problems, such as the problems of the relation of Italian capitalism to various political forces, were the heart of socialism. While in jail, *pro forma,* Morandi made some notes on the relation between philosophy and Marxism, but his conclusion—that idealist philosophy had nothing to offer Marxism—ran completely counter to the entire Marxist tradition from Labriola to Gramsci. But Morandi himself felt that he had better things to do than to elaborate that notion. As a first sign of his real skills and interests he had written, before his imprisonment, a *History of Italian Industry.* It was a guarded but unmistakeable indictment of a capitalism that was callously indifferent to all social values, and utterly incapable of solving the predicament of the South, an exploited colony of the North. Indeed, Morandi felt that Italian capitalism had made that problem insolvable. Capitalism had learned from its periodic crises only one thing: how to apply pressure and force the state to come to its rescue. These were the recurrent themes of Morandi's Marxism, and after his release from jail toward the end of the war, he came back to them in a number of ways—in 1945 with *Socialismo,* a cultural review; the *Bollettino dell'istituto di studi socialisti* (1945-47); and in 1946, the year of the Constituent Assembly elections, *Studi socialisti.* Along with Basso's *Quarto Stato,* these reviews gave socialism intellectual tone.

Despite differences in approach and outlook, however, Morandi's principal conclusion coincided with that of Gramsci: that the problem of the South, like the problem of recurrent capitalist crises, was due to the ineradicable class conflict, and that that conflict could be solved only by the party of the proletariat. Morandi did not have Gramsci's scope, and certainly lacked the poetry that occasionally sparked the pages of Gramsci (as a writer Morandi was hopelessly dull), but the two were not at all far apart, and Morandi was coherent in urging extremely close collaboration with the Communists, and working hand in glove with them to hasten the coming of the new order. The question remained, then, why Morandi did not consider the Socialist Party superfluous, and advocate that it incorporate itself into the Communist Party. The answer is that Morandi recognized the Communist Party as a highly centralized party organization in which orders and directives were issued from the top down, and was convinced that there was still a need for an independent, more democratic Socialist Party, that such a party, with its greater mobility and circularity of functions and orders was a useful corrective and an indispensable competitor.

For all the differences between the two parties, however (and this was a conviction shared by Morandi, Basso and Nenni), forty years of experience had taught Socialists what Labriola had seen so clearly —that a party that allowed itself to be diverted from its main objectives by clever capitalist concessions not only postponed but imperiled the final victory. In this conviction, at the first post-war Socialist Congress of 1945 Morandi had been instrumental in winning overwhelming approval for the continuation of extremely close ties with the Communists, and a plan to run with them on a fusion ticket.

Three years later, the combined Socialist-Communist force, which had reached its ultimate limit of collaboration with the opposition party in the Constituent Assembly, challenged the Christian Democrats in the April 1948 elections. Against that coalition, De Gasperi hardened his stand on several key points. To start with, from the point of view of the Christian Democrats, relations with the Communists had to take into consideration, if not accept as the last word, Pius XI's encyclical on atheistic communism. The party could never lose sight of the teaching of theologians that error had no rights. Needless to say, there were no tendencies, in the anti-Fascism of various Catholic groups ranging from the FUCI (Federation of Catholic University Students) to varied elements in Catholic Action, to the more conservative *Osservatore Romano* circle, that pointed to the possibility of any lasting collaboration with Communists. And in their preparations for the 1948 elections the Christian Democrats, like their opponents, did not shrink from using methods perfected by the Fascists. With their network of Catholic parochial societies, the organization of the Christian Democrats was a match for the Communists. In excesses, too, one was often a match for the other. The Communist claim that one could easily be both Catholic and Communist was countered by the assertion that there was nothing in communism even remotely Christian or acceptable to Christians. In addition to working among its own, the Christian Democrats also relied very heavily on help from other elements with no particular interest in Christian democracy—the Liberals, the Republicans (whose political program was virtually the reverse of the Monarchists') Bonomi's group, and above all the great amorphous group of unpolitical who had been tranquilly Fascist until Mussolini began to overextend himself.

While the Christian Democrats were equal and perhaps even superior to the Communists and Socialists in organization, as an intellectual force they were by no means as compact and united. Catholics could point to no champion with Gramsci's intensity and range of interests, no martyr of his stature. De Gasperi had limited prestige as a political thinker. During the years in exile in the Vatican, he developed the idea of a corporate state founded on Christian principles, but precisely what that implied for post-Facist Italy was not very clear. It was clear only that De Gasperi was to the left of Catholic Action groups led by Luigi Gedda, and also to the left of the former leader of the Popular Party, Don Sturzo, who had returned from America by 1946; and that he was to the right of Giovanni Gronchi, Amintore Fanfani and the *Cronache Sociali* group, headed by its editor Giuseppe Dossetti. Of all the groups of the Christian Democratic Left, the *Cronache Sociali* circle was the most appalled at the "Fascist" use by both Communists and Catholics of the "Rome or Moscow" dilemma; and of all groups in the Christian Democratic Left, they were the least influential in party deliberations.

But what De Gasperi lacked in prestige and the united backing of intellectuals, he made up for in daring. The dismissal of Communists from his coalition government in 1947, which was followed by the ouster of Nenni as foreign minister, demonstrated superb timing and analysis. It forced the electorate to take a stand before the elections on a government without Socialist or Communist representation.

Those dismissals were De Gasperi's boldest pre-election move, and would not have been possible without a sudden but not totally unexpected development, the first post-war split in the Socialist Party, distantly reminiscent of the Socialist crisis of 1922, when Turati's moderate Socialists were expelled. In spite of the sizeable Communist successes, and indeed in part because of them, the fundamental cleavage between Nenni and Saragat had not narrowed substantially. By 1946, after the CLNAI had made its last defiant attack, Saragat and the allies he had found on his return (not all Socialists who had remained in Italy were as revolutionary as Morandi's *Centro Interno Socialista*) were becoming increasingly restless. Saragat himself, who served as minister to France and then as president of the Constituent Assembly, did not personally direct the fight against Nenni, Morandi and Basso; his collaborator, Giuseppe Romita, took the initiative against them. As fiercely anti-monarchist as the most impassioned left-wing Socialist, Romita, then minister of the interior, had done his bit to insure a victory for the Republic in 1946 by manipulating election schedules so that the early anti-monarchist returns from the big cities would sway undecided voters; but anti-monarchism was the only conviction he shared with the Nenni-Morandi-Basso wing. Romita was no Turati in political skills or in political scope, but he had courage. He not only joined the De Gasperi government as minister of the interior, but he did not hesitate to suppress revolts and uprisings, particularly in Puglie and in Tuscany, even though he knew that the Communists would exploit the suppressions politically. He also defended the national police from left-wing Socialist insistence on radical epuration, and even fought, on grounds that they were technicaly competent and free of Fascist fanaticism, the epuration of many Fascist-appointed prefects.

In his opposition to the left-wing Socialists, Romita had the solid support of a group of Socialists headed by the editor of the new *Critica Sociale*, Ugo Mondolfo (the brother of Rodolfo Mondolfo, who had had some prestige as a Marxist theorist in Turati's group), and of the *Iniziativa Socialista*, which after 1945 joined the fight in

Socialist Congresses for the overthrow of the Nenni-Morandi-Basso leadership and for greater independence from the Communists. The large Socialist Initiative group, led principally by ex-Communists and ex-Action Party adherents, had more intellectual prestige than any other dissident group, counting among its members Aldo Garosci, formerly of the Giustizia and Libertà, and the ex-Communist Ignazio Silone who, with his publication, *Europa Socialista*, was an extremely convincing spokesman for a socialism that considered personal freedoms more important than doctrine.

Not quite unified among themselves, these groups were pushed aside at the Congress of 1945, when the overwhelming number of representatives had voted for fusion with the Communists, but they came back very strong the following year. The Socialist Congress of 1946 made no reference to the need of a Leninist guide-state to lead Italy to authentic socialism, and the Socialist Initiative group, controlling 300,000 votes, blocked further talk of fusion. Their questions at the same time became louder and more insistent. How, they asked, did Morandi expect his socialism to remain "open" in the event of a Socialist-Communist victory? How could any Socialist party retain its autonomy in an alliance with a victorious Communist Party, considering the latter's notion of "deviation," which quickly disposed of all heterogeneous elements? And in a cold war between America and Russia, and a polarized situation between the Communists and the Christian Democrats, if Socialists continued their common-front policy, how could they persuade a reactionary capitalism to dole out any but the most meager concessions to a working class branded as Communist?

These misgivings became more vocal after the local elections of 1946, and louder yet after the elections for the Constituent Assembly. Right-wing Socialists claimed credit for the surprising strength of the Socialist vote, greater than the Communist, and for Socialist victories in most of the principal cities. By January 1947, their discontent had reached the boiling point. If Basso continued to have a dominant voice, Saragat warned in an ultimatum, he and his followers would leave the party. The demands were not met and Saragat's group broke off and constituted itself as the *Partito Socialista dei Lavoratori Italiani* (Socialist Party of Italian Workers).

A significant break had been made in the Socialist-Communist common front, and De Gasperi did not let the occasion slip by. It was in the very month of Saragat's defection that the Prime Minister dismissed the Communist and left-wing Socialists from his Cabinet and offered a post to Saragat, who had been followed out of the party by 52 of the 115 Socialists in Parliament. Saragat accepted.

Saragat's group, collaborating with the Christian Democrats, Liberals and Republicans, was the furthest to the left of the parties represented in the government. It was the first indication that after the long years of Fascism, the Christian Democrats and the right-wing Socialists were willing to collaborate, and it put both in very vulnerable positions. After the appointment of Saragat, the Liberals and the right wing of the Christian Democrats kept a close watch on De Gasperi; and Saragat was consistently and viciously attacked by left-wing Socialists and, needless to say, by the Communist Party. The breakaway of Saragat's group, therefore, could not do too much to alter substantially the polarization of the political situation. Two developments further intensified that polarization: the Allied promise (obviously made with an eye to the elections) that every effort would be made to keep Trieste Italian, and the Communist *coup d'état* in Czechoslovakia. Two months before the elections, news of the Communist *coup*, in which the government was overthrown by Klement Gottwald (whom President Beneš had appointed to the Cabinet only after very strong Communist pressures), gave many shocked Italians pause. That development confirmed the fears of many Italians, and De Gasperi appeared prescient in having driven the Communists out of his government. Because of that *coup d'état* a great many independent voters with no taste for the extremes of either the Communist Party or the Christian Democrats felt that they had no choice but to give their vote to De Gasperi.

In the final vote of April 1948, the figures read thirteen million votes and 307 deputies for the Christian Democrats; eight million votes and 182 seats for the representatives of the Popular Front. The third force, represented by Saragat's Socialists, won two million votes and seated 33 deputies.

In the industrial North, the Christian Democrats won, 6,248,000 to 4,278,000, 22 seats to 14 for the Popular Front, a sign that the high-water mark of Communist-Socialist strength had begun to recede. In Lombardy, De Gasperi's party polled a vote of over two million, almost double that of the Popular Front. In Piedmont the same situation prevailed, with a Christian Democratic vote of over one million to some 700,000 votes for the Popular Front. Even in leftist Liguria, the Christian Democrats edged out the Communists and Socialists with a vote of 456,000 to 388,000. In Central Italy, the Catholic party made a surprisingly strong showing and edged out the Popular Front, 2,217,400 to 1,915,700, 50 deputies to 42. In Emilia the Communist-Socialist vote of over a million exceeded the Christian Democrat vote of 725,000, but in Tuscany and Umbria the Communist victory was close.

In the South the Christian Democrats also continued to roll up a large majority and outstripped the Popular Front, 2,900,000 to 1,310,000, 36 seats to 19. But the Christian Democrat majority would have been greater yet had the South not been the stronghold of the Extreme Right, accounting for 505,000 Liberal votes (more than half that party's total) and 400,000 votes of the *Partito Nazionale Monarchico*, the monarchist PNM (260,000 in Campania alone)—all votes that would otherwise have gone to De Gasperi's party. The South was also the strongest region for the minuscule neo-Fascist party, the *Movimento Socialista Italiano* (MSI)—the change of name was sufficient to circumvent the legal ban on the party—which continued to gain strength in Sicily. In the North, reminders of the Fascist debacle were still too numerous, the memories of the Nazi-Fascist alliance too fresh for neo-Fascists to be any kind of political force, and they won in all only 117,000 votes there (40,000 in Lombardy). But in the less devastated South, the party won over 200,000 votes and in Latium, around Rome, the bureaucratic capital of the country, they won almost 80,000.

Virtually a mandate, the victory was hailed as an endorsement of De Gasperi and his *quadripartito*. De Gasperi had taken a substantial risk in dismissing the Communists and Socialists from his Cabinet, and it had paid off. The way was now open, consequently, for the first Catholic prime minister in modern Italy to experience the varied and often contradictory implications of that massive support. As an initial hint of what to expect, the victory demanded that the Christian Democratic Party rule only with that very small *quadripartito*. Saragat's party had won almost two million votes, but its strength was limited principally to the North (in Central and Southern Italy its vote amounted to only 400,000). The Liberals won only slightly over a million, of which more than half came from the South; their entire vote was not much greater than that cast for the PNM. The vote of the Christian Democrats' third ally, the Republican Party, rather evenly distributed throughout the country, amounted to some 650,000 votes. These parties, moreover, were not consistently in agreement among themselves, and in the case of the Liberals and the Saragatian Socialists, there was even sharp opposition.

The Communists and Socialists, then, the second most powerful force in the country, were completely unrepresented in the government. The Christian Democrat victory seemed to many a rescue in the nick of time, and to an extent it was. It was not long, though, before it appeared quite clear that the magnitude of the victory was in direct proportion to the problems that it carried with it.

XV

DE GASPERI

The cold war manifestly accounted for a good part of the Christian Democrat victory of 1948, and continued to work to the advantage of that party afterward. In moments of heightened tension, in fact—as during the Berlin airlift, and the outbreak of the Korean War in 1950—the Christian Democrats were very much in command and many previously hesitant allies and supporters closed ranks with them.

There was less support, though, for that part of De Gasperi's foreign policy that aimed toward European federalism, a goal very dear to his heart. The concerted action of the Italian Prime Minister, Schumann and Adenauer, pointing to a luminous European possibility, was respected by most Italians as lofty political idealism, but there the matter rested. In political terms not even the anti-Communist aspect of federalism could make it a popular cause. The whole range of anti-Communists were lukewarm in their support. In twenty years of Fascism, they had been schooled in cynicism, and the realities of the cold war, the widespread conviction that the world was irreparably divided into mutually exclusive spheres, rubbed the musk off any budding hopes. In the first weeks of 1949, when the Marshall Plan was initiated and Parliament ratified the Atlantic Pact over violent Communist and Socialist protests, Italians of all anti-Communist parties rushed to the defense of the Christian Democrats and De Gasperi; but when De Gasperi tried to plod his way to European federalism he met at best with perfunctory and absent-minded approval and encouragement.

Violent debates on foreign policy, on the Atlantic Alliance and the Marshall Plan, however, could not obliterate the domestic crisis that loomed soon after the elections. Throughout 1949 and 1950, there were waves of strikes, reminiscent of 1919 but on a still larger scale, and widespread land occupations in Sicily and in Puglie. In Calabria demonstrations threatened to get completely out of hand. Destitute, land-hungry peasants had heard a great deal of talk of agricultural reform from all parties, and they were clamoring for action, particularly in the South. The greater part of the Monarchist and the neo-Fascist MSI vote came from that region, but the mood of the peasantry was revolutionary. Indeed, the MSI vote had a good deal to do with the outbursts; for after the Fascist defeat, the peasants were furious at the prospect that large landowners and urban middle classes might, in the name of anti-Communism, reinforce the old order, for which the peasants had no affection. Fascism had done very little for them; agricultural reforms had been limited to scattered land reclamations, some reorganization of the Sicilian *latifondi*, and the construction of "window-dressing" model cities in former marsh lands. Land reform, of course, may be no final solution in a land-poor country like Italy, but in any case, one could hardly expect the peasantry not to be embittered and painfully aware of the inequitable distribution, when one-third of the country was owned by some 24,000 landowners. With good reason, their mood was similar to that prevailing before the Sicilian revolt of 1896. It was the mood that had long characterized Italian history, and led to protests beginning in the South and rapidly spiraling up through the peninsula. The likelihood was that if Minister of Agriculture Antonio Segni's land-reform bill of 1950 had been the only reform measure in view, it would not have contained the protests. Indeed, in view of the mounting fury of those uprisings, it would have been surprising had even De Gasperi's *legge stralcio* (sample law), which heralded the real beginnings of land reform, been able to do much. The distribution of land to one-third of the 100,000 who applied could not provide a very strong breakwater.

But De Gasperi, appreciating the combustible aspect of the unrest, had prepared for it with something more than those two reform bills. The danger, he knew all too well, did not lie in anarchist peasant revolt but in the Communist exploitation of it. The Communists had already shown that the South was a citadel of the entire spectrum of the Right—from conservative Christian Democrats to Monarchists, Liberals and "Missini," as the partisans of the MSI were called; further advances of those parties among the upper and middle classes could only lead to a corresponding Communist gain among the peasants. The danger lay not so much in demonstrations or in the takeover of lands, but in an increase in Communist votes.

These were immediate political considerations with De Gasperi; but it was a sign of his genius and his boldness that he recognized that the old, persistent problem of the South demanded something beyond the calculating measures of party politics, that it required a virtual about-face from the traditional policy that the Christian Democrats had inherited from the Popular Party. The problem of the South could not be solved with the old measures that had failed time and again. The region required a totally new kind of aid, different in kind and quality from any previous assistance. The crisis had been long and sustained, and only an unprecedented degree of state aid would have a chance of altering the situation. De Gasperi planned to provide that aid, on a massive scale, with the *Cassa del Mezzogiorno* (the Fund for the South).

In effect, the Fund for the South was a clear admission that neither regional autonomy, nor private enterprise, nor the traditional spasmodic assistance that followed each emergency was adequate. There had been many programs of suggested agricultural reform in Italy since the Sonnino-Jacini report in the 1890's, but the trouble was not only that they were not implemented, but also that they were ill-conceived and inadequate. The time had come for the state to assume full responsibility for unprecedented agricultural reforms, for programs of reforestation, the construction of new aqueducts and highways, and the development of power.

No doubt the Fund for the South was a shrewd political move, but it was also an act of courage. De Gasperi had no illusions; he knew how many political allies the reform would alienate. In the 1950's as in the first decade of the century, the anti-South prejudices that had caused Salvemini to break away from Turati's Socialist Party some thirty-five years before were deep-rooted and pervasive. The rationalizations were familiar: the South, it was said, lacked initiative; its inhabitants had a dole mentality; they were lazy. Like a leech, the region attached itself to the North for survival and then complained that it was being exploited. Corrupt, irresponsible and dedicated to only one industry—a political bureaucracy—the South would drag the North down with it; its exorbitant demands would lead the country to bankruptcy.

These arguments illustrated the cruder form of prejudice; but De Gasperi also had to contend with the more insidious sophisticated argument that, after all, the Fund for the South might not be worth the risk. To believe that Communism had a following exclusively among the destitute (so ran the argument of his critics), among those for whom communism was what Don Sturzo called communism of the stomach, was naïvely Marxist. There was some truth in the contention; for the Red Belt in Italy indeed was not in the poorest but in the richest agricultural region, and the peasants and the members of the middle class there who gave the Communists their vote were incomparably better off than the peasants of the South. Was there any reason, then, to believe that Southern peasants would express proper gratitude for even substantial help? Wasn't it more likely that, like small neutral powers, they would learn to play Communists and Catholics off against each other, and transfer their allegiance now to one group, now to another?

There were similar objections from private interests. The long-range plans of the Fund for the South called not only for thorough agricultural reform, but for the beginnings of the industrialization of the South in an attempt to transform the region from a consumer to a producer economy. The aim was laudable, the critics conceded, but was it likely that the state could succeed in industrializing the area when private initiative had failed because of insuperable obstacles? And assuming that it could, in the very distant future, did De Gasperi think he would have a more tractable industrial proletariat there than in northern Italy? The final objection was the most immediate and forceful: Did De Gasperi fully expect the funds that the government would allocate to the Fund to reach their destination? The Mafia and the wily Southern *classe dirigente* were not things of the past.

The Prime Minister did not have the answers to all of these questions. Many of the problems involved are not solved today. Nonetheless, he had the will to act, and by 1950, the Fund for the South, involving an expenditure of a quarter of a billion lire annually for the entire region, including Sardinia, and calling for intensive work on the plateau of Sila in Calabria as a first concrete accomplishment, offered fresh hope to the Southern peasantry.

Nor did De Gasperi stop with the revolutionary Fund for the South. He moved with similar boldness in the industrial sector of the economy, through the IRI. Under De Gasperi's leadership, state-controlled capitalism saw an unprecedented development. In a matter of a few years, the state acquired about 30 per cent of all outstanding stock in Italy, between companies under direct control and others controlled by IRI holding companies or their subsidiaries. The essentials of industrial production were controlled by 350 of its companies: the Finsider subsidiaries, for example, produced 90 per cent of the country's pig iron and over 50 per cent of the steel output; Fincantiere accounted for 80 per cent of all shipbuilding. The IRI thus continued in the direction of the capitalism of Fascist Italy; but it went well beyond, including a part of the automotive and telephone industries, as well as Alitalia, the nationalized airline, and all radio and, eventually, television networks. In this gradual and steady amplification of IRI's powers, the organization ran into serious problems, and from 1945 to 1949, five presidents succeeded one another in the administration of the agency. By 1952, however, IRI was solidly entrenched, employing 300,000 people. (Fiat and Montecatini, the two most powerful independent corporations in the land, employed 63,000 and 50,000 respectively.)

The most momentous development of state socialism under De Gasperi, however, was not this steady increase in the power of IRI, but rather the sudden emergence of ENI, the National Hydrocarbon Board. The discovery of methane gas deposits to alleviate the country's dependence on imported coal had been one of Mussolini's ambitious dreams, and with this goal in mind he had organized an agency called AGIP. Nothing had come of its efforts, however, and after the war the government was having trouble selling the assets of the defunct agency for $100,000. At this point, Enrico Mattei, a former Catholic partisan leader who was responsible for disposing of the agency, disobeyed government orders and on his own initiative pressed on with explorations. After a few months, in March 1946, methane deposits were discovered at Caviaga in the Valle Padana. The discovery of the methane deposits revolutionized the Italian economy no less than the fund for the South. Although it would be years before the country profited completely from the discovery, it became clear as new deposits were gradually discovered that Italy was on the verge of entering a new economic era. Toward the end of De Gasperi's first term, methane deposits were discovered in Gela, in southern Sicily, and in Augusta on the eastern coast of the island.

ENI opened entirely new horizons for the northern industrial economy and offered a vision for the South. Working in conjunction with the fund for the South, which laid down the essential framework for southern industry, ENI gave substance to the hope that the industrialization that would follow agricultural reform was perhaps not too distant a prospect. At any rate, regardless of the pace of reform and of eventual industrialization, the South had the solid support of the strongest government agency in the country, which within the space of five years grew into a multi-billion lire enterprise and became, with De Gasperi's taut approval, something of an empire within an empire.

The enmities provoked by the ENI expansion, however, were even deeper than those provoked by the Fund for the South. The private enterprise capitalism that had survived the war—the great corporations that Fascism had favored, and that had played a key role in Parri's downfall—chafed under the restrictions and competition of the new IRI, and ENI, which was run by Mattei with professional competence (he used American big business as his model), further restricted their freedom of movement. Mattei, moreover, was imaginatively aggressive; by 1953 he was not only expanding in Italy but competing with American oil companies for contracts in the Near East, building ENI into an industrial empire with international assets.

These two programs, the Fund for the South and ENI, involved basic transformations, and the electorate gave the first inkling of its reaction in the local administrative elections of 1951, a victory for the Christian Democrats. In general, the northern cities showed a decrease in Communist strength and a corresponding increase in the strength of De Gasperi's party. But in the South, the parties of the Right continued to surge ahead. As a result of the two reform programs, the great bloc of votes that had buttressed the Christian Democrats in the polarized elections of 1948 veered further to the Right.

By 1950, too, the Prime Minister began to encounter steadily stiffening resistance within his own party. In July 1949, Pope Pius XII had excommunicated all Communists, and although there was some question as to who those Communists were (those who voted Communist or, more plausibly, those who worked passionately for the Communist cause), there was no doubt that politically the move helped conservative Christian Democrats and the parties of the Right more than it helped De Gasperi. For Luigi Gedda, the lay head of Catholic Action and leader of the Civic Committees (Catholic groups that had been in the thick of the 1948 elections with their activist proselytism), that condemnation was the signal to rally all believers to the defense of Italian Christendom, and in that crusade Gedda's forces were substantial. The Young Men's group, with 10,000 associations and a membership of some 360,000 in 1946, had grown to 15,000 associations and 550,000 members by 1953; in the same period, the Young Women's group went from 14,000 associations with 900,000 members to 19,000 with a membership of almost two million. Parades and athletic rallies were their forte, and in one major city after another vociferous assemblies of the green-capped youth of Catholic Action gave marching witness to their compact energy. At one point, some 120,000 youths marched in Red Bologna as a show of strength and a mammoth rally in the Colosseum in Rome compared favorably in number with those the Fascists had staged in front of Palazzo Venezia or the Communists in Red Square.

Toward the close of World War II, a spokesman for Catholic Action had insisted that the group had no political goals. As a body, Catholic Action was politically generic, with no party commitment. But during the polarized 1948 elections, even though it could be argued that the organizations still theoretically left its adherents free to vote according to their conscience, it was also obvious that conscience and a common-sense appraisal of the situation dictated that they vote for the Christian Democrats and against Communism. It was inevitable, in the light of its successes, that Catholic Action should conclude that it was called upon to do more than give witness to anti-Communism. At the summit of their ambitions, Gedda and a number of Catholic Action bishops, aflame with anti-Communist fervor, envisioned the possibility of a Catholic Action elite corps whose task would be to direct and offer sound doctrinal guidance to the Christian Democratic Party. Practical difficulties, however, and De Gasperi's deferential but firm independence soon made them rub that vision out of their eyes, and by 1951 Gedda had settled for the notion of Catholic Action as a watchdog force. Their mission was to see to it that De Gasperi returned to what Catholic Action would call "Christian principles"—principles which, translated into political specifics, allowed collaboration only with the parties of the Right, with Liberals and Monarchists. Even though De Gasperi had expelled Communist and left-wing Socialist ministers from his Cabinet, his inclusion of Saragat unnerved many in Catholic Action. They were also convinced that he had exceeded the limits of prudence with his mild policy toward the numerous Communist-led strikes. It was time that the crooked way be made straight; it was time for the Catholic Prime Minister who was "soft on Communism" to mend his ways.

Gedda and the Catholic Action group, already strong with the support of most of the hierarchy, would have had an additional advantage had they been able to enlist the aid of Don Sturzo. But Don Sturzo chose an even more isolated position in post-Fascist Italy than he had chosen in the last years of the Popular Party. He opposed De Gasperi, but he had little enthusiasm for the Catholic Action group. Since his return, the old Sicilian priest, like so many returning exiles, found little to his liking in the emerging Italy. This was not the new state he had fought for. It was an old Italy, he lamented, that perpetuated Fascist vices and compounded them with many of its own.

The old Populist leader felt that De Gasperi, under the guise of working for the common good, had strengthened the tyrannical, centralized state that he, Sturzo, had fought since the turn of the century. He lacked a Christian vision of man and politics; it was a compromising of principle, a well-meaning, tragic blunder. De Gasperi's policies won votes, no doubt, but they did so with criminal shortsightedness. In terms of pure efficiency, furthermore, not one of the major reforms proved its worth. The vaunted IRI bungled enormously, and the way in which its subsidiaries, oblivious to the commonweal, squandered their modest energies in competition among themselves was a scandal. Five presidents in four years proved that the entire baroque structure was basically an *ad hoc* improvisation, with remarkable skill in juggling accounts and proliferating a bureaucracy. In no way, Sturzo charged, was the IRI any different in structure or spirit from what it had been in Fascist Italy.

The ENI, even more, aroused Sturzo's wrath. He saw the organization as a state within the state, having virtually unlimited borrowing power, paid political representatives, newspapers and, within its sphere, full sovereignty. It could pressure Parliament to pass legislation to bar private oil companies from probing even where ENI had already searched unsuccessfully for oil, and in general could make it very hard for private enterprise to compete. Although Sturzo had often denounced industrialists for going to extremes in their stupid opposition to labor and their spineless acquiescence to the all-powerful state, he did consider the interests of private enterprise as insurance against an overcentralized state. For too many Italians, Sturzo lamented, Mattei's ENI was synonymous with growing prosperity, "the Italian miracle," and Italian successes in the international field, where Mattei had in fact successfully competed in the Near East with Goliath American oil interests. Its successes notwithstanding, Sturzo did not feel that the ENI lived up to its claims; where methane was discovered, it was being sold at excessively high prices, three times the cost of production.

But Sturzo's main objections to ENI and the Fund for the South were not derived from the weaknesses inherent in the programs, but from the principles on which these programs were based. The Fund for the South would inevitably become an elephantine bureaucracy, an occasion for petty and not very petty thievery, but its most vicious consequence would be its perpetuation of the peasants' dependence on the omnipotent state. Agricultural reform was obviously urgently needed, and the peasants' need of land and the tools to work it was beyond discussion, but the Fund for the South was not the proper means with which to accomplish those ends. Regional agencies could achieve those indispensable reforms much better than any centralized bureaucracy.

With respect to legislation for regional autonomy, Don Sturzo wholeheartedly approved the direction of the new Italy. He did not share the fears of Liberals and Monarchists that decentralization could be exploited by Communists, in particular the Liberal nightmare that in Emilia the granting of regional autonomy would lead to the establishment of an independent Italian Communist Republic. Only with a greater degree of regional autonomy, he argued, could agricultural reform become meaningful. The communism of Umbria, for example, could be more effectively checked with an increase in public works and industrial development under the direction of the regional administration than by any amount of agricultural reform directed by the centralized government. Regional legislation, reflecting a better understanding of the people's problems, could avoid many of the acknowledged defects of the centralized government's program. (The requirement that peasants receiving land grants remain on the land for twelve and in some cases up to thirty years was but one notorious example.) More important yet, with regionalism Italians would acquire needed schooling in the responsibilities of democratic self-government, the lack of which had so far crippled Italian political life.

This critique persuaded many. In the Senate, Don Sturzo sat not with the Christian Democrats but with the Independents, but his influence on a number of Christian Democrats (especially on Mario Scelba, very close to him) was notable. His arguments were entirely acceptable also to both northern and southern Liberals, to some out of disinterested persuasion, to others out of self-interest. Thus, though he did not give his approval to the mood and ideals of Gedda's Catholic Action, Sturzo did aid their cause indirectly, and his opposition to the government, together with that of Liberals, Monarchists and the minuscule MSI, coalesced into a substantial bloc opposing De Gasperi's "socialist" policies. These were small parties, true, but so were the Prime Minister's allies. In the 1948 elections, the Republican Party had won only slightly more than 650,000 votes; and though Saragat's party was the fourth-strongest in the land, the Liberals were not much weaker, and the Liberals in 1950 withdrew from the government. The departure of the Liberals underlined the obvious truth that since the second- and third-strongest parties in the country were unrepresented in the Cabinet, those parties that joined the government had an importance out of all proportion to their size or strength at the polls. Their support meant survival for De Gasperi, and the withdrawal of one demanded the search for support elsewhere. This floundering search was to continue for more than a decade.

But the opposition to De Gasperi was only in part attributable to the daring of the Fund for the South and ENI. Both programs, in the last analysis, required time to bear fruit, certainly more than the five-year interim between elections. In the meantime, though, there were many other developments between 1948 and 1953. The virtually one-party government repeatedly acted in high-handed and arrogant fashion. There was, as an inevitable consequence of the renewal of the Lateran Pacts, petty and irksome collusion between ecclesiastical authorities and the government. There were scandals and frequent evidence of corruption in high places. But above and pervading all, among many groups whose help De Gasperi could not do without, there was a growing dissatisfaction with and distaste for what Italians rather crudely call *puzza di sagrestia* (the smell of the sacristy)—the spiritual spectaculars of the time, the ceaseless religious processions, the public devotions to the Madonna, the miraculous visions, the performances of "god's microphone," Father Riccardo Lombardi. Even the much-admired and venerated Pontiff, showing signs of fatigue from his enormous labors, was losing popularity, and grumblings of clericalism and paternalism ceased to be *sotto voce*.

Against this peculiar form of discontent, De Gasperi had few defenses. The level of popular quasi-Fascist Catholicism was what it was, and there was little he or anyone else, for that matter, could do about it. The Third Generation (*Terza Generazione*), an extreme left-wing Catholic intellectual movement willing to work with Communists and Socialists, gave scandal and was almost immediately condemned by ecclesiastical authorities; and priests like Don Primo Mazzolari (whose newspaper *Adesso* was reminiscent of the *Catholic Worker* in tone) were generally considered eccentrics. Giuseppe Dossetti's *Cronache Sociali* group, including Giuseppe Lazzati, Amintore Fanfani and Giorgio La Pira, was articulate and had a certain following, but the soubriquet applied to them gave an adequate idea of the man in the street's view—they were *pesci rossi in acqua santa* (red fish in holy water).

The *Cronache Sociali* group did not mince words in denouncing the spirit of Gedda's Civic Committees—a tired, sterile anti-communism that was hardly inspired by a love of the poor or by the spirit of the Gospels. Dossetti's circle was shocked at how many Catholics made use of their religion in the crudest *instrumentum regni* manner; and they pleaded for a Catholicism reflecting the spirit of Maritain's *True Humanism*, that of Cardinal Suhard and of *Esprit*, the French Catholic publication dedicated to "the destruction of the present disorder."

Dossetti, in particular, made some very telling points as to the obligations of a party professing to be both Christian and Democratic. For that party, he argued, the problem of full employment could not be simply a technical economic problem, but a moral concern. Similarly, the question of an equitable distribution of wealth in a society with a small very wealthy class and many, many poor was not so much a problem as a scandal, and something had to be done about it. The ENI and the Fund for the South were applauded by the Christian Left but also criticized for not going nearly far enough. For Dossetti, there was still too much old Liberal leaven in De Gasperi's new bread, and he was particularly critical of the role of southern Liberals (in particular Epicarmo Corbino, Minister of Finance), and also of the frequent exploitation of the cold war issue by less scrupulous members of the Christian Democratic party.

Dossetti and Lazzati were not political men, but the help that the more political members of the *Cronache Sociali* group, La Pira and Fanfani, could offer De Gasperi was of questionable value to him politically. La Pira probably did De Gasperi more harm than good. The Sicilian-born mayor of Florence had no doubt won a remarkable victory in 1951 in that city, where the Communists were particularly strong, and his administration showed that his pamphlet, *L'attesa della povera gente* (*The Expectation of the Poor*) was more than a literary exercise. La Pira was a cross between an early Christian and a maverick, and terrified most Catholics even more than did Don Mazzolari or the *Terza Generazione*. He took the law into his own hands in public housing and interpreted the primacy of needs in an absolutist fashion, repeatedly turning empty buildings, with or without the owners' permission, into shelters for the homeless.

Fanfani, perhaps, a member of the Cabinet who had directed a low-income national housing program and many similar operations, came closest to offering unalloyed aid to De Gasperi. But the active professor of economics was also suspect of being paracommunistic, and in any case did not yet have a sizable following.

As a consequence, then, of the mounting general dissatisfaction, De Gasperi, in preparing for the 1953 elections, fell back less on his accomplishments than on the tried and proven issue of the previous elections—anti-communism. The Communists were still his strongest rival and their strikes and anti-American, anti-Marshall Plan foreign policy were vote-getting issues for De Gasperi. It was also to the Christian Democrats' advantage that negotiations for a peace settlement in the Korean War were coming to a close by the time of the elections, erasing the American imperialist warmonger issue.

But the Communists were strong. The party maintained a firm hold on labor in spite of the defection from the General Confederation of Labor of Catholic groups, who had formed a rival federation, the CISL, in protest against the general strike called by the Communists after an attempt on Togliatti's life in 1948. The Prime Minister's bold program had not stripped them of all issues. None of De Gasperi's innovations could cut into their following. In the South, the party merely exploited the bungling and corruption that was undeniably a part of the Fund for the South, and told the peasants that, all things considered, the Fund was a drop in the bucket in comparison with what they needed, and what they could get under the Communists. For the more demanding, in terms of an official Leninist-Gramscian explanation, it was easy to label the Fund as the last and most subtle instrument of imperialistic northern capitalism to keep the South a colony. In the Communist strongholds of Central Italy, the party needed only to repeat its slogans and stress the undoubted efficiency and honesty of Communist municipal administrations there. With respect to the industrial proletariat, after five years of De Gasperi's rule the party following was still persuaded that the Atlantic Alliance was an instrument of aggression and that the Marshall Plan was designed to serve American economic interests. As for the implications of the ENI and the enlarged IRI, Togliatti had but to repeat that these agencies were precisely what the Liberals and Sturzo said they were—instruments designed to perpetuate the Christian Democrats in office.

The Socialists, still bitter over the 1948 defeat, were for all practical purposes one with the Communists. Nenni was in the thick of the parliamentary battle against ratification of the Atlantic Pact, and his ties with Basso and Morandi were strong. Ever since Romita and other moderate Socialist splinter groups had gone over to Saragat's PSDI, the Italian Socialist Party—the PSI of Nenni, Basso, and Morandi—had closed ranks.

Whatever De Gasperi had accomplished, the PSI leadership in general agreed with Togliatti that it was too little and too late; and their close alliance with the Communists continued even though they decided not to run again on the Popular Front ticket with them in the 1953 elections.

In view of this unchanged situation between the PSI and the

Communist Party, De Gasperi's strategy in falling back on the issue of anti-Communism had undeniable merit. De Gasperi relied completely on Saragat's inclusion in the government to prove that the Christian Democrats were willing and ready to collaborate with Socialists who were not compromised body and soul with the Communist Party. But De Gasperi also needed support from Saragat's party, and just at this time that group was giving signs that it was neither very powerful nor indeed united. It had failed to unite firmly the various anti-Nenni Socialist groups and had itself suffered a schism of Center-Left elements. As a result of this internal dissension, Saragat's Social Democrats, as a member of the government coalition, gave De Gasperi at best erratic support. It became increasingly doubtful as the elections approached that the party would be able to win over any large bloc of Socialist votes.

The rallying cry of anti-Communism in this setting could not produce the results it had achieved in 1948. Subject to pressure from the Communists and the PSI on the left, and with only intermittent support from the Social Democrats, conservative Christian Democrats, Monarchists and Liberals on the right, De Gasperi (with the approval of the *quadripartito*, the four-party ruling coalition) played his last card with the passage of an electoral-reform law designed to give a greater stability to Christian Democratic rule if the party emerged victorious in the 1953 elections. The reform, in effect, was designed to give the party winning more than half the votes a greater share of representatives in the Chamber of Deputies. Superficially reminiscent of the Acerbo Law, a rigged-up election law that the Fascists used for assuring their election victory after the march on Rome, it was by no means as extreme or unfair. Nonetheless, denounced by many as a fraud, the measure became a burning issue in the elections. When the results were tallied, it could not even serve its purpose, since De Gasperi's party did not win more than half the votes.

The Christian Democrats' representation in the Chamber of Deputies dropped from 307 to 263; the Communists elected 143 deputies and the PSI 75. The situation did not change in the traditional strongholds, but all along the line parties of the Right, who opposed De Gasperi's program almost as much as did the Communists, made steady gains. In the South in particular, the combined vote of the rightist parties was about the equal of the national Communist vote.

But the big disappointment of that election was the very poor showing of the PSDI, on whose help De Gasperi had counted heavily. That party dropped from 33 to 19 seats, and this loss of support spelled the end, in De Gasperi's words, of the Christian Democrats as "a party of the Center moving toward the Left." In 1948 the Christian Democrats' allies in the *quadripartito* had added 61 deputies to its strength in Parliament; in 1953, without the Liberals, the collaborating parties could add only 24. From another point of view after the 1948 elections the Christian Democrats had the opposition of only 20 deputies of the Right to contend with; after the withdrawal of the Liberals from the Cabinet the number rose to 39. After 1953 it had to face the opposition of 82 Rightist deputies—40 Monarchists, 13 Liberals, and 29 Missini. Only eight years after the military defeat of Fascism a sizable number of Italians in the South and in Central Italy around Rome were no longer reluctant to admit nostalgia for a part of the Fascist past. And just as these Italians effortlessly distinguished between a good pre-war Mussolini and a bad wartime dictator, so with equal ease they distinguished between the Fascism that overstepped proper limits and that which had maintained order and put an end to strikes and party squabbling. As long as it appeared that De Gasperi acted as the savior of the country against the Communist threat they had given him their vote; but after five years they considered his brand of anti-Communism itself a threat.

The elections of 1953 thus marked the failure of De Gasperi's vision and the tactics with which he tried to implement that vision. The failure was not that of the Christian Democratic leader, though. In its brief history as a modern state no Italian prime minister tried to do and did so much with so little. After the 1953 elections, after De Gasperi tried and failed with a new government (it lasted only twenty-one days), the rapid succession of one Christian Democrat prime minister after another gave a proper idea of the dimensions of what he had managed to achieve.

Italy in 1953 was still in the mood for outright confrontation with Communists and Socialists, only this time following not the "leftist" De Gasperi but the rising forces of the Right. In this overall mood no one paid much attention to the election slogan of Nenni (whose party ran a poor second to the Communists) that this was the year of the *alternativa socialista* (the socialist alternative). In an Italy in which the sole Socialist allies of De Gasperi had suffered a serious setback at the polls, and in which the PSI and the Communists were firmly allied, that notion seemed—and *was*—preposterous.

XVI

THE LAST LIBERALISM

OF BENEDETTO CROCE

Croce survived Fascism and witnessed the emergence of the new Italy, but the octogenarian philosopher did not live to see the 1953 elections. After he stepped down as president of the Liberal Party (an office he held from 1943-47), he dedicated himself completely to interrupted studies in history, literature and philosophy, his vocation, and in this work died on November 20, 1952. All of Naples, and certainly the most distinguished part of Italy, attended his funeral, and there were few present who in the solemnity of the moment did not sense with apprehensive nostalgia that Croce's death marked the end of an era, and that theirs was the responsibility of doing justice to a magnificent heritage. Croce's contributions, however, lay more in his theory of political liberalism than in his practical leadership, and even that theoretical liberalism, all in all, seemed less important than his work on historiography, philosophy or literature. As a consequence, soon after his death there began a devaluation of Croce's liberalism and political philosophy that has continued down to our day.

At its extreme point, this criticism, voiced with characteristic sharpness by Salvemini a few years before his death, has called into question the very value of Croce's anti-Fascism during and after the Fascist period. It would seem, then, that Croce's little known last Liberalism bears reconsideration, to see whether or not it is authentically anti-Fascist, a meaningful alternative to various Socialist or Catholic political philosophies.

In Fascist Italy, of necessity, politics for Croce had been politics in the widest sense of the word. For twenty years, with a prodigious output touching on all the areas of his wide range of interests, Croce managed to dispel to some extent, at least for himself and the happy few, the emptiness, the oppressive boredom of the low level of intellectual life under the Fascist regime. But with the collapse of Fascism and the catastrophic condition of liberated Italy, Croce, oblivious to the weight of years, threw himself into the thick of the practical politics of reconstruction. He was convinced that he had to do something for that Italy in which he had never lost faith; and quite as much for the South, which, he was fully aware, still sorely lacked a widespread civic sense, a truly politically committed intelligentsia.

From the day he addressed the first congress of partisan forces in Bari in January, 1944, to the day he handed in his resignation as minister without portfolio in the Badoglio government, he did not spare himself. He was of key assistance to De Nicola in winning the King's promise to step down in favor of his son, and in his counsels had helped to give the Badoglio government's dealings with the Allied powers a tone that was deferential and cooperative but not servile; the latter accomplishment was no doubt as important as the former.

Yet though Croce showed skills as a man of politics and a diplomat in attaining certain immediate goals, primarily the removal of Victor Emmanuel III without destroying the monarchy, his principal concern was not with immediate ends. He considered it his obligation to help in the emergency, but his real mission was to give heart and ideas to the Liberal Party, the political party that for him most fittingly expressed the tenets of his Religion of Liberty, in 1943 as in 1924.

Needless to say, the make-up of this party immediately after the fall of Fascism was not what it had been some twenty years earlier. There were a few survivors of that distant epoch, members of that old party—Nitti back from exile, De Nicola, and Victor Emmanuel Orlando—and they wanted the party to be what it had once been, the party of the "golden mean" in politics. For the older generation, the Liberal Party, committed neither to the Right nor Left, was the defender of the primacy of lay culture against Catholic and Marxist rivals, of sane nationalism that avoided all excesses, of moderate state socialism that did not seek to take over all of the economy. In the

South, in particular, where memories of Amendola and Nitti had never died out among the older generation, these Liberals could count on the support of the middle class.

In view of its defense of lay culture, it would seem that this Liberal group would have little in common with Christian Democrats of the Right. But in spite of this difference, the two groups were only moderately apart. The followers of Don Sturzo, who certainly did not see eye to eye with the Liberals on several crucial issues, were not so far from them that they could not form a united front on more than one occasion; and among Sturzo's group, Croce had some of his closest friends, such as the old Populist minister, Guilio Rodinò.

There was a second group of Liberals, though, for whom liberalism was something quite different—primarily the rights of private initiative against state interference, and even more important, the defense of nationalism against international atheistic Communism. For years this group had listened intently to Mussolini's warnings against the Communist threat and the need for an anti-Communist crusade. During World War II and especially toward the end, when the CLNAI became increasingly powerful, they found all their fears confirmed. Composed of elements from the middle class, liberalism of this type was more often than not barely distinguishable from crypto-Fascism, and the conservative *Uomo Qualunque* party quite understandably made its greatest gains among this group.

This was the tone and structure of the Liberal following in the South. In the North, it was equally varied. There, too, there were groups for whom liberalism verged on crypto-Fascism and others that were akin to the Christian Democrats. There was even, though more attenuated, a very class-conscious liberalism reminiscent of that of the South. In addition to these varieties, though, there was a sturdier and more disinterested liberalism, best represented by Luigi Einaudi, the *Corriere della Sera*, and the more-to-the-left journal, *La Stampa*. Especially in the field of journalism, northern liberalism was far superior to that of the South, which very soon became the refuge of many Fascist journalists.

A very motley following, the Liberals nonetheless had had little trouble in expressing a common stand on a number of issues. On the cold war, for example, Croce and Liberals of the most varied persuasions were unflinchingly anti-Russian. During the war the philosopher had occasion to talk with a number of Russian dignitaries, including Vishinsky, and with many enthusiastic supporters of the USSR, and none of them persuaded him to revise his estimate of Communist Russia, which dated back virtually to the founding of that state. He acknowledged that Russia was a power, and its government had popular support. It had fought well. But Croce saw nothing in the thirty years of Communist rule that had anything to offer for the Religion of Liberty, the Liberal Party or Italy. He admired the Russian people and did not doubt that, considering their past, their lot under communism was an improvement. As a religion, however, Leninist-Marxist philosophy was nothing but an accumulation of old errors; not philosophy, but another version of state-enforced ideology. Political, military and economic successes could not alter this fact; and therefore Croce did not hesitate to make common cause with the Christian Democrats in considering anti-Communism of the essence.

Accordingly, in the short interim from the end of the war to the first national elections for the Chamber of Deputies in 1948, Croce gave his authoritative support to De Gasperi and his foreign policy. He approved of the declaration of war against Japan, which would serve, he hoped, to alleviate the predictably harsh terms of the peace treaty. He was happy over De Gasperi's successes in handling the delicate situation in the Alto Adige, and he backed De Gasperi completely, as did all men of his generation (and not they alone), for his insistence that Trieste be returned to Italy. De Gasperi's removal of Communists and Socialists from the Cabinet naturally met with his staunch approval. Like millions of Italians, Croce was sure that De Gasperi had merely anticipated what Togliatti would have done in the same position.

Croce's agreement with the Christian Democrats on questions involving the anti-Communist issue won the strong support of the Liberals he led, but it was not as easy for him to win a consensus in his party on other issues. In crossing the bridge from political theory to political practice, Croce, like many before and after him, found himself on unfamiliar terrain, and more often than not alone.

With respect to the question of the monarchy, it was known to most Italians that the matter was not a subject of debate in the South. That region, for many reasons, was solidly monarchist. On the highest level of conscious political articulation in the *ceto medio*, there was a moderate Liberal tradition, to which Croce himself adhered, that made no fetish out of the monarchy but considered it an extremely useful stabilizing force in a still very divided nation, all the more necessary in view of the Communist-Socialist threat. On a lower level there was the monarchism of the disillusioned elements of many classes, people convinced of the ineradicable veniality and malicious incompetence of all party government, who clung to the monarchy as the tower of stability and common sense. There were also monarchists whose convictions were based quite simply and unequivocally on a tenacious mistrust and antipathy for the republican North, and for them the King was the last defender of an exploited South. There was even, at the very bottom of the hierarchy of pro-monarchist convictions, a remnant of an old throne-and-altar mentality, for whom the monarchy was the one fixed point in a changing world, a bulwark against the enemies of God and country. In terms of that minimum political realism without which parties cease to be, the Liberal Party *had* to take into consideration the overwhelming pro-monarchist sentiments of the South. But under Croce's leadership, that reality was not considered decisive. Croce held that it was debatable whether or not the retention of the monarchy would make for a better Italy, and on debatable questions party unity was not required.

Croce himself, like De Gasperi, whose party followed a similar neutral policy albeit for altogether different reasons, had open monarchist leanings; but those preferences, he insisted, were personal. The gist of his more abstract arguments was that history had seen high-principled monarchies and corrupt republics and vice versa. In more immediately relevant terms, he reiterated his conviction that since Fascism was not traceable to any one cause, group or institution, responsibility for it should not be concentrated on the royal house. Italy stood to gain with a royal house that would return to the traditions of the Liberal Risorgimento, that would embody the cause of constitutional liberal government and of moral-political values that, prior to their betrayal by Victor Emmanuel III, had made Italy great.

But Croce insisted that his defense of the monarchy was not and should not become an official party stand. The Liberal Party was to remain neutral, keeping the argument on a higher level than that on which most southerners, and certainly most Liberals, placed it; and this was but the first sign of the unique way in which Croce conceived of the nature and function of the Liberal Party. There were others, and in most instances they, too, failed to win a consensus within the party.

On one all-important question, that of decentralization and increased regional autonomy, however, Croce concurred completely with the majority of the Liberal representation, though not quite for the same reasons.

"To my beloved Naples," he had written pointedly in the dedication of his diary for 1943–44, "which has never distantly thought of seeking autonomy or separation, religiously faithful to that ideal of national unity of which the revolutionaries of 1799 were the heralds." A united Italy was to remain so, and this was not a "debatable" matter. It was a matter of debate whether the monarchy could do the new Italy more harm or good, but there was no doubt in Croce's mind that the problem of decentralization allowed of no legitimate doubts. There might have been real injustices in Italy's past that explained requests for regional autonomy (Croce himself, though, was never convinced), but such injustices, Croce argued, could be rectified by other means. Italian unity was still too frail, too precarious for decentralization, and on this stand Croce allowed no concessions, no compromise, unswayed by the fact that regionalism and decentralization were very popular issues in the South. The wrongs suffered by the South or any other region of Italy at the hands of a despotic central government, Croce insisted, were not to be compounded by weakening the central authority, which was still wobbly after nearly a century of political life.

The conclusion was shared by other Liberals, not so much out of concern for Italian unity (a farfetched fear), but because they were afraid of the rise of independent Communist enclaves (a still more farfetched fear). Croce did not succumb to these exaggerated fears of communism, but in his last years the ideals of the Risorgimento appeared to him particularly luminous and he felt called upon to defend as all of one piece, as a seamless robe, that national unity he had extolled in the *History of Italy* as

. . . . an admirable work such as only Italian political genius, daring and sensible, idealistic and yet realistic, could conceive and create, in the spirit of its great works of art, the hallmark of an innate classic sense of form.

Regionalism was a cause championed by Don Sturzo and the Christian Democrats, enemies of Liberal Italy, and that was enough to persuade Croce that the defense of Risorgimento unity was not an idle Quixotic cause; and if that had not been enough, the unanimous agreement of all parties of the Left in their endorsement of decentralization made him completely intransigent in his opposition.

The matter of regionalism, though, was virtually the only issue on which Croce and the party saw eye to eye; on all others, the Neapolitan philosopher urged policies that were *not* popular among the Liberals. In his opposition to the renewal of the Concordat, the philosopher stood virtually alone. His position was that of 1929, when he was the only one to stand up in the Senate to protest against it—not out of anti-Church sentiment but out of the deep conviction that it was to the best interests both of the Church and Italians to maintain the status quo. His arguments were as applicable in 1945 as they had been in 1929, indeed much more so. To make the Concordat and the Lateran Pacts a part of the Constitution was to put old wine in new wineskins, and Croce was particularly distressed and upset at the cynical acquiescence of the Socialists, Communists and many Liberals. Opposition to the Concordat, like opposition to decentralization, was for him a matter of principle, but in 1945 as in 1929 he stood alone. In post-war Italy, most Liberals were persuaded that, given the cold war and the coming showdown between Communists and Catholics, to go against the manifest wishes of the Pontiff and of De Gasperi was out of the question. Anticommunism needed all the support it could muster, they felt, and this Paris was well worth a mass.

The stand that made Croce most unpopular with the Liberals, however, was that which he took on the Fund for the South, IRI and ENI; and here, in particular, Croce paid a heavy price for consistency with past convictions and theories.

Basic to Croce's political creed was the notion that true, authentic liberalism was not indissolubly tied to economic liberalism. The two were separate and distinct. In a continuing polemic with Einaudi, in which Croce had made his point for the last time in 1940, the philosopher had insisted that the question of state intervention in the economy did not involve principle. Measures taken by the state to intervene in the national economy were a technical, neutral means toward ends that had nothing to do with an overall philosophy. In abstract theory, Croce argued, a regime based on Communist economics could still be "liberal," provided it did not infringe on the autonomy of the individual, the right of the person (within the limitations imposed by the historical moment) to live according to the dictates of his conscience, and make his own way to basic truths, uncoerced by the state. Croce was moderate, however, when it came to the concrete application of this approach. Wilhelm Ropke, the economist-advocate of "the third way," an economy that sought to avoid the extremes of unbridled private enterprise and state socialism, seemed to him the most sensible of Liberals and economists, and there was a place in Ropke's theory for measures such as De Gasperi's economic reforms.

It was precisely on this point, on the indifference of "means," on the "neutral" aspect of state intervention in the economy, that Croce met with the strongest opposition within the party, and not only from those obviously arguing the case for vested interests, but also from those who, agreeing with Einaudi, felt that economic policy was not neutral ground, and that in its opposition to state socialism, traditional liberalism was concerned with moral values, with a defense of liberty; that in an economy completely dominated by the state, liberty would become an empty abstraction. This group felt that Croce pushed his thesis too far when he maintained that a Communist economy could be "Liberal"; they felt that it was straining plausibility to believe that a state that completely dominated the economic sphere would permit or tolerate the meaningful intellectual liberty that Croce considered of the essence.

More often than not, then—on the matter of the referendum on the monarchy, on the renewal of the Concordat, and on the new state socialism of De Gasperi—Croce, the head of the Liberal Party, was at odds with a substantial number of its members as he attempted to apply his theoretical principles to concrete situations. The price for principle was high. Because of the party's neutrality on the referendum on the monarchy, a substantial group left the Liberal Party and moved over to the *Partito Nazionale Monarchico*. Later, after Croce had stepped down as party leader, the entire party, under the new leadership of Marchese Lucifero, rejected his stand on state socialism, and over the philosopher's strong objections, formed an alliance with the conservative *Uomo Qualunque* party in the 1948 elections.

But not all of Croce's difficulties were traceable to an intransigent commitment to well-founded principle. His arguments were not always cogent, his case for what was and what was not of the essence was not always persuasive. He made a very good case against the renewal of the Concordat and a rather bad one against regionalism and decentralization; and with regard to state socialism, he became enmeshed in an impossible position. Modern capitalism was reformable, he maintained, pointing to the economic policies of the British Labor Party and of the New Deal as examples that could be particularly meaningful to the new Italy; but in keeping with his notion that economic policy was neutral ground, he balked at endorsing any specific economic program for the party. At one point Nicolò Carandini, a leader of the left wing of the party, proposed that the Liberals adopt such an economic policy, in order to make it perfectly clear that the party was not a tool of conservative interests. But Croce would not hear of it; and even when Carandini's faction followed others and broke off, protesting that Croce's liberalism was incoherent in not moving closer and forming an alliance with Saragat, Croce held his ground.

By this time it was amply clear that Croce's idea of a party was completely at odds with the usual one. It made no concessions to principle for the sake of unity and was not concerned at all with retaining or increasing its following. If principle demanded that an inflexible stand be taken, the obligation was fulfilled regardless of consequences. The Liberal Party, in a word, was a practical failure —and the reasons for its failure strikingly paralleled those that accounted for the downfall of the Action Party, the party Croce most abhorred.

During Mussolini's tenure, Croce made it a policy not to give aid and comfort to the regime by criticizing the work of anti-Fascists with whom he strongly dissented, and because of that he made few references to Rosselli's or Gobetti's ideas on politics. Adolfo Omodeo, however, who replaced Gentile as Croce's right-hand man on *La Critica*, did review Gobetti's *Risorgimento senza eroi* (*Risorgimento Without Heroes*), a debunking history of the period, and said all that Croce himself thought on the charge that the Risorgimento was a failure. The harshness of that review, significantly, was not softened by the awareness of the quality and meaning of Gobetti's anti-Fascism. After the fall of Fascism, once the liberal Marxism of Gobetti and Rosselli became incarnated in a political party, Croce could speak out clearly, and he lost no occasion to point out that, in the last analysis, the Action Party wittingly or unwittingly served the Communist cause. He denounced the Action Party for its anti-monarchism, its republican mystique. He ridiculed it for its political intransigence, the political "purity" in the name of which it had first hesitated to join the Badoglio government and later refused to join the second Bonomi ministry. He heaped scorn on it for its lack of party discipline. He vehemently accused it of perpetuating two of the worst aspects of Fascism, the cult of action as a good *per se*, and the cult of "irrationalism;" and he made repeated sarcastic jibes at its moralism, and its claims as a supraparty.

At no point throughout this long and passionate indictment, however, did Croce notice how very close his own party was to the Action Party. As leader of the Liberal Party he, too, considering the price he paid in party losses for principle, was certainly open to the charge of political obtuseness. In insisting that the party would ally itself only with those parties that showed complete respect and deference to democratic liberalism—that is, with Bonomi's *Democrazia del Lavoro* and Nitti's group—he was certainly "pure" and intransigent, as he was in arguing that the Liberal Party was not at all interested in being a party of the masses. It was obvious to even the most detached observer, furthermore, that if Croce's Liberal Party was anything at all, it was a supraparty and that some of its weaknesses were due to frequent excesses of moralism.

But the most striking coincidence of the positions of both parties was on the key issue of the meaning and extent of state socialism. The Action Party had splintered because of disagreements on the relation of private capitalism and state socialism, and Parri had failed completely to check mass defections to the Left. Croce's Liberal Party had also fallen apart on that problem, in spite of the very elegant dialectic notion of the philosopher, who argued that the party would always adhere to a vital center through the fusion of democratic elements that kept it from lapsing into conservatism, and liberal elements that protected it from demogoguery. The fusion of the two notwithstanding, one segment of the party went with the

Uomo Qualunque group, another with the Saragatian Socialists, and still another with the Action Party. There were good reasons, after all, why so many of Croce's closest associates—the group around Croce's publishers, the Laterza family in Bari, Omodeo, Federico Chabod, the Liberal historian who had actively participated in the Resistance in Piedmont—had gone over to the Action Party. In spite of its undeniably fuzzy concepts, it was the only alternative for those Liberals impatient with the stand-pat policy of the Liberal Party.

With respect to the most serious charge that Croce made against the Action Party, its cult of action, there was in Croce a peculiar weakness for its opposite. If it was true that in the Action Party there was an excess of "action," it was also true that in Croce there was at least a tendency (witness the timbre and quality of his monarchism and his anti-regionalism) to preserve continuity and avoid anything that resembled a clear break with the past.

But in most other respects the failure of Croce as a party leader was paradoxically very similar to that of Parri; and in this unexpected convergence of opposites, the failure was heavy with meaning. It meant that the leaders of a potential third force, in the heat of the struggle against the Communists and Christian Democrats, could not see how much they had in common. It meant that any leftist-oriented liberalism in the aftermath of World War II, such as that of Croce or even that of Parri, that sought to maintain a position distinct from and yet friendly to even as vaguely Marxist a Socialist Party as that of Saragat, could run into enormous difficulties. With this ultimate convergence of Croce's liberalism and the Action Party in mind, Croce's failure as leader of the Liberal Party is something more than an incident of anecdotal value in the declining years of the grand old man of Italian philosophy. It highlights a key unsolved problem of contemporary Italian politics—the problem of contributing to a pluralistic democracy by implementing in party terms a liberalism that seeks to do justice both to the religious dimension of political commitment, and to the just economic demands of a Marxist left.

Croce failed as a party leader to make much progress toward this end. He did succeed, though, in a more general approach to the problem. The Religion of Liberty, which Croce elaborated to his dying days with studies in literature, philosophy and history, was not something that would or could be defeated with the Italian electoral returns of the next decade or so. The flaws or inadequacies in his anti-Fascism (which gave rise to further polemics with Salvemini that added no dignity to either of the disputants) did not detract substantially from the richness of the legacy that he bequeathed his country. Croce's historicism may well lead to a *"tout comprendre c'est tout pardonner,"* as some of his critics then charged; but if the accusation carries weight, it is with respect to his treatment of other periods, not Fascism. On that score, in view of the old philosopher's claim that Mussolini was no more than an "adventurer," Fascism no more than a "passing weakness," it would be more plausible to charge Croce, not with an excess of understanding, but with an absolute paucity of it.

It was not these polemics, though, but the elaboration of his Religion of Liberty that absorbed Croce in his last years, and that religion, even when not recognized as such, still has much to offer Italians. In most respects it has far more to offer than the more orthodox aspects of Gramsci's Leninist-Marxist rival religion, which also failed to bind together intellectuals and non-intellectuals. To this day, Gramsci continues to be the official symbol, the most brilliant representative of the new Italian Marxism, but even before Croce's death, it was evident that perhaps Gramsci was not what Togliatti made him out to be, and that perhaps his Marxism was not as orthodox as had been believed. It required an enormous act of Marxist faith to believe that the highly centralized Communist Party was in any way the embodiment of Gramsci's vision of a democratic Marxist party in which a previously unrepresented peasantry and industrial proletariat were to determine party policy. In the light of Gramsci's earlier thought and of Togliatti's mode of maintaining discipline among intellectuals, it seemed plausible to many non-Communist admirers of Gramsci that his manuscripts and letters had indeed been carefully edited and censored before publication. It even seemed plausible, as some close ex-Communist associates alleged, that before dying, Gramsci had confided to intimates that he no longer considered himself a Communist.

The question of Gramsci's Marxist orthodoxy apart, however, by 1952, with the waning of that initial enthusiasm that had drawn many intellectuals to the party, the judgments on Gramsci from within the party were changing perceptibly. The Russians had never really approved of the great enthusiasm of Italians for Gramsci or his proposal for a revision of Lenin's empirio-criticism along Crocean idealistic lines; and by the 1950's, Italian Communist intellectuals were also beginning to have second thoughts. It did not seem very wise or prudent to consider Croce, as did Gramsci, the high point of the bourgeois philosophical culture of the times. True, Gramsci did offer Italian Marxism continuity and an autonomous tradition, but there was a real possibility that in working so much within the idealist tradition he had fallen into a *cul de sac*, that Italian Marxism had followed philosophical idealism to a dead end. Perhaps reform was needed in the philosophical basis of Leninist-Marxism; but if so, the argument ran in the 1950's, it was in a completely different direction from that suggested by Gramsci.

Criticism of this sort was pushed even further, of course, by readers of Gramsci who had never been of the Communist persuasion. Just as the idea of continuous development from Marx to Lenin appeared contrived, more or less obviously "ideological," so did the idea of a corresponding development from Labriola to Gramsci. Labriola had placed the whole emphasis on the priority of the industrial proletariat and that was sufficient (in spite of the stress some party intellectuals put on a passing admiring reference of Labriola to the Sicilian uprising of 1896) to keep Labriola as distinct and far removed from Gramsci as Marx was from Lenin. From the standpoint of these critics, Gramsci had little in common with Labriola beyond a few doctrinal essentials. But it was obvious to them as to others that the two, if they shared little else, shared the same weaknesses. Like Labriola, who saw Marxist adversaries as conscious or unconscious agents of the reaction (he had spread it about among his friends that vested interests had had a part in the Kautsky-Bernstein polemics of the late 1890's), Gramsci had trouble in believing in the good faith of opponents. He was not content, for example, to point out what was no doubt dubious Marxism in Turati, but let it be understood that in all likelihood the moderate Socialist was in the pay of the northern electrical trusts.

With respect to Croce, indeed, he went much further, and in doing so was far less persuasive than the Neapolitan Marxist of the 1890's. Labriola had been upset and distressed at Croce's "obtuseness" in not seeing the point of Marxist philosophy, but he never questioned Croce's motivation. According to Labriola, Croce believed in all good faith that we can know more than we actually can. Gramsci's explanation of Croce's anti-Marxism—that Croce was a conscious or unconscious pawn of southern agricultural interests— was several notches lower, and his notion that Croce was in effect a cowardly humanist like Erasmus (an affront to both Croce and the Renaissance thinker) was lower yet. Possibly Gramsci was right in arguing that Croce, in pursuing humanistic cosmopolitan culture, distracted some southern intellectuals from dedicating themselves to solving urgent economic-social problems of their region. It is likely, though, that those that were so easily dissuaded could not have been very strongly drawn to economic-social problems in the first place. Besides, by 1953, there was already at least one conspicuous Croce-oriented group in the South that dedicated itself completely to the economic-social problems of the region—that of Franco Campagna and his publication, *Nord e Sud.*

Aside from his interpretation of Croce, however, Gramsci left much to be desired in his elaboration of the central doctrine of class conflict, which Croce rightfully saw as the essence of Marxism. Gramsci's ultimate demonstration of that doctrine, indeed, was just as circular as Labriola's: modern society was explainable only in terms of the class conflict, and the class conflict alone explained modern society. The difference was all in the tonality of the demonstration. Gramsci's interpretation was less speculative in character and lacked Labriola's fascination for a deterministic philosophical system, but it was not more plausible. It was not a demonstration of the primacy and truth of Marxist "law," but a poetically powerful crystallization of the peasant stoic acceptance of struggle as the law of life, reminiscent of the world of the novelist Verga.

Gramsci no doubt was among the most perceptive observers of the Italy of his time. His observations, however, were not exclusively Marxist. The notion of the needed union of the peasantry and the industrial proletariat had been advanced long before Gramsci by the not very Marxist Salvemini. No one could quarrel with Gramsci's exposé of the hollowness of Fascist culture, but again, such criticism was not made by the Marxists alone. Croce had said quite honestly that "in reading the many opinions of Gramsci, I find myself in agreement with almost all, and perhaps with all of his opinions on men of letters of the times," and Croce could do so without subscribing to one single exclusively Marxist insight. Nor did one need to be Marxist to recognize, as did Gramsci, that in 1950 as in 1900, Croce was more concerned with preventing proletarian and peasant tendencies to revolt than with alleviating the conditions that gave rise to revolution—the dehumanizing character of modern industry and the plight of the southern economy. This deficiency in Croce was real, but it did not require the canons of Marxist economic determinism to recognize it.

The fact remained that in spite of the great political advances of Marxist parties in Italy, Marxism as a totalitarian creed with a demonstrable philosophical basis had its first and last great champion in Labriola. Croce's rebuttal of that Marxism was just as persuasive in the 1950's as it had been at the turn of the century, Gramsci notwithstanding. There were, of course, valid insights in Marx himself that Croce did not deal with, but in terms of Marxism as Labriola and Gramsci envisioned it, Croce's critique was unanswerable.

More persuasive than Gramsci's Marxist religion, Croce's Religion of Liberty continues today to be a strong rival to Italian Catholicism. There had never been a compact unity between intellectual Catholics and the mass of believers in Italy (in this sense all three religions are failures), and Catholicism has no thinker the equivalent of Croce, or for that matter of Gramsci. In certain quarters, such as Dossetti's group, there exists a bold, fresh commitment to Catholicism as a perpetually renewed dialogue between Christ and the world, with Christians and non-Christians; but even as late as the accession of Pope John XXIII to the Chair of Peter, that movement was in its mere beginnings.

Thus, as an operative conviction, as a general belief, Croce's Religion of Liberty is very much alive. While not primarily political, it has something particularly relevant to say for the political situation as it developed in Croce's last years, with the threat of polarization between a Christian Right and a Marxist Left with mutually exclusive "religious" claims. That polarization undid all the daring of Parri, as it undid Croce's dreams for the Liberal Party. A common ground was and still is urgently needed—a lasting basis on which Christian Democrats, moderate Liberals and Socialists can work together for the commonweal. Unity of action cannot be achieved by dismissing as ideology the contrasting religious dimensions of liberalism, Catholicism and Marxism, but by testing, prudently but boldly, in order to distinguish between religion that cannot allow of compromise, and politics that can.

In the furtherance of that end, Croce left Italians a long, valuable meditation on what could and could not be of use. This peculiar, unwitting contribution to the next decade's "opening to the Left," was not among the least of the riches he left his country.

XVII

THE OPENING TO THE LEFT

The best commentary on the failing power of the Christian Democrats and on the political unrest in Italy from the fall of De Gasperi until the decisive change of direction initiated in 1962, is the number of governments and prime ministers and the rapidity of their rise and fall during this period. In the five years between the elections of 1953 and those of 1958, five prime ministers succeeded each other. Giuseppe Pella, a Liberal-oriented economist, was prime minister from August 1953, to January 1954, when Amintore Fanfani succeeded him with a *monocolore* (one-party) government that lasted for only a month. Mario Scelba, an independent-minded Sicilian protégé of Sturzo, achieved some stability (remaining in power for sixteen months) by including Saragat's PSDI in the government, and his example was followed with even greater success by Antonio Segni, a professor of law from Sardinia, who for almost two years (from July 1955 to May 1957) headed a government that was further broadened to include not only Saragatians but Liberals as well. But his government, too, succumbed to pressures from both Right and Left, and his successor, Adone Zoli, again resorted to a *monocolore* Cabinet, managing to hold power for thirteen months.

With the exception of Fanfani, the Christian Democratic leaders of these years, known as the *dorotei*, had been members of De Gasperi's circle, though as a group they were a bit more to the right than he. Their unity by and large lay more in a common hostility to a leftist-oriented rival group within the party, the *morotei*, than in any common positive policy. The *dorotei* were by no means a caricature of conservative capitalism. (For Don Sturzo, indeed, who died in 1959, some were quite dangerously leftist.) They were convinced that De Gasperi had gone as far to the left as was feasible, and that, given the circumstances, the *morotei*, led by Fanfani and Aldo Moro, another southern professor of jurisprudence, advocated policies dangerous to party and country, imperiling the continued and rising prosperity that they, the *dorotei*, had nurtured in these years. Any further concessions to the Left, in the light of continuing close collaboration between the Communists and the old-line Socialists, amounted virtually to sabotage and treason. The Christian Democratic Party would lose ground, they charged, if they were highhanded in their dealings with the entire spectrum of the Right. De Gasperi's policy of being careful not to alienate indispensable anti-Socialist, anti-Communist allies, they were sure, was the only proper course.

Their accusations expressed some very popular convictions. Things were going quite well, according to the general persuasion, and in the prevailing prosperity the Christian Democrats would do well to refrain from making any radical changes, and to let Communists and Socialists run out of issues. Furthermore, in defending themselves against the Communists and Nenni's PSI Socialists, both seeking to bring down the government by attacks from without, by strikes and demonstrations, the government had every right to use tactics such as those of Scelba's *celeri*, riot police who effectively broke up demonstrations by charging into the crowds in jeeps at breakneck speed. Such measures were called for to check protests that were unjustified. Even though Pella's successful anti-inflationary measures, for example, temporarily slowed down the economy and made for increased unemployment, inflation *had* been checked. The economy *did* pick up again.

The prosperity issue was, then, the central point stressed by the *dorotei*, and they emphasized it with a vigor worthy of the most militant advocate of economic determinism. All through the 1950's, the economy sustained its momentum and continued to climb, and the *dorotei* used that prosperity to answer virtually all charges of the opposition, within and without the Christian Democratic Party.

It was not surprising, therefore that these claims goaded the Socialist Basso to complain in a moment of exasperation and rancor, that Italian capitalism was puny and sickly. It lacked all the essentials of a vigorously expanding capitalism. It had insufficient accumulated capital, no viable credit system, no spirit of initiative.

There was no adequate network of roads and communication facilities, and certainly no expanding domestic market. Post-Fascist capitalism in every way was old and tired, continuing to lean on the state for subsidies and aid for survival. In effect, Basso argued, there was nothing new under the sun.

Basso's diatribe was a refreshing counterpoint in years in which the exaltation of capitalism on purely technical grounds reached new heights; and it was interesting to note that at least one Socialist had inherited the spirit of Labriola, who more than fifty years before had bitterly lamented Italian capitalism's lack of scale and its petty pace. But Basso, like Labriola, let his bitterness run away with him. The *dorotei* were right and he was wrong: the economy *was* booming, and Italian capitalism *was* making prodigious progress. For the first time in modern Italian history, slightly more than half of the national income was based on industry, not agriculture; and the rise in the production of industrial essentials was noteworthy. Iron production in 1955 (1,343,000 tons) passed the high point of 1941. Output in steel rose to nearly five and a half million tons, and in aluminum to over 60,000 tons. The chemical, snythetic rubber and plastics industries set new records in production and profits, and automobile production, the internationally recognized symbol of affluence, passed the 230,000 mark by 1955. In oil and methane, the discovery of which revolutionized the Italian economy, progress was equally striking. In crude oil, production rose to 203,000 tons a year, and between 1951 and 1955 methane production rose from 966 million cubic meters to over three and a half billion cubic meters a year.

The picture, of course, had to be put into proper perspective relative to other European economies; but even then the Italian miracle was impressive. Italian private capitalism, which had to compete with state capitalism and foreign competition, was doing extremely well. Italian captains of industry had a right to feel that they were doing a good job, particularly in the light of a tax structure that badly needed overhauling, and a bureaucratic jungle that assured that only the most robust would survive.

By itself, however, the rising affluence could not solve the political problems of the country. Indeed, the boom was accompanied by heightened opposition from political adversaries and quite as much, and for the first time, from unions. Fascist "corporatism" had been made to order for industrial interests. Unions were stripped of their

only weapon (Fascist law forbade strikes) and were headed by leaders completely subservient to Fascist directives. In Fascist Italy,
then, Italian capitalists, unlike their counterparts in other parts of
Europe, had not learned the give and take of the management-labor
struggle that is an essential characteristic of a modern democracy.

The situation had not changed completely since the fall of
Fascism. Understandably, management preferred not to learn the
difficult skills of collective bargaining, and in all justice, industrialists had been given fresh justification for their anti-unionist spirit by
the fact that the country's strongest union, the CGIL, was led by
the dynamic and extremely competent Communist, Giuseppe De
Vittorio. Even De Gasperi, who had tried to follow a leftist-oriented policy, was adamant on the concessions to be made to unions.
In a polarized situation, the idea of neutral, unpolitical labor unions.
was out of the question, he argued, and the government—and im-
plicitly, industrialists—had to be particularly on their guard in dealing with the Communist-dominated CGIL, making as few concessions as possible.

Capital, of course, concurred completely with De Gasperi. In the
first years after the war, when negotiations for the renewal of contracts were set up on a national level between representatives of
Confindustria and Confiagricola, representing management, and the
CGIL, representing labor, the policy of Confindustria was very
clear-cut. The industrialists' representatives refused to bargain with
the Communist-led union, and were as intractable with respect to
the union's more moderate and sensible demands as they were with
respect to its most extreme ones, preferring to make one package
out of some very obviously disparate demands. In 1953, for example,
Confindustria absolutely refused to negotiate on *conglobamento*, the
compound factors that determined wages—base pay, family allowances, cost-of-living allowances. The representatives of Italian capitalism continued this policy even with the formation of the CISL,
the union that broke away from the CGIL and stressed its anti-
Communism and "non-political" nature. The CISL, especially in
its first years, was extremely reasonable in its relations with management, readily assenting to management's contention that there
were times when an increase in the wage scale could have catastrophic consequences in spiraling inflation that was to everyone's
disadvantage.

As long as the much weaker CISL continued in this stance and took no part in what it considered the CGIL's "political" strikes, the representatives of Confindustria ran into no big problems. It was relatively easy, under these circumstances, for management to drive some very hard bargains with the CISL and, in the midst of general prosperity, to minimize the political problem of two million unemployed. But in 1954, this very comfortable period for Confindustria was coming to an end. As head of the moderate union, Giulio Pastore concluded that CISL had become too vulnerable to charges of being a "company union," and that Confindustria was benefiting more than the CISL from the union's anti-Communism. Toward the end of 1953, consequently, he joined the CGIL and a minor third federation, the UIL, in strikes, and even played a leading part in them. In the following year he reaped his reward: Confindustria was ready to bargain and to come to a settlement with all three unions. Moreover, in 1955, the labor unions at Fiat, the aristocrats of labor in Gobetti's vision, broke from the stronger union and joined the CISL.

But under Pastore, the union's change in attitude was not restricted to its dealings with Confindustria. The union leader began to fashion a new and stronger policy with respect to the Christian Democratic Party, with which it was allied in a very unofficial, informal way. It was an open secret that Pella, because of his economic policies and his alleged sympathies for large landowners, was not acceptable to labor unions, and it was also an open secret that in calling for strikes during his tenure, CISL was acting to precipitate a crisis, to force Pella to step down. By 1954, a new situation prevailed in relations between the Christian Democratic Party, the CISL, and Confindustria—for the first time the new capitalism found that not all union problems could be settled by a tough anti-Communist policy, and the *dorotei* Christian Democrats found that the CISL was no more a "government union" than it was a "company union." The following year, too, CISL strikes protesting Segni's slow pace of reform helped hasten Saragat's decision to break with Segni and consequently helped to topple that government.

Labor-union strength, therefore, a new factor, was having its effect on Confindustria and on the center Christian Democratic group, and in particular on its alliance with Saragat, needed perhaps more than ever after the death of De Gasperi. But the repercussions were still more far-reaching with respect to the perpetual problem of the South.

In general, Christian Democratic policy toward the South had not changed under the *dorotei*. In spite of acknowledged blunders and shortcomings, and in spite of the political risks involved, the party renewed the Fund for the South, and indeed pressed on with programs of reform. Perhaps the Fund for the South did spend too much money to reclaim an unredeemable, arid hinterland, and no doubt bureaucrats had had a field day in the administration of the program. It was also true that many large landowners were more than amply compensated for lands expropriated by the state. But these shortcomings notwithstanding, and in spite of the disillusionment that invariably follows Utopian expectations, the Fund for the South had proven itself, and the question was no longer whether or not it should be continued, but rather the extent to which help should be increased. The *dorotei* felt that aid should be increased considerably, and toward this end helped pass the Vanoni Plan, that of the close friend and collaborator of Mattei who had previously reformed the tax structure and elaborated the first workable progressive income tax. The plan, basically concerned with a more equitable distribution of national wealth, sought to increase still further the role of the state in those areas where private intiative was not very active because of low returns. Over a ten-year period, by means of an austerity program, the investment of a higher percentage of the national income, and a policy which favored foreign investments, the Vanoni Plan sought to raise the national income by 5 per cent a year, and concurrently provide for four million new jobs that would wipe out unemployment. The implications of this plan for the South, with its recognition that as long as the South remained primarily agricultural its problems were virtually unsolvable, were obvious.

The IRI and the ENI, of course, had for some time been acting on the same assumption and toward the same end, and by the end of the fifties, had drawn up plans for a huge industrial complex in the South between Taranto, Brindisi and Bari that was to be the southern equivalent of the Genova-Turin-Milan triangle of the North. To facilitate the Vanoni Plan, the *dorotei* passed significant legislation to induce light industry to settle in the South (granting tax exemptions, cheap credit and the like), and special laws providing designated industrial development areas with roads, water and basic necessities almost entirely at the expense of the state. Another basic law required that 40 per cent of the investment capital of state-owned industries be invested in the South. Soon after the discovery of oil in Sicily, legislation was pushed through to allow joint exploration by government and private enterprise (largely American companies) and the areas near Catania and Siracusa took on the appearance of boom towns.

The Vanoni Plan, however, which quickly ran into stiff opposition and was never effectively implemented, required time for its effects, and in the meantime, the situation in the South continued to worsen. Prosperity continued to be largely limited to the industrial North, and the South's vast surplus of labor became increasingly restive. Land reform notwithstanding, great numbers of peasants continued to emigrate. The requirement that those who received land under the reform program were in some instances not to leave it for thirty years accelerated the emigration of the younger generation, and between 1951 and 1963, it has been estimated, some 750,000 emigrants left the South, most of them settling in the northern industrial triangle. The great waves of emigration that periodically swept the South, those figures emphasized, had not come to an end with the relative prosperity. The difference was that now the bulk of the emigration went North instead of leaving the country.

This made for a staggering problem. Even the boom was not enough: industrial expansion *had* to accelerate regularly to absorb the southern immigrants. According to the estimates of the economist Pasquale Saraceno in the early sixties, more than a million and a half new industrial jobs must be created in 1973 to absorb the immigrants if emigration proceeds at its foreseeable pace. In political terms the consequences of failure could be grim. Upon settling in the North, peasants who in the past deferred to the judgment of the local priest or the landowner when they voted, more often than not deferred to the judgment of the Communist Party, since that party offers more than any other group to the immigrant. Communist unions help find him a job, a place to live, friends; they give him a sense of "belonging." Paradoxically, the Communists, who failed to win over the peasantry in the South, are making great progress in capturing the loyalties of the "industrialized" peasant.

The prosperity issue, then, on which the *dorotei* and their supporters counted heavily, made for and did not settle political problems. Indeed, according to some Liberals and monarchists, that prosperity was more to the credit of Italian industry than to the credit of irresolute government, irresponsible labor unions and Communist blackmail; and from the Socialist and Communist point of view, it was nothing more than the continuation of a boom-and-bust economy that increased the profits of a few monopolies and let the problem of unemployment and the problem of the South remain largely on the planning board.

Caught in the crossfire of these charges, the *dorotei* could only repeat that as much progress was being made as was possible—an answer, of course, that satisfied none of their opponents. By 1956, therefore, the Christian Democrats' popularity was steadily decreasing, despite some very real achievements. Indeed, they were more and more considered an irritant, a government which maintained one-party rule and, like the Liberals of the 1890's, appeared impervious to any and all attacks. As the 1958 elections approached, the party's prospects were not bright, but the sudden outbreak of the Hungarian Revolt in late 1956 modified a good many things on the Italian political scene, including the growing hostility toward the Christian Democrats. The Russian intervention in Hungary had a shattering effect in Italy, which had the strongest Communist Party in Europe. There was little that Togliatti could do about the situation in Hungary or the way the Russians dealt with it; and for all of his protestations of the independence of Italian Communists, Togliatti, who was no Tito, did not condemn Russian intervention in Hungary. He followed the party line, and as a result, suffered his most serious reversal since he advanced the plan to resolve the problem of Trieste by striking a bargain with Tito. A substantial number of Italian Communist intellectuals left the party and, most serious, many pro-Communist Socialists, including Nenni (who had shortly before received the Stalin Peace Prize) broke their close ties to Togliatti's party. Domestic issues were temporarily forgotten, a war mood swept over the country, and since many Italians remembered that at the height of the debates on the Atlantic Pact, Togliatti had declared that in case of war Italian Communists would not hestiate to fight alongside of the Russians in Italy, there were numerous clashes throughout the peninsula between Communists and anti-

Communists, and demonstrations and counterdemonstrations galore.

In a Europe seemingly on the brink of war, the increasing dissatisfaction with the Christian Democrats' domestic policy seemed a
small matter. The conviction grew that in the coming showdown
there was no point in giving the vote to any but the strongest anti-
Communist party. The Suez crisis, which followed soon after,
heightened this mood. It seemed even more certain that the political
struggle had once again reached a confrontation between communism and anti-communism.

Despite these dramatic developments and the return of a part of
Trieste to Italy (the great achievement of Christian Democratic
foreign policy in 1953), there were still many Italians, as the results
of the national elections of 1958 showed, who found it hard to
suppress strong feelings against the ruling party, and preferred to
find other ways to express their anti-communism than by support-
ing the Christian Democrats. The Christian Democrats won again
by a sizeable majority—twelve million votes, two million more than
in 1953—and they captured 273 seats in the Chamber of Deputies; in
the North the party won more than six million votes, and it went
ahead steadily in central and southern Italy. But the rest of the
election results provided a number of surprises.

The Communists were not very badly beaten at all. They ran
second again in Lombardy, Piedmont, and Liguria; they still won in
Emilia, and they advanced also in central and southern Italy. In all,
Togliatti's party won over six and a half million votes and dropped
only slightly in their representation in the Chamber of Deputies, to
140 seats.

In the North, moreover, there was a new development, the phenomenon of Liberal strength. For with the 1958 election that party,
winning more than 500,000 northern votes, ceased to be a party of
the South. With its total national vote of slightly over a million, it
approached the strength of the PSDI, which won 1,345,000 votes.
In the South, the elections marked a slight neo-Fascist advance and
the beginnings of the break-up of the monarchist vote with a schism
in their ranks. The new PMP (*Partito Monarchico Popolare*) of
Achille Lauro, a wealthy Neapolitan shipowner, won 440,000 votes,
and the PNM was reduced to some 220,000.

The decisive aspect of the election, however, did not lay in the
surprising strength shown by the defeated Communists or in the

rapid progress of the Liberals, or in the stationary position of the PSDI. The surprise was the showing of the old-line Socialists, for that party won an increase of almost a million votes and its representation rose to 84 seats. As a Socialist party numerically it towered more impressively than ever over Saragat's group.

In the light of this new distribution of political strength, a continuation of the rule of the *dorotei* presented all sorts of difficulties. Both Right and Left were stronger; both Liberals and Saragatians demanded a higher price for collaboration, and there was no one strong personality among the *dorotei* willing or able to find the needed support for something resembling a stable Cabinet. The situation obviously—and especially considering the increase in PSI strength—prepared the way for the accession to power of the *morotei*, who were more or less committed to working with the Socialists. But they came to power only after a parliamentary impasse (in which all parties were to a greater or lesser degree responsible for their doctrinal intransigence) was climaxed by the short-lived government of Ferdinando Tambroni. Before Tambroni, Segni had headed a government (February 1959 to February 1960) with the support of the Liberals, both monarchist parties, and the neo-Fascists. But Tambroni's *monocolore* Cabinet was supported in Parliament by only one outside group, the neo-Fascists.

This was a startling development. During the impasse, while Liberals and Saragatians held out against collaboration and *morotei* and *dorotei* fought each other, the Fascists, or so it seemed, making the most of party divisions and irreconcilable party demands, had slipped back into a position of some power and won a decisive say in the government. For outraged Socialists and Communists, this was the last proof that the Christian Democrats were crypto-Fascists and for the Liberals and monarchists this was the dead end to which the monopoly of power had brought the Christian Democrats, the point the party had been driven to in order to defend itself against Communists and Socialists. Some fourteen years after World War II, it seemed, Fascism, though insignificant as a party, was once more a threat. For those who remembered the impasse of the early 1920's that had played such a large part in Mussolini's takeover, the moment was terrifying. Up to now those Italians were aware that a degree of Fascism was behind a good deal of the anti-Communist, anti-labor, anti-pluralistic party feeling—the deep persuasion that anything was better than the undisciplined, disorderly state without any firm authority to regulate all—but few had expected to witness, so soon after the collapse of Fascism, another political verification of that mood. The Tambroni government was the expression of that "other Italy" with no taste for the pluralistic party Italy. And that "other Italy," it appeared, was as strong as the politically conscious party Italy, which had brought the country to this impasse.

Despite the ominous aspect of this development, it was not true that Italy had come full-circle politically, and was again approaching Fascism. Fascism was inconceivable without a forceful leader and a propitious historical situation; there was no one strong leader among the *Missini*, no one with a national following, and conditions in the country and in Parliament were altogether different from those that had prevailed in the years in the 1920's.

Not all *dorotei*, certainly, were happy with the Tambroni government. Some looked upon it as a desperate solution to an impossible situation; and no leader among them thought even distantly of aiding and abetting the Fascists, as Giolitti had before he recognized the scope of their ambitions. There was, furthermore, no pervasive want of confidence in Parliament, no popular sentiment that the only meaningful political action had to be outside of Parliament. There were no armed Fascist bands, no collusion between Fascists and local governments. About the only real similarity between 1922–25 and the sudden re-emergence of Fascist strength was a polarized situation between the Catholics on one hand and the Socialists and Communists on the other; and the Hungarian revolt had perceptibly modified the position of the Socialists in that polarization. Lastly (and this showed how utterly different the times were) the neo-Fascists in 1960 were caught in the white glare of hostile publicity and had no chance at all, as Mussolini and his followers had had, of coming to power almost surreptitiously.

Nonetheless, the fact remained that it was unnerving to have a Christian Democrat *monocolore* Cabinet relying on the parliamentary support of the Fascists and only the Fascists. There were still many Italians, after all, with very vivid memories of partisan warfare and of the Republic of Salò with its *Bande Nere;* and when the Fascists in 1960 designated Genoa, a stronghold of Communists and Socialists, as the site of their annual Congress, the move was taken for what it was, a challenge, and the response was immediate and

violent. Genoa became the scene of demonstrations and clashes between *Missini* and Socialists and Communists, and the situation became so tense that the mayor of the city was forced to ask that the
Congress be held elsewhere. A wave of demonstrations and violence
then swept through the peninsula, and a general strike called by the
Communists resulted in some eleven deaths. Balked and furious at
Tambroni for not intervening in their behalf, the neo-Fascists withdrew their support from his government and in July, after four
months in office, he stepped down.

The fall of Tambroni was a definitive blow to the dwindling
fortunes of the Christian Democratic Right. It was obvious that a
right-oriented policy, with or without an alliance with the PSDI,
had exhausted its possibilities. This was the hour of the *morotei*,
whose only notable success in the post-war years had been the election of Giovanni Gronchi to the presidency in 1955, with the indispensable aid of Socialist and Communist votes; fittingly, Fanfani
headed the new government that took office in July 1960. The
morotei were the only Christian Democratic group capable of elicit-
ing enough support from other parties, and Fanfani managed to win
for his *monocolore* Cabinet the parliamentary support of not only
Saragat's PSDI and the Republicans, but somehow even that of the
Liberals. In the not very auspicious beginnings, every step Fanfani
took was an extremely cautious one. But in a wide sense, the political atmosphere of the 1960's could not have been more propitious for
the *morotei*, for things had been changing for almost two years,
since John XXIII acceded to the chair of Peter.

In the last years of his pontificate, Pope Pius XII had been too
sick and exhausted to dedicate as much of his time and energies to
Italian matters as he had previously. It was known, though, that
the austere, ascetic Pontiff had rejoiced in the Christian Democratic
victory of 1958, and that particularly after the Hungarian revolt, his
main preoccupation had been to find the energies with which to
battle communism until the end. He had spent himself in this work,
and in his declining years there was certainly nothing to indicate
that he would have given wholehearted approval to any plan of left-
wing Christian Democrats to draw closer to the Socialists.

His successor, who smiled much more often than Pius XII, was in
an altogether different position. Cardinal Roncalli had not been
known primarily as a great diplomat, and indeed there were very

few Italians who had any real idea of his political leanings. But even before he took a specific political stand, the whole tenor of his pontificate affected the political situation. The style of Pope John's Christianity was fresh and even startling, and for him religious convictions became politics in the highest sense. "It will take the Church fifty years," one cardinal remarked, "to repair the damage." That opinion was not confined to conservative prelates. John's awareness of the need of the Church to be more catholic (and that obviously was the point of calling the ecumenical council) had its repercussions on the political climate of his years in the papacy. Most Italians were not aware of any such need, and as a group they did not feel that relations with Jews, Protestants and unbelievers needed to be improved. In underlining the need for coexistence and cooperation among differing groups, and breaking out of the mold of hardened attitudes, Pope John rendered Italy a signal political service, as important and decisive as any move on the Italian political checkerboard during these years. The Pope's ecumenical work was an immense work, of course, the political impact of which may not be felt for several generations; but in a narrow but very real sense that work was a practical schooling for a most difficult political maneuver, the *apertura a sinistra* (opening to the left), toward which the *morotei* and Nenni's Socialists were quietly working. Even then, this radical change appeared to be the only way out of a situation that was rapidly being ringed about with signs reading "no exit."

Pope John's invaluable contribution acquired a sharper contour with the publication of his most celebrated encyclical on politics, *Mater et magistra*, in 1961. In a number of ways this encyclical, so unusual in its absence of anathemas, was more relevant to contemporary Catholic political thought in Italy and elsewhere than any that preceded it. Even with its generic language, it came out with an unequivocal condemnation of *laissez-faire* economics, a condemnation to warm the hearts of Catholics who had pondered on the lesson given by De Gasperi. In an industrial society, the encyclical taught, "just as wages cannot be regulated only by laws of a market economy, neither can they be fixed arbitrarily; they ought to be determined according to justice and fairness." For Pope John, economic progress unaccompanied by social progress was not progress at all.

The same sentiments, of course, were to be found in *Rerum novarum* in 1891, but Italian readers who still had hopes for the radical reform of capitalism noticed that there was a distinctly sharper edge to certain views. Industry "could not reduce its daily collaborators to the level of simple, silent executors of orders without any possibility of having their experience become something of value, entirely passive with respect to decisions that govern their activities." There was also, again very relevant to the Italian situation, an approval of the entire program of De Gasperi, of the IRI and of the Fund for the South implicit in Pope John's defense of socialization as a good which worked toward an equitable distribution of goods and services, and implicit in his defense of the duty of the industrial sector of economies to offer substantial aid to the invariably weaker agricultural sector. Even more important was the encyclical's view of the future. The Pontiff did not believe that technology was pushing the world toward an increasing depersonalization, that man would become subject to machines. He made a tranquil act of faith that this would not come to pass.

The Pope's views on the problems of peace in *Pacem in terris* of 1963, published two months before he died, were equally fresh and no doubt equally disconcerting for many, believers and non-believers, who had concluded that to take the initiative for peace was to allow oneself to be used as an *"utile idiota"* by the Communist propaganda apparatus. Coming not too long after the Hungarian revolt, and especially in a country in which uncompromising anti-communism had become the *sine qua non* of Christian Democratic policy, accounting for some of its worst blunders and miscalculations, the views expressed in *Pacem in terris* prepared the way for a slow change in climate, for the relaxation of tensions that was absolutely indispensable for any progress in building understanding between *morotei* and Socialists.

Thus Pope John XXIII, with his immense personal popularity, unmatched in the recent history of the papacy, and with ecumenical views that were as applicable to the political as to the theological sphere, bolstered prodigiously the position of the *morotei* and of all groups working with them—including, significantly, a good part of Catholic Action, which had changed radically in outlook since the high point of Gedda's power. It was the first time that a political move to the left had been sanctioned by the papacy, and certainly the first time the papacy had directly inspired part of its theoretical basis for a party based on Christian principles, willing to work with those of differing views. The timing of Pope John's contribution was also well chosen; a more "prudent" pontiff would no doubt have waited for a more "propitious" time, a safer political climate in which to manifest his views.

Favored by John XXIII's teaching and practice, the *morotei* in Fanfani's administration had some very concrete issues to work on together with the Socialists, issues on which there already was substantial agreement. Both Socialists and *morotei* wanted a continued expansion of aid to the South through the Fund for the South and the Vanoni Plan. They also wanted to take up the work of regional autonomy, which, after an initial firm commitment and planning, had been perpetually postponed. They were similarly united on the nationalization of a number of industries, in particular the electrical industry, a move that was strongly opposed by the *dorotei* and above all by the Liberals.

From Nenni's point of view, however (and for the purposes of collaboration Nenni and Socialism were synonymous, since he was the most pragmatic of Socialists and, particularly after the Hungarian revolt, the Socialist leader most interested in collaboration), agreements in theory were idle as long as the Christian Democrats offered no tangible evidence of their willingness to pass mutually acceptable measures. Fanfani took the necessary step. After a second and last reshuffling of his Cabinet in February 1962, with Liberals protesting that Italy was being transformed into a Poland or Yugoslavia, and with Socialists in Parliament abstaining (the best Nenni could do, since feeling in the party against the infamous compromise of "state socialism" was still strong), the Prime Minister pushed through the most hotly debated bill of his administration, the nationalization of the electrical industry.

For the purposes of the *apertura a sinistra*, Fanfani and the *morotei* could do no more. They were fairly united among themselves, in spite of a strong rivalry between Fanfani and Moro; they had a benevolently disposed Pontiff; they had enough power to push through Parliament a very controversial measure; but at this point the rest was up to Nenni. And Nenni's task within the PSI was no easier than that of the *morotei* within the Christian Democratic Party, for the left wing in the old-line Socialist Party was still strong. Indignation at the Russian suppression of the Hungarian revolt understandably led to a change in the Socialist policy of a common front with the Communists on matters of foreign policy; but to abruptly switch from a pro-Russian foreign policy to a generally pro-American one—an indispensable condition laid down by the *morotei*—was no easy reversal. It was one thing to be anti-Russian, another to be pro-American; and in arguing for such a radical change on grounds of convenience and principle, Nenni sparked a civil war in the party with the old Morandi-Basso faction and its substantial following. To Nenni's good fortune, Morandi died suddenly in 1955, long before the struggle reached its high point. Yet even with this development, Nenni had a very tough fight on his hands, for Basso and his sympathizers were a power to be reckoned with.

Nenni was regarded with increasing suspicion by the left wing of his party since 1955, when he had met with Saragat for a conference on eventual Socialist unification, and by 1960, the temper of the debates within the PSI were reminiscent of those between Communists and Socialists in exile during the Fascist era. Now, however, the polemics were within the party, and the Communist charge of *petit bourgeois* betrayal of Marxist-Leninism was leveled by the Socialist Basso against the Socialist Nenni. The arguments were furious and interminable, and in justice to Basso, he could not be accused of advocating a servile policy toward Italian Communists who were consistently deferential to Russian directives. Yet although the left-wing leader saw the dangers, he was not able, any more than Morandi, to fashion a policy that could maintain the independence of the Socialists while working very closely with Togliatti's party.

It was precisely this dilemma, in fact, that accounted for Nenni's victory in the struggle. No doubt there was something upsetting, if not ignominious, in the required turn-about in foreign policy, and there was in Nenni a very practical politician with a flair for pragmatic considerations; but the fact remained that Nenni's arguments were compelling. Russian communism *had* become less and less of an ideal for most Socialists, and the attempt to work closely with Communists but independently of them had *not* worked. The Christian Democrats, in spite of their weaknesses, had managed to keep the Communists, the country's second-largest party, out of the government for more than a decade, and there was every reason to believe that as long as Socialist policy remained generally pro-Communist, the ruling party would treat Socialists in the same way. The *apertura a sinistra*, therefore, Nenni argued, was the one hope, a coalition with the Christian Democrats was the one way in which the Socialist Party could break out of the impasse and work toward its goals, for it could not be denied that in domestic policies the *morotei* and moderate Socialists saw eye to eye on many matters.

The argument was persuasive, and when Nenni was able to substantiate his claims with Fanfani's display of good faith in the passage of the legislation nationalizing electricity, he carried the day. Both parties had reached the point of no return, and indeed, even after the setback registered in the elections of 1963, the movement toward collaboration continued to accelerate on both sides.

Those election results spelled out very clearly that the electorate at large had no great enthusiasm for the *morotei* and for Nenni's Socialists. There were no surprises in traditional strongholds, but there was a drop in the Christian Democratic popular vote to some 11,700,000 (260 seats) and a slight rise in the Communist vote to 7,700,000 (166 seats); the Socialists' vote was stationary at four million (87 seats). Most damaging for the opening to the left, Liberal strength, particularly in the North, rose prodigiously (they won 39 seats to the 17 they had won in 1958), and in central and southern Italy, though the two monarchist parties virtually disappeared from the national scene, Communists made steady progress.

The elections of 1963 revealed that both the Communists and the Liberals had gained strength and both, though for utterly different reasons, needless to say, vied with each other in their denunciations of the idea of a center-left coalition, which they felt sure would bring the country to ruin.

The setback at the polls was grave enough to force Fanfani to step down, but by May, Aldo Moro won approval to form a new government, and Nenni took his place as deputy prime minister. For the first time since 1947, old-line Socialists and Christian Democrats shared the responsibilities of government.

The political history of Italy from that time to ours is the history of the opening to the left. There have been many moments when it seemed that the coalition government was about to collapse, that it

could not survive the divisions within it or the attacks from without. The center-left, however, has shown that it is far more resilient
than was believed. In one way or another, it has survived scandals,
an economic recession and the unremitting attempts of Liberals and
Communists to convince Italians that any other government would
be preferable to this impure hybrid, this trasformismo that dwarfs
any trasformismo of the past.

In surviving, the coalition government has posed a number of
pivotal questions for itself and for the opposition. The future of the
new Italy depends on the answers. With respect to the Socialists,
the center-left collaboration has precipitated a Marxist crisis such as
has never been experienced in Italy, and in contrast to which the
crisis of Marxism of the 1890's is a puny thing indeed. As long as
Socialist schisms were limited in size and scope, as they were with
Bissolati's and Bonomi's groups and later with that of Saragat, the
Italian Socialist Party could dismiss them somewhat nonchalantly
and not even bother very much to elaborate its doctrinal dissent.
But when the main core of the Socialist Party joins the "deviationist" Socialist parties, a number of consequences cannot be avoided.
Under such circumstances, Socialist collaboration implies that most
Marxist Socialists no longer believe in the traditional Marxist thesis
that the state is irremediably corrupt. They no longer consider the
class conflict the be-all and end-all of the political struggle. In a
word, they renounce the totalitarian aspect of Marxism, and are
quite willing to let that aspect of socialism fall entirely and exclusively to the Communist Party. In a word, the collaboration of the
PSI with the Christian Democrats logically called for their reunification with Saragat's party, a unification that has most recently come
about.

The Communist Party, as a consequence, is caught in a very
difficult position. Under Togliatti it maneuvered brilliantly, but
after his death the Communist leader's political testament showed
how much he had chafed under Russian direction of the Italian
Communist Party. Still, in his lifetime Togliatti did not find it in
him to set up an autonomous Italian Communist Party, and there is
no evidence that today his heir, Luigi Longo, is so inclined. In this
sense, the Achilles' heel of Italian communism is more exposed
today than ever. This weakness is not simplified by the party's
retention of its totalitarian or "religious" heritage, which has no

thinker of stature to defend it today. Communists have suggested all
sorts of amplifications and emendations of their basic tenets, but
such changes remain in the discussion stage. Togliatti, for example,
took enormous pains to remove from the party the onus of being an
atheist party, tirelessly arguing that there was nothing intrinsically
anti-religious in communism, but that it fought religion only when
religion became the tool of vested interests. To be completely persuasive, however, the argument would have to be reinforced by
Russian approval, and again and again, while Italian Communists
have tentatively probed toward coexistence with the Church, Moscow has taken a very tough, uncompromisingly anti-religious stand.
Similarly, Italian Communists have gone to great pains to explain
how authentically democratic Italian Communist society could
eventually be, how free of any type of coercion of artists and intellectuals, and at the same time they have had to contend with a
Russian political apparatus that allows only a bare minimum of dissent and does not hesitate to use repressive measures of varying
degrees and subtlety. There are numerous points of doctrinal Marxist-Leninism on which Italian Communists run into similar troubles.
The most exasperating problem is that no matter how much Italian
Communists might be tempted to jettison the whole Marxist-Leninist heritage, they cannot, since they dread that they would thereby
make the party superfluous.

For the Communists to remain compact and united, therefore,
they will be forced to a large extent to hold on to an ideology in
which most adherents of the party do not believe. There is every
reason to believe that for a long time the party will continue to win
a large number of votes—protest votes alone are enough to assure a
degree of success in the foreseeable future. But in all probability, its
leadership will decline, for at best, that leadership will only be able
to mouth what were once intense convictions with Gramsci and
Labriola, and to succeed only with the least politically alert and
sophisticated groups. To survive as a totalitarian Marxist party, Italian Communists will be forced more and more to deck themselves
with the plumage of the past in order to conceal the poverty of the
present. The prospect is not one that particularly distresses world-
weary, disillusioned intellectuals, a type that abounds in Italy today
—for them, in a false world the falsity of Communism is, inexplica-
bly, preferable to others. Nor does it distress political hacks. But it is

hard to see how it can ever draw to the party men of the spirit and stature of Gramsci and Labriola.

But the Socialists, too (and as of 1966, reunification with Saragat's group is a reality), will also have to put their house in order. The monumental common sense of Nenni notwithstanding, Socialists will have to be on particular guard against succumbing completely to pragmatic trasformismo. They will have to further elaborate the fundamental assumptions that separate them from the Christian Democrats and make clear what Marxist and Socialist outlook gives their party the consistency and structure without which political parties in Italy crumble.

Much the same can be said of the Liberals. If they continue the endless elaboration of the apocalyptic consequences of nationalization, their righteous denunciation of the proliferation of bureaucracy and, paradoxically, their opposition to regional autonomy, they too, like the Communists, will for a foreseeably long time find voters, but not a young, inspired leadership.

The Christian Democrats will also have to work out some of the insistent consequences of the opening to the left. As long as Communists remain a compact, united party, it is unlikely that Catholics in politics will think seriously of forming more than one party. But just as the Liberals, to survive, will sooner or later have to advocate something more than a variant of economic liberalism, so Catholics will have to consider seriously the dangers of succumbing to a trasformismo reminiscent of that of the 1890 Liberals, in which moves to the right or left were but means of assuring self-perpetuation in power. Catholics will also have to give increasing thought to the desirability of solving church-state differences on some basis other than that of the Concordat, which in the future could well cause more friction than it has in the past.

These are some of the immediate consequences implied in the opening to the left. It will take years, though, to know whether the experiment will succeed, and in the meantime, Italy, in a very real sense, will hang in the balance. There is the possibility that the demands made by the center-left will be too strenuous for Italians in an increasingly affluent society. It is possible that, instead of working to resolve exhaustingly intricate issues that keep parties apart, they might yet prefer political conformity, a subtle form of neo-Fascism of either Liberal or Communist coloring. But there is also a good chance that Italians will recognize that, of all alternatives, the opening to the left is by far the most meaningful, that the present coalition of parties has the best chance to deal equitably with the problems of church and state, decentralization, the South, the form of capitalism and labor unions—problems that have shaped the history of Italian politics and parties for over a century. The election of Saragat to the presidency after President Segni (who succeeded Gronchi in 1962) stepped down for reasons of health, is a good step in this direction. Should the *apertura a sinistra* succeed in solving such tangled and unique problems, it would be a remarkable accomplishment, in many respects more remarkable than the Risorgimento itself, when so many disparate elements were implausibly woven into one surprisingly resilient national state.

BIBLIOGRAPHY

The following is skeletal bibliography for the reader who would like to check certain facts, consider divergent interpretations, or just browse. The author would have preferred to list more books in English, but since there is a great deal in the field that has not yet been translated, he has listed indispensable works that are not available in English with the hope that a dictionary or two and abundant good will might combine to do wonders.

I. General Histories of the Period

BONOMI, IVANOE. *La politica italiana da Porta Pia a Vittorio Veneto, 1870–1918.* Turin: Einaudi, 1946.

CHABOD, FEDERICO. *L'Italia contemporanea (1918–1948).* Turin: Einaudi, 1961.

GRINDROD, MURIEL. *The Rebuilding of Italy, 1945–1955.* London: Royal Institute of International Affairs, 1955.

MACK SMITH, DENIS. *Italy; A Modern History.* Ann Arbor: The University of Michigan Press, 1959.

MAMMARELLA, GIUSEPPE. *Italy after Fascism; A Political History.* Notre Dame, Indiana: Notre Dame University Press, 1965.

NOLTE, ERNST. *Three Faces of Fascism.* New York: Holt, Rinehart and Winston, 1966.

SALAMONE, ARCANGELO W. *Italian Democracy in the Making, 1900–1914.* New York: Oxford University Press, 1960.

SALVATORELLI, LUIGI and GIOVANNI MIRA. *Storia d'Italia nel periodo fascista.* Turin: Einaudi, 1957.

VALERI, NINO. *Da Giolitti a Mussolini.* Florence: Le Monnier, 1956.

——. *Lotta politica in Italia dall'unità al 1925.* Florence: Le Monnier, 1945.

II. More Specialized Histories

ALATRI, P. *Origini del Fascismo.* Rome: Editori Riuniti, 1956.

BERSELLI, ALDO. *La destra storica.* Bologna: Il Mulino, 1965.

BISSOLATI, LEONIDA. *La politica estera dell'Italia dal 1897 al 1920.* Milan: Treves, 1927.

CATALANO, FRANCO. *Storia del CLNAI.* Bari: Laterza, 1956.

CHABOD, FEDERICO. *Storia della politica estera italiana.* 2 vol. Bari: Laterza, 1965.

CORBINO, EPICARMO. *L'economia italiana dal 1860 al 1960.* Bologna: Zanichelli, 1962.

COMPAGNA, FRANCESCO. *Lotta politica nel secondo dopoguerra e il mezzogiorno.* Bari: Laterza, 1950.

DEGLI ESPINOSA, AGOSTINO. *Il Regno del Sud; 8 Settembre, 1943 – 4 Giugno, 1944.* Rome: Migliaresi, 1946.

DELZELL, CHARLES F. *Mussolini's Enemies; The Anti-Fascist Resistance.* Princeton: Princeton University Press, 1961.

DENKIN, F. W. *The Brutal Friendship.* New York: Harper and Row, 1962.

DIPIERO, MICHELE. *Storia critica dei partiti italiani.* Rome: Internazionale, 1946.

GRINDROD, MURIEL. *The New Italy.* London: Royal Institute of International Affairs, 1947.

HOSTETTER, R. *The Italian Socialist Movement.* Princeton: Van Nostrand, 1958.

HUGHES, H. S. *The United States and Italy.* Cambridge, Mass.: Harvard University Press, 1953.

KOGAN, NORMAN. *The Government of Italy.* New York: Crowell, 1962.

———. *Politics of Italian Foreign Policy.* New York: Praeger, 1963.

LA PALOMBARA, JOSEPH. *The Italian Labor Movement; Problems and Prospects.* Ithaca: Cornell University Press, 1957.

LOTTI, LUIGI. *La Settimana Rossa.* Florence: Le Monnier, 1966.

MALVEZZI, P. and G. PIRELLI, ed. *Lettere dei condannati a morte della Resistenza.* 8th ed. Turin: Einaudi, 1953.

MANZOTTI, FERNANDO. *Il socialismo riformista in Italia.* Florence: Le Monnier, 1965.

MORANDI, CARLO. *I partiti politici nella storia d'Italia.* 9th ed. Florence: Le Monnier, 1965.

ROMANO, S. F. *Storia dei fasci siciliani.* Bari: Laterza, 1959.

ROMEO, ROSARIO. *Breve storia della grande industria in Italia.* Bologna: Cappelli, 1961.

ROMITA, G. *Dalla Monarchia alla Repubblica.* Pisa: Nistri-Lischi, 1959.

SALVADORI, MASSIMO. *Brief History of the Patriot Movement in Italy, 1943–1945.* Chicago: Clements and Sons, 1954.

SPADOLINI, G. *Lotta sociale in Italia.* Florence: Vallecchi, 1948.

——. *I radicali dell'Ottocento* (*da Garibaldi a Cavallotti*). Florence: Le Monnier, 1963.

TREMELLONI, ROBERTO. *Storia dell'industria italiana contemporanea.* Turin: Einaudi, 1947.

VALIANI, L. *L'avvento di De Gasperi.* Florence: Sansoni, 1949.

——. *Dall'antifascismo alla Resistenza.* Milan: Feltrinelli, 1959.

ZANGRANDI, RUGGERO. *Il lungo viaggio attraverso il fascismo.* Milan: Feltrinelli, 1962.

III. On the History and Problems of Italian Socialism

ARFÉ, GAETANO. *Storia dell'Avanti!* Rome: Editori Avanti, 1956.

BULFERETTI, L. *Le ideologie socialistiche in Italia nell'età del positivismo evoluzionistico, 1870–1892.* Florence: Le Monnier, 1951.

——. *Introduzione alla storiografia socialistica in Italia.* Florence: Le Monnier, 1949.

FROSINI, VITTORIO. *Breve storia della critica al marxismo in Italia.* Catania: Bonanno, 1966.

HILTON-YOUNG, WAYLAND. *The Italian Left: A Short History of Political Socialism in Italy.* New York: Longmans, Green, 1949.

LOVECCHIO, ANTONINO. *Il marxismo in Italia.* Milan: Bocca, 1952.

MICHELS, ROBERT. *Storia critica del movimento socialista italiano dagli inizi fino a 1911.* Florence: "La Voce," 1926.

ROMANO, ALDO. *Storia del movimento socialista in Italia.* Milan: Bocca, 1956.

VALIANI, LEO. *Questioni di storia del socialismo.* Turin: Einaudi, 1950.

——. *Storia del movimento socialista.* Florence: La Nuova Italia, 1951.

IV. On Church-State Relations

BINCHY, D. A. *Church and State in Fascist Italy.* London: Oxford University Press, 1941.

FALCONI, CARLO. *La Chiesa e le organizzazioni cattoliche in Italia, 1945–1955.* Turin: Einaudi, 1956.

HOWARD, EDITH PRATT. *Il Partito Popolare Italiano.* Firenze: La Nuova Italia, 1957.

JEMOLO, ARTURO CARLO. *Chiesa e stato in Italia negli ultimi cento anni.* 4th ed. Turin: Einaudi, 1955.

WEBSTER, RICHARD A. *The Cross and the Fasces.* Stanford: Stanford University Press, 1960.

V. On Problems of the South and Regionalism

COMPAGNA, F. *Labirinto meridionale*. Venice: Neri Pozza, 1955.

GALASSO, GIUSEPPE. *Mezzogiorno medievale e moderno*. Turin: Einaudi, 1965.

RODANÒ, CARLO. *Mezzogiorno e sviluppo economico*. Bari: Laterza, 1954.

SALVEMINI, GAETANO. *Scritti sulla questione meridionale*. Bari: Laterza, 1955.

SERENI, EMILIO. *Il capitalismo nelle campagne (1860–1900)*. Turin: Einaudi, 1947.

VI. Writings of the Leading Thinkers in this Study

CROCE, BENEDETTO. *Conversazioni critiche* (serie prima), 3rd ed. Bari: Laterza, 1942.

——. *Croce, the King and the Allies; Extracts from a Diary, July, 1943–June, 1944*. New York: Norton, 1950.

——. *Due anni di vita politica italiana, 1946–1947*. Bari: Laterza, 1948.

——. *Historical Materialism and the Economics of Karl Marx*. New York: Macmillan, 1914.

——. *History, its Theory and Practice*. New York, Russell and Russell, 1960.

——. *History of Europe in the Nineteenth Century*. New York: Harcourt, Brace and Co., 1933.

——. *A History of Italy, 1871–1915*. Oxford: Clarendon, 1929.

——. *History as the Story of Liberty*. London: Allen and Unwin, 1941.

——. *Philosophy, Poetry and History; an Anthology of Essays*. New York: Oxford University Press, 1966.

——. *Politics and Morals*. New York: Philosophical Library, 1945.

GOBETTI, PIERO. *Rivoluzione Liberale*. Turin: Einaudi, 1948.

GRAMSCI, ANTONIO. *Gli intellettuali e l'organizzazione della cultura*. Turin: Einaudi, 1949.

——. *Letteratura e vita nazionale*. Turin: Einaudi, 1950.

——. *Lettere dal carcere*. Turin: Einaudi, 1947.

——. *Il materialismo storico e la filosofia di Benedetto Croce*. Turin: Einaudi, 1948.

——. *The Modern Prince and Other Writings*. London: Lawrence and Wishart Ltd., 1957.

——. *Note sul Machiavelli, sulla politica e sullo stato moderno*. Turin: Einaudi, 1949.

——. *L'Ordine Nuovo (1919–1920)*. Turin: Einaudi, 1955.

——. *Passato e presente*. Turin: Einaudi, 1951.

——. *Il Risorgimento*. Turin: Einaudi, 1949.

LABRIOLA, ANTONIO. *Essays on the Materialistic Conception of History*. Chicago: C. H. Kerr and Co., 1904.

——. *Scritti varii di filosofia e politica*. Bari: Laterza, 1906.

——. *Socialism and Philosophy*. Chicago: C. H. Kerr & Co., 1912.

ROSSELLI, CARLO. *Socialismo liberale*. Milan: Giustizia e Libertà, 1945.

SOREL, GEORGES. *L'avenir socialiste des syndicats*. Paris: Jacques, 1901.

——. *Réflexions sur la violence*, 10th ed., followed by the *Plaidoyer pour Lenine*. Paris: Librairie Marcel Rivière et Cie., 1946.

——. *Saggi di critica del marxismo*. Palermo: Sandron, 1903.

STURZO, LUIGI. *Le autonomie regionali e il mezzogiorno*. Rome: Edizioni "Il Commento," 1944.

——. *Italy and the Coming World*. New York: Roy Publishers, 1945.

——. *Italy and Fascismo*. New York: Harcourt, Brace and Co., 1926.

——. *Pensiero antifascista*. Turin: P. Gobetti, 1925.

TURATI, FILIPPO. *Carteggio di Filippo Turati e Anna Kuliscioff*. 6 vol. Turin: Einaudi, 1949.

——. *Critica Sociale, 1891–1926*, ed. Giuliano Pischel. Milan: Gentile, 1945.

——. *Critica Sociale*. ed. Mario Spinella. Milan: Feltrinelli, 1959.

——. *Le vie maestre del socialismo*. ed. R. Mondolfo. Bologna: Cappelli, 1921.

INDEX